GANGSTA IN THE HOUSE

MIKE KNOX

Momentum Books, Ltd.
Troy, Michigan

Printed in the United States of America

97   96   3

Momentum Books, Ltd.
6964 Crooks Road
Troy, Michigan 48098

ISBN: 1-879094-46-0

Library of Congress Cataloging–in–Publication Data

Knox, MIke, 1958-
    Gangsta in the house / Mike Knox.
        p.   cm.
    ISBN: 1-879094-46-0 (alk. paper)
    1. Gangs--United States.   2. Juvenile delinquents--United States.
    3. Juvenile delinquency--United States--Prevention.   I. Titles.
HV6439.U5K68   1995
364.3'6'0973--dc20   95-12717

To Jennifer, Jackie, Bo, Cedrick, and the hundreds of other young men and women who have died from gang violence. Perhaps in death your lives can teach others how to live.

Contents

PREFACE

Most police gang investigators spend months, even years, trying to determine what separates one gang from another. What does a specific hand sign mean? How is this gang different from another? These are important questions that are relevant to solving crimes committed by gang members. Answers, however, are unlikely to give one an understanding about how children become gang members.

I have taken a different approach to understand the gang phenomenon in this country. I began by looking for similarities among the various gangs. The gang members became my teachers. I listened to their words and to their intent. I watched them interact with one another, the police, and the communities where they live. Gang members want what every person wants: security, fellowship, and respect. What they crave is external discipline. They have no one to teach them and so have turned to one another.

Discussion about graffiti and other signs and symbols of gang life is included because these external trappings are important to the gang member. Understanding of them may help the reader identify gang activity in his neighborhood; however, these issues are not the primary focus. My goal has been to try to take the mystery out of the gang myth and bring reason to madness.

I began writing this book with an idea that I could share information with other police gang experts and school administrators. It did not occur to me that anyone else would be interested. I began speaking publicly about gangs and learned that a wide variety of people want to know more about gangs; parents, teachers, counselors, hospital personnel, and even corporate America are interested in this problem. Such broad-based interest should suggest the level at which gangs have begun to influence America. What my book offers is more than mere identification of the problem; it offers practical common sense solutions.

The reader should know that the prologue is a graphic account of a drive–by shooting. The names and specific circumstances are fictional, but the story is based on a compilation of several drive–by shootings I helped investigate. I felt it unfair to present one actual case history. People tend to rationalize violence. We like to think it happens to "those" people, but gang members exist in every socioeconomic strata in the country. Consequently all members of a community are at risk of falling prey to gang violence. I felt it appropriate to give the reader a peek into the real world of that violence.

I have used masculine pronouns throughout because constantly referring to gang members as "he and/or she" becomes unwieldy and confusing. I am fully aware that there is a growing number of female gang members and that they are in as much, if not more, peril than their male counterparts. I have dedicated chapter 4 to their specific problems. My experience with gang members who are committing crimes that bring them to the attention of the police is predominantly with males. I ask the reader to forgive any unintentional appearance of sexism in my writing.

I hope that those who read this book will become inspired with a sense of urgency to make changes in the way they and those around them view street gang members. Many gang members are salvageable. I have pulled no punches but my message is not gloom and doom, rather it is a message of hope. Perhaps, if we all work together, we can prevent the tragedies being caused by street gang violence in America today.

ACKNOWLEDGMENTS

I used to think that a book acknowledgment was the hokiest thing on earth. When I began writing this book I told Helen, my wife, that I was not going to write a syrupy acknowledgment. Again, I have learned to never say never.

Many people contribute to the successful completion of a book. Some provide support and encouragement when you need it the most. Some provide technical information, and some just keep being your friends no matter how crazy you act. I cannot possibly name all those who have helped me in preparing this book; however, several persons deserve some special recognition.

Michael L. Howard, my friend, is one. His friendship and candor is invaluable to me. Mike provoked me into becoming involved with gang investigations, and we have spent many happy and exciting years working on the gang problem in Houston. I look forward to his friendship for many more years.

Another friend and coconspirator is Manette Schaller. Manette is the principal of a school dedicated to delinquency problems. I spent many afternoons at her facility. Manette and I made several of the observations recorded in this book while discussing specific problems of individual gang members in her charge. She encouraged me to begin sharing information with parents and "civilians" about the gang problem.

Susan Huff and Claudia Kemendo, both professional writers, offered constructive criticism of my first feeble attempt at writing. I credit them with helping me prepare a first draft of the manuscript that piqued the interest of my publisher.

A book that remains unpublished remains unread. An unread book is a waste indeed. Momentum Books, Ltd. and Kyle Scott have taken a great risk on a first-time author. I appreciate their courage and confidence in me.

Finally, and most important, my wife, Helen, and son, Jason, have had to endure hours of my staring blankly into a computer screen. I am guilty of ignoring their needs for days on end and yet they have never complained. Their support, and gallons of coffee and tea, helped me struggle through the writing of this book.

See? This kind of stuff is incredibly hokey but I mean every word of it. Thanks to all who helped.

PROLOGUE

Albert and Sandra were in the living room, waiting for their eldest son to come home from his usual Friday night prowling. They were watching television. Neither was interested in the show. They were using the noise of the television as cover. They didn't want Toby to hear them while they discussed their concerns about Mark and his new friends.

Several years ago, when Mark was just starting middle school, they were concerned that he wasn't going to make any friends. It seemed to them that Mark was distracted when he started the sixth grade. He had seemed unusually shy and quiet. As the year progressed, however, things worked out. Mark seemed happy enough and he had made a few friends.

At first they had chalked it up to hormones and growing pains. Then they decided that Mark was in a "phase" and would grow out of it. But lately, well, things seemed to be getting bad.

Albert and Sandra talked about how Mark had become very secretive. He seemed to want to argue about everything with them. At times, Sandra told Albert, she was afraid Mark was going to hit her. Albert commented that he had the same feeling only last week. Both thought Mark had learned a lesson after his arrest on that assault charge. He had received probation and seemed to improve awhile. These past two weeks, though, had been tough.

Two weeks ago Mark came home from high school with a black eye and a busted lip. Sandra could not get him to tell her what had happened. All Mark would say was, "Me and my boys will take care of it. It ain't nothin', Mama!"

Sandra had decided to do Mark a favor and clean his room on Monday of last week. She found some disturbing things. Among them were drawings that looked to Sandra like gang graffiti. She also found several neatly pressed and starched blue bandannas in one of his bureau drawers. Sandra confronted Mark about her discoveries and the two had gotten into a terrible argument. During this argument Sandra was unsettled by the look of anger and violence in the eyes of her eldest son. It had so unsettled her that she left the house to stop the argument.

Toby woke with a start. That noise, a sort of popping sound—he recognized it. It was a gun. He was sure of it and it was firing close to his house. Toby jumped out of bed and ran into the living room, where his mom and dad were still watching television. He couldn't believe they hadn't heard the noise, it was so loud.

Sandra interrupted Albert in midsentence and said, "Did you hear that?"

"What?" asked Albert.

"It sounded like some gunshots outside," said Sandra. They sat still for just one second. Then their world exploded.

While he was running toward them Toby heard another noise, one he had never heard before; it sounded like angry bees, a kind of ZSZING sound. He also heard himself yelling at his mom and dad. He felt as if he were running as fast as he could but things seemed to move so slowly.

A scream of terror reverberated through the house as Toby came tearing into the living room. Over the noise of Toby's panicked screams and the sound of his little feet running frantically toward them, Albert heard a noise he could never mistake. He recognized it from his Vietnam days—the deadly ZSZING of bullets passing close enough to hear. He recognized the danger at once but could not get up fast enough to protect Toby.

As Toby made it into the living room, something hit him from behind and knocked the wind out of him. He took a short skip–step and fell on his face. Toby didn't know what happened. He thought he had tripped on the rug but he couldn't get up. He tried to roll over but he couldn't. He tried to call for his mother but could only manage a soft whimper.

Albert could only watch as the bullet passed through Toby's back and exited through his small chest. The exiting bullet sprayed him and Sandra with a fine red mist. Toby hit the floor like a damp rag. Albert was over him in a flash and ripped Toby's nightshirt open. His war training and experience told him that the young boy in his arms was going to die. He refused to believe it.

Had he survived two tours in Nam and been wounded three times to come home and watch his youngest son die on the living room floor? Fear gripped Albert's heart. He screamed at Sandra to call an ambulance. Sandra stood there and screamed and shook and wrung her hands and finally ran to the phone. Albert tried desperately to keep little Toby from bleeding to death.

Someone rolled him over and Toby saw his mother and father screaming at each other to "call an ambulance, somebody call an ambulance, for Christ sake!"

The pain started about that time. His entire back was throbbing as if twenty bass guitars were playing at full volume. He couldn't breathe. His chest felt wet. Toby looked at his nightshirt and saw the blood...gallons and gallons of blood pumping out of his body. His father was pressing on his back and his chest and he just could not breathe.

Toby's streetwise eight–year–old brain kicked into overtime and told him he had been shot. He looked at his father, who was holding him so tightly, and said, "Daddy, I don't want to die!"

That one phrase would haunt Albert the remaining days of his life.

The last thing Toby saw was his mother and father. They were crying and looked scared. Toby was frightened too. Then Toby could not feel anything. Toby couldn't see anything or hear...anything. Toby died as his daddy gently rocked him back and forth.

Sandra was hanging up the telephone when she heard Albert's roar. It sounded angry, pained, and frustrated at the same time, as if something had ripped the soul from Albert's body. The sound of it sent chills through her being. She ran back into the living room and knew in an instant that her baby was dead.

The ambulance arrived, about three minutes after receiving the call, to a home in turmoil. The attendants reported their observations to the first police officer on the scene.

"The parents were sitting on the floor of the living room cradling the dead body of an eight–year–old male. Both parents were covered with blood splatters. We checked the child for vitals and found none. He was dead. We called you guys."

Mark was out "playing" with his friends. He liked that they called him Crazy–D and he worked hard to make the nickname fit. He had earned the nickname when he had fought the leader of a rival set of gang members several years ago. His opponent then was two years older and much larger, yet Mark had prevailed. He had become so mad that he had fought like a crazy person. Mark liked to remember that fight although he had long ago forgotten what had made him so angry. Ever since then his friends had called him Crazy–D.

Lately Crazy–D had become the unofficial "official" war chief for his set of the B.D.s. Just last week he had arranged to do a drive–by on one of those "punk Cholos." He was proud of that, it had gone well.

Things started to calm down about two in the morning and he figured his parents would be asleep or too tired to argue with him, so he caught a ride home with one of his Homies, Shooter–D. When they pulled onto his street they immediately saw all the police lights and knew something was up. As the two came closer to his house, Mark realized all the excitement was coming from his home. Shooter–D let him out about a half block down the street. He didn't want to get "popped" in a stolen ride. Mark ran the rest of the way and was stopped by a cop standing inside a plastic "crime scene" tape.

He wrestled with the officer for a brief moment and then explained that he lived in the house and wanted to know what was going on. About that time the mortuary people were leaving the house with a bundle wrapped in a plastic body bag and draped with a cover bearing the name of the mortuary facility. Mark was stunned.

"Hey, man! Who's that they takin' out my house?" Mark asked, not really wanting to know.

One of the neighbors told him more than he really wanted to know. "Some Cholo dudes come by here a couple of hours ago. Man, they lit up yo house like the Fourth of July. Too bad 'bout yo brotha, man. He was a cool little dude." It was said without any real feeling and Mark got the idea the neighbor didn't care. Mark walked to the front door, looked in, and saw the large pool of blood on the floor. He saw his mother sitting in a chair, her head rocked back, staring at nothing. His father sat in a chair next to his mother, his head bent over. For some reason, Mark was fascinated that his father was resting the bridge of his nose against the backs of his thumbs with his hands folded together. Mark noticed his father was crying, softly. Mark had never seen his father cry. The sight of it frightened him.

Mark, the tough guy gangsta who lived in this house, couldn't take it. He left. He didn't know where to go but he knew he had to go. He found a spot under a loading dock, behind a grocery a few blocks away. He cried all night long for his brother. Later he would boast that no one saw him cry.

Three days after Toby's funeral the Homicide Division again contacted Albert and Sandra. A detective explained how the case was progressing. Albert was relieved to know that the police had not forgotten Toby and were working on the case. The detective explained that cases like Toby's usually take longer than usual to resolve because of the gang involvement.

At first Albert and Sandra tried to argue that Toby was no gang member. In their minds there was no reason for a gang to shoot at their house. During the next thirty minutes, however, their minds began to see the probability of gang involvement in Toby's death. The detective seemed to know a lot about Mark and his friends. More important, he seemed to know about Mark's enemies—something Sandra realized she had never asked Mark about. Sandra was finally convinced when the detective showed her and Albert some photographs of neighborhood graffiti. The photographs looked exactly like the kind of "art" she had found in Mark's room last week. The detective read the messages and explained them to her. Albert resisted but Sandra brought him around.

What they learned frightened Sandra and angered Albert: Mark was a member of the Black

Disciples (B.D.s); he had been "jumped in" the gang when he was in middle school. The gang he belonged to was suspected in several recent drive–by shootings of houses, cars, and people. Albert was angry because he realized that Mark's association with this gang was the reason Toby had been killed. Sandra was frightened because she did not want to lose another child to violence.

"You see," the detective said, "there were no eyewitnesses to the shooting, other than the people in the car that shot him. We will have to rely on physical evidence, or we have to find someone in the car to be a witness." The detective continued, "Another problem we face is a lot of people are claiming responsibility for killing your son." The detective explained that gang members were bragging about it at Toby's and Mark's schools. Albert and Sandra were horrified that anyone would want to brag about killing their precious little boy.

"I can't fully explain the evidence and leads we're developing at this time," said the detective at the end of the meeting. "We're withholding certain information so we can determine which of these kids who are bragging may be involved in the death of your son." Albert and Sandra talked about the detective's visit for a long time after he left.

Mark had come home the morning after his brother had been killed. He did not explain his absence and his parents did not ask. He tried to comfort his mother and father but could not. He was uneasy around them because he felt they blamed him for Toby's death. Sandra would not look at him directly and only spoke to him in cursory tones. "Mark, come to breakfast." They ate in silence. "Mark, get dressed and clean your room." His father didn't speak to him at all. He just glared. Mark decided that he would help discover who shot his brother. Maybe that would help his parents get over Toby.

The first day after Toby's funeral, Mark and some of his friends hit the street. They talked to a lot of "witnesses" who told them that the Cholos were saying that they killed Toby. That made a lot of sense to Mark because he and his friend had done several drive–by shootings on some Cholos just before his brother was killed. Mark and his friends decided on a course of action and set out to determine which group of Cholos killed his brother.

One week had come and gone since Toby had been buried. Mark and his friends were no closer than they had been to discovering who had shot Toby. Mark was frustrated. The police, he believed, had given up, because no one had been arrested and he was not aware of any actions by the police. He became more convinced that he would have to punish those who had killed his brother. Mark decided he would have to retaliate on any and all Cholos to avenge his brother.

Mark met with two of his closest buddies, Shooter–D and Psycho–D.

"We just gonna have to do some Cholos, man," said Mark.

Psycho–D agreed. "Yeah, but which ones and how we gonna do it, Cuz?"

Shooter–D volunteered, "I know where I can get

a gat and maybe a gauge. We could just go down to Cholo town and pick one and just do him!"

Mark laid out his plan. He liked the idea of the randomness of a drive–by. It seemed like poetic justice to punish an unsuspecting Cholo for having the audacity to shoot up his house and kill his little brother. He told his "boys" to go ahead and get the guns and that he would steal a car to use.

Mark's plan was simple: steal a car and then drive around until they saw a Cholo and kill him. Mark insisted that he would be the one with the gauge, or shotgun. Psycho–D volunteered to carry the gat, or pistol, as backup. Besides, he was getting the guns so he ought to carry one of them. Shooter–D settled for the driver position. Shooter–D hadn't told his friends, but he had a 9 millimeter pistol he had stolen the other day. He would carry that just for fun. Besides, he hadn't got the name Shooter–D because he liked to drive cars. They all agreed that Friday night would be the best time to find some Cholos on the street.

Saturday morning television and newspapers reported another brutal murder, a result of an apparent gang war. Two Hispanic males were gunned down by several people in a car. One of the Hispanic males, a sixteen–year–old, was dead at the scene. The other, though seriously wounded, was expected to recover.

The homicide detectives were hard at work and had narrowed their search to six members of a gang called La Raza 13. This gang was relatively new to the neighborhood. The police had recovered several shell casings and determined that a .45 caliber pistol, a 12–gauge shotgun, and a .223 caliber rifle were used in the drive–by shooting of Toby's house.

A thirteen–year–old boy finally came forward and told the detectives that he was in the car at the time of the shooting. Francisco, also known as Luna because of his round face, told the detectives that he and his friends had driven by and shot up Crazy–D's house to show the B.D.s that they were players too. Francisco said that he sat in the back seat and didn't do anything. He explained that he was afraid he might go to jail if he didn't tell what he knew. Besides, he had known Toby and had thought he was okay, for a little kid. Francisco told the detectives that "they told me we were just gonna have some fun. No one was supposed to get hurt. I been havin' nightmares about what we did to Toby. I just want to sleep without them nightmares."

Luna told the detectives who was driving the car, where the car was parked, and who shot which gun. Search warrants for the other suspects' residences were obtained and two of the three weapons were recovered. Three suspects were arrested and charged with Toby's murder.

On Monday, three weeks and two days after Toby was buried, another detective spoke with Albert and Sandra. He told them the case had been solved and that the suspects had been arrested and charged with murder. The detective told them that two of the weapons recovered were positively identified, through ballistic evidence, as the ones fired into their home. In addition, one of the shooters had confessed. All the suspects were members of a rival gang called La Raza 13.

Albert and Sandra felt relief that someone was going to be held accountable for the murder of little Toby. Although they did not want to relive the experience in the courtroom, they both had strong feelings about what should be done with the scum that shot and killed their baby. Neither had any indication of the suffering they were soon to encounter.

Six weeks after little Toby was buried, two detectives and four police officers barged into Albert and Sandra's house at 2:30 in the morning. They were screaming "POLICE, POLICE" and literally pulled everyone out of bed. They made them lie on the floor in the family room. Albert was confused and angry. Sandra was terrorized. Mark was silent.

One of the two detectives handed Albert an arrest warrant for Mark. The charge on the warrant was murder. When things calmed down, one of the detectives explained that they were from the local gang unit and had been investigating a murder case. They believed that Mark and two of his friends had killed a sixteen–year–old Hispanic male. Albert could not believe this and demanded to know why the police thought Mark had killed anyone. The gang–unit officer looked directly into Albert's eyes with a calm and steady gaze. He told Albert that Mark and his friends had killed the Hispanic boy in retaliation for the death of Toby. Albert began to shake. His knees felt weak. He looked at Mark and asked him if what the officers said was true. He followed Mark and the police to the waiting police car, begging Mark to tell him it wasn't true. The police left with Mark, who never said a word.

It took several hours to calm Sandra down and get back into bed. Albert and Sandra lay in their bed and watched the shadows brighten into a new day. Both stared at the ceiling, lost in their thoughts. Albert wondered how Mark had come to this and what he could do to help him. Sandra imagined how the mother of the sixteen–year–old Hispanic boy would feel about her son when the police told her about Mark's arrest. She had not considered her son scum, yet she knew the Hispanic boy's mother would. It occurred to her that she had lost both her sons to the "hood."

1
MIND OF A GANGSTER

There are those who believe that gang members are animals, without conscience or moral values, and that gang members should be locked up for the rest of their lives or, worse, killed on sight. These people are falling victim to a prejudice. They are assuming that all people possess the same moral and ethical value systems.

Naturally, you cannot hope to understand another individual or group unless you are willing to "walk a mile in their shoes." To understand how a gang member thinks, one must look through the eyes of that person and see the world as he sees it. Gang members want the same things that we want out of life but they don't know how to get them. Understanding how kids who are in gangs think requires you to look into yourself. Most people will admit that they desire success. How we define success is debatable.

Consider a Catholic order of nuns who sacrifice financially, and occasionally physically, and live a spartan existence to benefit others. They will argue that their success will result in the supreme success:

everlasting life in heaven. One is not likely to convince many nuns that material possessions are anything more than a measure of the common person's failure to meet God.

Some find success in causing the earth to produce a bounty of food; others are successful in marketing these products at great profit. The farm owner/operator sees success in helping his crops grow and produce a bountiful harvest. He sells these crops to merchandisers and wholesalers who in turn view success as financial gain.

Generally, we define success as work that produces some benefit for humanity. A result of work is that we develop a sense of success and accomplishment that leads to a feeling that we have contributed and that we belong. We find our niche in the world and become satisfied. After some time, our skill levels become quite high and we begin to develop the respect of our co-workers and family members. Respect of one's co-workers, family, and friends builds respect for oneself. Self–respect produces well–grounded persons living a good life. At least that is what we strive to achieve.

Most people learn to succeed by practicing successful behavior in school. Generally, every student has one or more subjects that he enjoys, at which he becomes proficient, which can lead to excellence. The child begins to feel good about himself as various successes occur. If the child has at least one parent who is well grounded, who can teach the child the value of success, the child will likely grow into a successful and responsible adult. He will, in turn, become respected in his own right as an adult and will teach *his* children the lessons of success.

The same process applies to gang members. They are attempting to develop a sense of personal success. They want the "respect" of their fellow gang members and of the population surrounding them as well. If, however, membership in a gang is an attempt to find a place in society, to belong somewhere, how can it produce such violent and mean–spirited persons?

Apparent random acts of violence committed by today's youth are common newspaper headlines. The newspaper accounts of Toby's death and that of the Hispanic youth killed by Mark and his friends would likely have been reported as random acts of youth violence. The vicious, apparently unprovoked attack on someone by a gang, who later report they did it for fun, is incomprehensible when viewed from conventional morality. From a gang viewpoint, however, the more violent, vicious, brutal, or cold–blooded the act, the "better" it is for the gang perpetrator. Being bad enhances the gang member's image. Failure becomes success.

I have never met a gang member who felt good about himself, despite the claims of "no fear" or the fatalistic approach to life: *When my time comes, it comes, ain't no big deal, you can't live forever.* From my experience, I can also say that all gang members are living a life based on lies. As such, they create a false persona. The bravado, the bluster, the apparent lack of concern for the pain of humanity, and the rest is a facade to hide their fear of becoming a failure.

Because the human mind will not tolerate repeated failure, a person must find a level of success to survive. Repeated failure will force anyone to begin to rationalize why he is failing. Failure becomes the fault of another person or group. Ultimately these rationalizations fail and the person must reorganize his belief about why he is failing. Typically gang members focus the blame on the system. The rules of society prevent our success; therefore we should ignore the rules and create our own.

We all associate with people who share similar beliefs. Gang members are no different. They begin to associate with others who share their view that failure within the system is success. These persons begin psychologically reinforcing the correctness of their distorted view of success. The gang member becomes a person committed to success through what most consider conventional failure. His sense of morality becomes the direct opposite of the rest of what they consider the "system." He is, in effect, displaying a mirror image of conventional morality. After continued failure, he begins to take pride in his ability to fail. Failing spectacularly becomes a means of achieving success.

Most kids who have trouble with self–esteem first show this difficulty in the first year or two of middle school. Many parents miss the signs and signals during this period and allow the deterioration to continue beyond their ability to correct the problem. A result is a frustrated parent who does not know how his child got to the point of being arrested or, worse, gunned down in a drive–by shooting. I recommend that you, the adult reader, open your mind and attempt to view the world through the eyes of your child.

Many grown–ups have difficulty with imagination because we work so hard at living in the real world. However, in this chapter, it is important that you imagine what it is like graduating from the fifth grade and arriving at middle school on the first day of school.

When Mark was in the fifth grade he was B.M.O.C. (big man on campus). He knew where all the classrooms were and the names of most of the teachers. Mark had become an old hand at changing classes. He also knew almost every kid in his grade by name.

Remember how class changes were accomplished? The teacher directed everyone to line up outside the door in single file. Then she led the way to the next class and everyone went in and found their seats. After this class the procedure was repeated. It was a comfortable routine. The class moved together as a unit and you knew everyone in that class.

This year things are different. A homeroom teacher takes roll call and hands out class schedules, which have teacher names and room numbers on them. Mark looks around the room for a familiar face and sees only one or two. Mostly he notices that the room is filled with strangers. After some effort the kid setting next to Mark strikes up a conversation with him. Mark discovers that Matt is from another school that Mark has never heard of.

The bell rings and everyone goes into the hallway to find their first class. Mark walks the halls looking for his first classroom. The older students laugh and poke fun at him because obviously Mark doesn't know where to go or how to get there. Mark is lucky today and finds his classroom quickly. There is no one in this class that he recognizes.

The day wears on and out of seven classrooms, Mark recognizes only four of his fellow elementary schoolmates. Two of them Mark considers nerds. One is a geek and the other is the younger brother of a gang member. None of them are friends of his and he is not interested in them.

Mark spends the day learning where his classes are and watching the older kids, trying to discover what is acceptable or not acceptable in apparel, manners, and conversation. It is absolutely required, as far as Mark is concerned, that he fit in as soon as possible. There is a problem. There are so many different kinds of kids from so many backgrounds that there doesn't seem to be any pattern. In which group does he fit? He begins to worry about his situation while time passes.

Several weeks go by during which Mark can never quite fit into the mainstream of the school. He tries harder and harder to fit in, which causes him to spend less time studying. Grades fall as study habits deteriorate. Pressure at home is increased and Mark becomes argumentative and hostile toward his parents over minor irritations. Tension builds at school until Mark lashes out at a teacher and lands in the assistant principal's office.

Mark decides that the less time he spends with adults the better, and starts skipping classes. He becomes an expert at hanging out in the hallway, until the last minute, and then scooting into his chair as the tardy bell rings. More time passes.

One day, while Mark is standing by his locker preparing to rush into his third–period science class, which seems like an incredible waste of perfectly good frog guts to him, four gang members walk toward him. The crowds in the hallway part before them as they pass. Mark tries to act like he doesn't see them and does his best to blend into the wall. However, he can only pretend to have trouble with the lock on his locker for a few minutes.

Mark can feel them standing behind him. He thinks, Well, if I just don't turn around maybe they will go away. They don't. He turns, convinced that these guys are going to rob him of his new Jordans or his lunch money. A sick feeling begins in the pit of his stomach and his legs feel suddenly weak.

The tough–looking one in the middle introduces himself as Kilo–D and says that he and his "crew" have been watching Mark and they like what they see. Kilo–D invites him to lunch with them at "their table." Mark is dumbfounded but agrees immediately. Quite frankly, Mark is glad they didn't want to beat the crap out of him and that they didn't try to steal anything. It occurs to Mark, suddenly, like a bolt of lightning. They said that they liked his style.

Mark has lunch with them. They call themselves the Black Disciples. He is introduced to the other members of the crew: Mac–10, Hitman, Shooter–D, Moneyclip, 8:30 (because his mommy makes him come in at 8:30 p.m.), and Stonecold. They seem nice enough and pretty soon Mark is joking around with them and they are kidding him back.

On the way home after school, Mark walks through the park. He is thinking about how good it was to let loose a little and joke around with the guys. Hey, they didn't seem to mind that he had been screwing up at school and at home. Matter of fact, most of them told him similar stories about their problems with teachers and parents. They seemed to understand what was going on. Mark is pulled out of his thoughts by one of his new friends calling his name by the basketball court.

Things are looking up, he thinks. I'm beginning to make friends. Then Stonecold looks across the park and notices a kid with a Raiders jacket on. He and several other B.D.s huddle and then run over to the kid. They surround him and take his jacket. Stonecold hits him a few times and then they let him run home, crying. The whole crew tries on the jacket and discovers that it fits no one. They hand it to Mark, who stood and watched the whole thing. "Go ahead, Mark," Stonecold says. "That guy won't say shit! He knows if he does we'll kill him, besides you'll look good in it."

Mark thinks about it for a few seconds and decides that he'll wear it for the moment but he'll give it back tomorrow. Mark recognizes the kid as one of his fifth–period classmates. Mark's parents are relieved when Mark comes home and tells them, "Oh, this jacket? A friend of mine at school let me wear it. I'm going to take it back to him tomorrow." His parents have been worried that he did not seem to be making any friends. They take this as a good sign.

The next day Mark does wear the jacket to school. He sees the owner in front of the school and starts to walk over to him. The kid looks at Mark. The color drains from his face and he runs away from Mark like a scared rabbit. Mark decides that the kid doesn't want his jacket back. I guess I'll just have to keep it in my locker so my mom won't know, he thinks. Later he runs into several members of the Black Disciples and they explain the jacket owner's response.

"Man, he musta thought you was one of us," says Hitman. "You know, it's like this. People 'round here respect B.D. They ain't gonna say nothin' to no-body cause they know whuz up. That's why people get out the way when we walk by. Respect!" Mark thinks about this awhile and accepts it as fact. He decides that maybe he could get some of that respect if he hangs out with these guys.

Mark starts to spend more time with his new friends and talks his parents into buying him new clothes. He begins to dress like his gang member friends. People in and around the school begin to look at him differently and most seem impressed with him. Some of the girls begin to take an interest in Mark and he gets the idea that he is beginning to find his place in the school.

As his new friends begin to demand more of his time, Mark starts arguing with teachers and his parents more often. He seems to enjoy defying the authority of adults. He runs away from home and returns a couple of days later. He becomes involved in petty theft and starts a small record with the police for shoplifting. After a time Mark gets into a few fights at school and calls on his new friends to help him. They do and severely injure one boy. The police arrest Mark, Hitman, and Stonecold for assault. Later they are all placed on juvenile probation and returned to their parents for supervision. Because of his argumentative reputation and newfound propensity for violence, the B.D.s start calling him Crazy–D.

Shortly after he gets his new nickname, Crazy–D gets invited to a very special party. He shows up at Mac–10's house, whose parents are not home. One of the guys hands Crazy–D a cold beer. He sits next to Deirdre and tries to talk some trash. He does a little dancing and some more drinking. After about an hour he notices that many older guys are starting to show up at the party. Everybody seems friendly, so it is no big deal.

About midnight, his friend Stonecold asks him to go to the bedroom with him. The door to the bedroom opens on a room with five or six older guys in a semicircle around the bed. There is an AK–47 on the bed surrounded by several semiautomatic pistols and two revolvers. Mark gets a sick, heavy feeling in the bottom of his stomach.

One of the older high school–aged guys tells Mark that it is time to make a decision. Mark is told that he has seen too much, shared too much, and knows too much about the Black Disciples. He must either join or....

Mark is young but he is not stupid. He sees the guns on the bed and realizes that he is surrounded. His mind is a bit foggy from the beer but he remembers all the stuff he has seen. He remembers his friend Stonecold beating up that first guy for the jacket that Mark still wears. He remembers watching his friends rob some people at a shopping mall and he remembers helping eat the pizza they bought with the money. He remembers the time his new friends beat up some kids for him because he asked them to do it. Mark also recognizes that his friend Stonecold has his arm loosely around his shoulder and neck and could hurt him if he tried anything stupid. Mark decides to join the gang.

Everyone in the room slaps him on the back and escorts him to the front yard. He is again surrounded by all the members of the Black Disciples, young and old. They congratulate him on his decision and explain the "jump in" process to him. Mark is told that he must defend himself against two groups of three gang members selected by the leadership present. Stonecold is selected as one of the first group of three. Mark is told that he must stay on his feet for sixty seconds. The entire group recites the Black Disciple "prayer" and then the circle expands.

Stonecold rushes Mark and hits him on the head as hard as he can. Mark's eyes blur but he recovers and strikes back at Stonecold. Then Mark realizes that he is being hit by two other boys from the circle and he attempts to fight back. Shortly Mark stops fighting back, stands, and covers his face with his clenched fists and raised arms. The blows pick up in strength and intensity; three fresh B.D.s are hitting him now. Mark reels back and forth between the attackers. He prays that he can last the full sixty seconds. Finally the beating stops.

Mark looks out from between swollen eyelids, through the meager defense provided by his up-raised arms, and sees that it is over. One of the older guys lays three fingers on the top of his head and proclaims Mark a Brother of the Struggle. Mark is officially named Crazy–D and will be referred to only by that name from now on. Crazy–D has embarked on a journey that will destroy him and his family.

Mark's story is based on hundreds of interviews with committed, hardcore, lifetime members of various gangs. The jump–in process contains elements like those in all gang initiations. Some are more violent, some less violent, but they are all violent. Gang membership does not occur overnight. It is a slow process that progressively erodes the value system from the potential recruit.

All new gang members are eventually confronted with the apparent futility of resisting and succumb to the pressure of the group. There has never been a gang member who woke up one morning, stretched, and said, "By golly, I think I'll join a gang today." None of them want to join the gang at first, because gang membership is a bad thing. Until the moment they decide to join the gang they can claim that they are not gang members. This helps assuage their guilt and helps them rationalize their association with the group. Once they join, however, they believe that there is no turning back. "You must do or die!"

The more time the potential gang recruit spends with members of the gang, the more negative behavior is reinforced. The adventures of the gang members are elaborated on and embellished until they become legend. The glorification of such crimes as assault, robbery, burglary, and murder, committed, of course, with absolute justification, reduces the conviction the recruit has in the mores of his parents. This erosion leaves the potential recruit ripe for remodeling into a gang member. Once he joins, the process begins in earnest.

New gang members are expected to prove their loyalty by performing whatever tasks are given them. Many gangs require new recruits to memorize their gang history, coat of arms, code of conduct, and the like. All gangs are interested in changing the way the recruit views the world. The new recruit must change his perspective of the world to accept the false premise on which all gangs are formed. This change in perception will allow the gangster mind to assimilate information and place value on that information that is 180 degrees opposite that of the conventional social morality. What is good becomes bad; what is bad becomes good. In this way the failure of the child to succeed within the system is how he becomes a success.

A parent, teacher, police officer, counselor, or any adult authority figure is not likely to influence the average gang member, because such persons attempt to apply their logic and value system to the life of a gang member. They are busy looking for complicated reasons for the existence of gangs. They fail to see the convoluted logic behind the apparent lack of appreciation for values they consider common decency. Gang members tell themselves that they are the fools and the gang members are the success. The gang members do not believe it but they want to very badly.

Adults who successfully deal with gang members understand that gangs provide basic needs that the child does not feel he is getting: security (protection), a sense of belonging (family), and success (social acceptance/independence). To understand the world of gangsters and the ideas presented in this book, you must be willing to open your mind to their reality. We all need to remember that security, belonging to a group, and success are things we all strive to achieve. They are worthwhile goals.

I sometimes make the analogy that a gang member is like a southbound train on a northbound track. Instead of allowing the train to continue forward, we must get the train off that wrong track. We should also return to where the train was misdirected to prevent future accidents.

Although we do need to hold the individual gang member accountable for his actions, we must also try to redirect as many of these youths as we can. To effectively accomplish this task, we need to understand how they got on the wrong track.

2

THE BIG LIES

All street gangs are founded on a false premise. There are three big lies and one big myth on which all street gangs are formed, all of which need to be scrutinized to understand how they work within the gang.

Lie no. one: The gang will provide protection to the member. "We got each other's back. We look out for each other. If something happens to my homeboy, then he knows we'll take care of it for him."

Unless we feel safe we cannot eat, sleep, or do productive work. Children are increasingly concerned about their safety in the community and in the school. Fear for their safety, whether the threat is real or imagined, is a legitimate concern. Unfortunately some kids are convinced that they must seek out the protection of a street gang to survive. The protection lie is a recruiting tool.

Many kids have told me they got into gangs because they felt threatened at school. Rather than turn to adults for help, they turned to their peers. Some kids look for the toughest gang or the one perceived as the largest in the area. Unknowingly the kids are enlarging the problem and creating the unsafe environment from which they are seeking protection. The theory among some students is: the bigger the gang the more protection afforded the members. The reality is that gang membership increases the risk of violence directed toward the member. Larger gangs have more enemies; therefore the larger the gang the more likely violence will occur to its members.

During conversations with gang members, I explain how this works by drawing a diagram, which consists of ten large circles. Within each circle I write "2" and enclose all the circles in a rectangle. Outside this rectangle I draw another circle with "2" on it. The gang member I am speaking with is represented by the circle outside the square. The "2" represents the number of enemies that each gang member brings with him to the group. Do the math.

I point out that if he has two real enemies he at least knows who they are and can recognize them if they should show up. He can flee, seek help from a competent authority, or try to deal with the threat on his own. However, when he joins the gang he has twenty–two enemies, of which he only knows two. That leaves twenty enemies unknown to him. Any of those twenty could walk up and "do" him—kill or severely beat him—without his having the slightest indication that he is in danger.

This recognition factor is, by the way, one of the reasons gang members hang out in groups. A group increases the chances that someone will recognize one or more enemies. Most gangs consist of many more than ten members, and reality dictates that many of these will have more than two enemies each. The point is that regardless of the size of the gang, the enemy pool is larger by at least twice the membership of the gang the child joins.

The child who joins a gang must help "back up" his new friends when they go on retaliatory missions against rival gang members. This action rapidly increases his personal enemy pool and adds to the

violence, on and off the school campus, which caused him to join the gang in the first place. The new gang member increases personal risk in geometric proportion instead of reducing his personal risk.

Lie no. two: Membership will garner the respect of the community. "Yo, man. When we walk, people respect us. They get out the way. Nobody gonna dis me 'cause they would be a fool. You know, they know we don't play. I'd bust a cap on them, cuz."

Respect. Gang members eventually get tired of the constant threat to their personal safety and attempt to gain some peace through their idea of "respect"—something we all want from our fellow man. However, gang members do not know what respect means. Typically gang members will mistake fear for respect.

When you respect another you are not likely to invade that person's space. You respect his privacy and give him room. Likewise, you are not interested in stealing from someone you respect. Certainly you wish no harm to those you respect. Fear is much like respect in many ways.

We are not likely to want to get to close to someone we fear. We give them plenty of room and try not to get into their space. No doubt the person we fear can physically harm us so we are not likely to draw this person's attention by taking anything that belongs to him. The difference between fear and respect is that fear repels and respect attracts. Because this difference is not understood by gang members, they tend to overreact to perceived disrespect.

Eventually the gang member must react violently to any perceived threat to his "respect." That is, when someone doesn't appear to fear him to a satisfactory degree, the gangster must do something to strike fear, or "respect," into the person "disrespecting," ("dissing") him. The least violence is a physical assault. The most is murder.

Police tend to believe that most murders occur because of conflicts over money, drug deals gone sour, or uncontrolled passion or anger. Many are rethinking their positions on this subject, particularly as more homicides are caused by what seems to be minor provocation.

Things like "mad doggin'," which is the practice of "looking mean" at someone, "flashing," or "throwing," a hand sign, and the wearing of wrong colors are all good reasons for a gang member to combat and kill another person. Many of these homicides are committed under the cover of darkness with few witnesses who can testify against the gang members who commit these crimes.

The apparent randomness of gang–related violence makes it difficult for the police to tie the victim to the murderer. It also makes it difficult for the community to comprehend the crime itself. Many times gang–related homicides are reported by the news media and some police agencies as senseless acts of violence.

Why do gang members respond so viciously and forcefully to relatively minor provocation? If they do not so respond they believe they will lose the "respect" of the gang culture, and bring more violence to their gang. Gang members fear becoming victims themselves and do not want to appear weak because rival gangs may see their weakness as an opportunity to commit violence on them. More to the point, the violence may be directed against their own person.

This point was brought home to me while discussing the 1992 movie *American Me* with several gang members.

In the movie the main character transforms from being the leader of a prison gang to finding love and having a will to live within the system. The character is tragically thrown back into the prison where he resumes his role as the gang leader. However, he is changed and shows some compassion toward a rival by not killing him. His fellow gang members end up stabbing him to death.

The message in this movie is brutally portrayed and points out the futile life of gang membership. The intent is to show that gang membership is nothing for a young man or woman to strive to achieve. The gang members I know who saw this movie had a much different perspective. To them, the main character became weak and therefore he deserved to die. The moral of the story, as reported to me by one gangster, was, "You have to be hard to survive. When you get weak you die." Another gangster agreed with the first and said, "If he had stayed hard and cold, he wouldn't have died. His boys would have had more respect for him."

The reality is there is no respect possible for a gang member, except from a fellow gang member. Most gangs specifically require their members to show no respect to other gangs. Violation of this requirement can result in a serious beating by one's own gang. Consequently when two gang members confront each other they have no avenue to acknowledge each other without confrontation. After all, only one gang can "rule" a neighborhood, right?

These rigid rules of mistaken respect and the gang members' misunderstanding of the reasons for joining the gang also mean that gang members often mistake kindness, courtesy, and giving the benefit of the doubt as signs of a weak person. Understanding this is important to the teacher, parent, or other responsible adult who attempts to persuade gang members to do the right thing by showing them how kindness and courtesy work. Inevitably, this kind of approach to gang members results in the victimization of the well–meaning adult.

A strong, firm approach is preferred when dealing with gang members. An attempt should be made to point out to gang members that when one person respects another, the company of that person is sought out. Fear, on the other hand, repels most people. No one wants to be around a person they fear. The public openly fears gangs and will avoid confrontation, but will eventually require the police to protect the community. Debate on this issue between a strong adult personality and several gang members will result in a very interesting exchange of ideas.

Lie no. three: The gang will become a family. "Well, like when I am with my gang we are family. We do more fun things and get closer to each other than we do with our own real families. We are a family and we take care of each other!"

Gang members like to propagate this lie. Rhetoric such as "when he's hungry, I'm hungry" abounds and is occasionally syrupy enough to make one slightly nauseated. When pressed about what it means to be a gang member, most can answer only vaguely.

A friend, to a gang member, is someone who will let him drive the car that was stolen yesterday. A friend is one who knows where to get the best dope, girls, or guns. Friends who rob together stay together, right? Outwardly, gang members stick together and "back up" one another. Inwardly, each of them is getting as much as he can from the other members, emotionally and physically, while trying not to give too much himself.

Inside a gang, members are constantly trying to achieve a higher status, a greater degree of "respect." Internal rivalries develop and sometimes lead to extreme violence. Contrary to the facade, there is no real sense of family. Most gang members will give up their "homeboys" to the police, especially if it will mean an opportunity to take that person's position in the gang. Mostly, gang members are simply groups of persons better able to commit crime together than individually.

Some gang members do experience a brother- or sister–like relationship with another. These gang members grew up together and would be friends without the gang. Usually one of the friends is recruited into the gang and then persuades the other to join as well. The immaturity of these gang members prevents one from exercising his right to dissociate from another that chooses to commit criminal acts; therefore these friends end up going to prison or watching the other die in a gun battle. Hey, but they were there for each other.

Friendship is a misunderstood phenomenon among gang members, much like fear is mistaken for respect. Children often view friends by the toys they possess: Johnny has a cool video machine so I need to be friends with him to play his video machine. Gangsters really do view their friends in that manner. They never fully grasp the difference in having a real friend, such as an associate, schoolmate, or co-worker.

Friends are an important part of each person's life. They help define who we are as individuals. Friends will tell each other the truth and will give good advice. However, gang members cannot develop a good method of selecting real friends. They do not understand that friends do not engage in activities that would place another in jeopardy or danger. They settle for playmates, school buddies, and others who are "fun" to be around.

Gang members don't even trust their own friends. The phenomenon of street names for gang members is more than a cute little affection from gang friends. Often gang members will know each other only by their street name, or "moniker." When Hitman, Crazy–D, Mac–10, Kilo, and Money–Clip get together they have a good time. They drink a few beers, blow some smoke, maybe go see their girls, and later rob a convenience store. Crazy–D gets caught several days later and tries to tell the police who was with him—Hitman, Mac–10, Kilo, and Money–Clip.

Joe Cop asks Crazy–D, "So you've known these guys for six years, what are their real names?"

Crazy–D says, "Man, I don't know their real names! We just call ourselves by our street names."

Joe Cop says, "Well, surely you know where your friends live."

Crazy–D says he doesn't. "We just always meet each other in the park next to the jungle gym shaped like a rocket."

The advantage of the street name becomes clear. Even if your friend tries to snitch you off, the cops won't believe him, or, if they do, they won't know who you are. If you happen to be Crazy– D, you are left holding the bag and doing the time...alone.

Myth: Once you're in, you're in for life! "Once you're in, man you are in. There ain't no gettin' out. Unless, you die. You could be jumped out if you want, but man that's rough."

The myth that there are only two ways out of a gang is a useful disciplinary tool and helps hold the gang together. The first way, dying, seems rather permanent and final. I agree. If you die while you are a gang member you would definitely get out of the gang. Of course, when they say die, they mean killed.

One interesting lie often told to support this myth is that if you don't hang with the boys enough, you are "dissing" your "set." The concern is that the other homies may get to thinking that you are talking to the police or another gang. (They trust you so much because you are like a family!) So they have to kill you because you are now a threat, you know too much.

The elements of this myth are told in variations

from gang to gang. Although it is true that gang members will occasionally kill members of their own set (usually for those old–fashioned reasons of money, women, or dope), it is not likely that a member would be killed for not hanging around enough.

The other way to get out of the gang is called a "jump out," which occurs when the entire gang lines up and forms a gauntlet or another equally imaginative gathering. The person wanting out must run the gauntlet while the entire gang beats the member with whatever and wherever they want. Sticks, pipe, chair legs, chains, guns, knives, whatever are approved for this purpose. You are not likely to survive the experience. The gang member interested in leaving the gang imagines the pain and injury and is therefore afraid to leave. There are several variations of this scenario but they all seem to follow the same pattern: member wants out, member faces entire gang and is beaten severely.

The beauty of this myth is that it promotes participation by the member in the gang. It also tends to encourage one to do whatever tasks the "leadership" wants done. The consequence of this myth is that it becomes a reality in the mind of the gang member. Sometimes, when he has never witnessed a jump out, a member will claim to "remember" being present when someone was jumped out early in his gang career. The telling of this myth often enough that it becomes reality to the member functions as "proof" that one cannot leave a gang. Jump outs do exist, but they are rarely as brutal or as permanently damaging as the one in the imagination of the gang member.

I can't count the times I have been told by gang members that they want out of the gang but can't because they are in for life. Once a gang member opens his mind enough to face the truth, he realizes that getting out of the gang is fairly easy with the proper help. That is the trick: getting them to open their minds and see the truth. It is a hard thing for any person to discover that he has been living a lie. The ultimate failure, for anyone, is a false life. Unless someone who can be trusted offers hope for success, it is dangerous to face that reality.

Most kids work hard at getting into a gang. They will dress the part for months, hang out where gang members hang out, attempt to develop friends among the gang, and occasionally will commit a public display of contempt for authority to draw the attention of gang members. Once the attention is obtained, the potential recruit is usually tested in some fashion and then, if everything goes well, the child is invited to join the gang. Once in the gang, the child works constantly at trying to elevate his standing in the gang. For him to leave the gang successfully, he must be willing to work at least as hard as he did to get into the gang.

There are ways to get out of a gang without the injury associated with the jumping out or the finality of death. The most successful ways will use a social safety net for the child while demanding that he take responsibility for his own actions. Requiring him to dissociate from his friends and changing his physical appearance is essential. The participation of one or more parents is necessary, as is that of at least one teacher or assistant principal (the more the better). A police officer, familiar with the gangs in the area, should be recruited to help as well. All the participants in this safety net should know how to reach one another and have a good working relationship. Each is important in removing the child safely from the gang.

Gang members tend to believe what they see (actions) over what they are told (words). When a gang member stops hanging out and stops dressing like a gang member, the other members start to believe the child wants out. Left to its own devices the gang will attempt to entice the child back into the fold. Failing that, they may target the child for victimization and begin a harassment campaign. Protection from these enticements and the harassment is the purpose of the safety net.

The parent is the base of support for the child and must be fully aware of the extent and implications of his child's gang affiliation. Knowing the full extent of his child's involvement will help him decide what threat exists when six "friends" show up at the front door looking for Li'l–D.

The parent may then call the law enforcement out and contact their "gang cop" or may simply run the "friends" off and report the incident to a school connection. Ultimately the parents' responsibility in this safety net is to reteach the child how to make good friends. They must be willing to get back into their child's life and reteach him about respect, friendship, and responsibility. The other members of the safety net are there for support, because the parent cannot be with the child every minute of every day.

The second most important area of impact is the school. At least one teacher or, preferably, an assistant principal is vital to the safety net. The child that wants out of the gang will be the most vulnerable to harassment and violence going to school, while attending, and returning home. Someone must be at the school who understands what is going on with the child. The child will need someone already aware of the problem and available for immediate help. This person, ideally, should possess some knowledge of the gang involved and can protect the child by authorizing class schedule changes for him or other gang members who might be bothering the "wanna–be–out." This person should also be able to enforce school policy and be able to recognize the difference between a criminal event and a deviation from school rules.

The police officer is the last and weakest link in this net. He is the weakest because there are many restrictions on what can be accomplished within the boundaries of federal and state laws. However, the officer does represent authority and can be quite helpful in this process. The officer must have knowledge of the gang involved and must be able to effectively talk with gang members.

His role will be to notify the gang that the child no longer wants to participate in the gang. The officer must also inform the gang that any attempt to harm the child will result in swift investigation and prosecution to the full extent of the law. The officer must be prepared to carry out such a promise. Remember, gangs believe what they see, not what they are told. Again, having an officer already familiar with the situation will prevent a loss of time while the situation is being investigated.

Absolutely no effort should be made to force the child to get out of the gang. A halfhearted attempt by the gang member will probably result in violence focused on the child. Therefore one should not attempt to remove the child from a gang unless all parties agree that the child is dedicated and willing to work hard to get out of the gang. Tell the child in specific and graphic terms what is required. If he is not ready, all that can be accomplished is to continue to counsel the child and try to deal with the problems generated by gang membership, one at a time.

3

THE FAMILIES

Many adults have a vision of the American street gang as a group of young men who engage in harmless pranks, or they view them as misguided youths, who will, given time, grow out of this foolishness. Most Americans visualize street gangs with a bit of romanticism as portrayed in the musical *West Side Story*, which revolves around a boy and girl who fall in love. The boy belongs to one gang, the girl to the rival gang. Both gang names are almost laughably juvenile: the Sharks and the Jets. Ultimately there is a confrontation and a fight in which the boy is wounded and then dies in the arms of the girl.

Street gangs are being romanticized throughout this country in the theater, in movies, on television, and in the newspaper. Movies such as *Colors* and *New Jack City* can make gang life seem exciting. Television talk shows are always interested in having gang members on their programs. Newspapers report on the violence involved with the gang lifestyle. In this book I try to show that the gang problem is a mainstream American problem and therefore worthy of mainstream American interest. Reality is not a tragic play. Real kids are being shot with real guns and their deaths are horrible and gruesome. The crimes committed by these youths are costing each of us dearly in increased insurance premiums, lost wages, and increased taxes to support charity health care facilities, prisons, and youth offender facilities.

There are many different types of criminal organizations in the world today. The Italian and American Mafia, or La Cosa Nostra, springs to mind. The Japanese version of the Mafia is called the Yakuza and has existed for generations. China has various tongs, such as the White Tigers and Flying Dragons. These organizations started as groups of businessmen and evolved into crime syndicates.

Criminal terrorist organizations, who operate outside the law in a paramilitary fashion, are considered very different from the American street gang, yet some argue persuasively that these groups are a form of criminal gang. Terrorism is found around the world. The crimes committed by terrorists, for the various causes they represent, are usually high profile and very violent. Terrorist organizations generally have a group of leaders and use a sign or symbol to represent their organization. The French Red Beret and the Symbionese Liberation Army, with their red berets and the multiheaded cobra, are two examples. These same groups also commit other crimes, less visible to the public, for money to purchase weapons and explosives. The one thing shared by all these groups is commitment.

All organized crime and terrorist groups share a commitment to their cause or chosen profession. This commitment to crime as a business opportunity or political cause prevents their members from advertising their individual membership in the group. The leaders of truly organized crime or terrorist organizations, whoever they may be, understand that secrecy is vital to the maintenance of their freedom. Should anyone discover who they are and link them to various crimes, they understand that they could be jailed. The game, for these mobsters, is to live the good life through crime, without getting caught, as long as possible. For the political terrorist the game is to cause radical change in a government without getting caught.

The motivation for criminal organizations, such as the Mafia or the Yakuza, is entirely profit oriented—it is a business. It is good for business that the community knows about the activities of the organization. This general notoriety increases the likelihood that some business owners and others will be susceptible to influence by organized crime. Once such a business is identified and infiltrated it can quickly be controlled by the gang and either used as a front for an illicit business, such as gambling or prostitution, or to launder moneys obtained from these illicit sources.

One of the lessons learned by organized crime leaders is that violent death brings with it the attention of the police and the concern of the community. This attention is bad for business. Organized crime leaders usually must sanction a killing before it is committed by a member of their organization. That is not to say that all killings by members of the various organized crime groups are sanctioned. Certainly many of these members are capable of murder for personal gain. The point is that the organization itself does not endorse these acts and will not protect the errant member from the police in the event of an unapproved homicide. All of these organizations are, nowadays, generally temperate in using deadly force against a rival group.

Other organizations have less control over their members but do engage in orchestrated acts of violence and larceny. Prison gangs fall into this category.

Prison gangs engage in crime for the good of the group; however, the motivation for these groups seems to be less organized and more opportunistic. Prison gangs use violence to achieve the primary goals of safety and financial security. A prison gang strives toward physically and psychologically dominating the prison population. The successful prison gang achieves financial security and safety. Physical safety derives from the fear of retaliation by members of the dominant gang. The motivation for most prison gang members is survival. They group by ethnic, racial, or some other common bond to protect themselves from one another and other inmates in the prison. Financial gain is an opportunistic offshoot of this association and one that the gang enjoys. Financial security derives from the ability of the more powerful prison gang members to demand "tribute" from other inmates.

Unlike the organized crime gangs that are secretive about their membership, the prison gang member often tattoos his membership affiliation on a prominent part of his body. It is important that the other inmates know to which gang the inmate belongs, particularly if it is the dominant gang in the prison. Prison gangs are much like street gang members, except they are more, let's say, sophisticated—they are more aware of the law and the consequences of law violations. This similarity enables street gangsters to assimilate quickly into prison gangs, once they land in the prison population. Despite this similarity, however, prison gangs are different from the common American street gang.

Organized crime groups are motivated by greed. Prison gangs are motivated by survival. American street gangs are populated by persons who want to succeed and who crave discipline.

Most young people who join gangs say that the reason they joined was for protection but what they respond to is the discipline provided by the gang. The "discipline" is not the same as punishment. Punishment is sometimes used as a tool for discipline but it is not discipline. Discipline is, to the gang member, being at all the parties, backing up your homies, participating at jump ins, recruiting new members, and the like. Discipline is the reminding of a person where the boundaries are and requiring him to adhere to those boundaries.

Many police agencies try to separate all the little details that distinguish one gang from another, which helps identify one gang from another. A result is that gangs are listed as they appear in the community as if each gang were not connected in any way with any other gang. I happen to believe that there is nothing new under the sun and looked for similarities. I believe that all street gangs are alike in providing certain things to their members, chief among which is discipline. They all say that they provide protection, a sense of family, and respect for their membership. In reality the only difference among the various "families" is their external facade.

Although individual gangs may create their names, most fall into one of the five families or groups in America. These are the Crips and the Bloods from the West Coast; the Folks and the People from the Midwest; and the Low Riders from throughout the United States. Each of these families has its own quirks and peccadilloes that all gangs who align with them share. Some identify with a color, some with symbols; each uses certain language cues, and each has adopted certain styles of speech. Within each family, however, the individual gangs remain autonomous and create specific styles and symbols incorporated within the national symbols demanded by the family to which they belong.

I should point out that there are other types of "homegrown" local gangs. Certainly there were a lot of gangs before the Crips and Bloods. However, these other gangs were mostly in poor sections of town and were not considered a major problem by most residents, for they wielded no power in the community. These more traditional gangs were motivated by misguided pride in the community and operated on a geographic "turf."

The West Coast–influenced gangs, the Crips and the Bloods, got started in the mid–1970s. No one really knows how the Crips and the Bloods got their

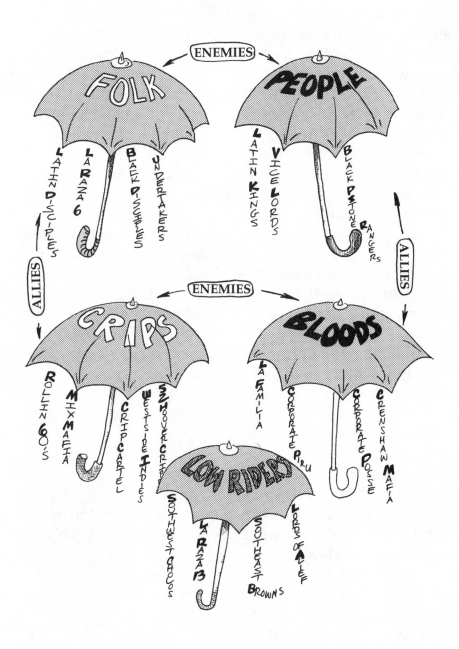

names but stories abound. If you asked a Crip family member about the name, you would likely be told how Crips always leave their enemies crippled. Likewise, if you asked a Blood family member, he would tell you that they leave their enemies bloody. One story that I have been told I choose to believe, because it sounds like what probably happened. This story was related to me by a California police officer who has many years of experience with the gangs and was working in the Los Angeles area in the mid–1970s.

A group of about eight kids who went to a high school in South Central Los Angeles liked going to a particular movie every weekend. This movie was titled *Tales from the Crypt*. The boys liked the movie so much that they began to call themselves "cryptsters." They decided to dress similarly so that they would recognize one another and so that others would recognize them. They chose blue because it was their school color.

The boys grew closer and would defend one another from members of other gangs at school and in the community. They began to write their names on the wall and the name of their "set," as was the fashion of the traditional neighborhood gangs. The problem was that none of the boys paid attention to the spelling of *crypt*. Instead, they spelled it "Crip" and added an *s*. The Crips were born.

The story that I prefer to believe about the beginnings of the rival Blood gangs is equally inspiring. About the time the Crips were being started, another group of young black males from the rival high school got together. These boys all lived on Piru Street, in South Central Los Angeles. Their high school color was—you guessed it—red. This group began calling itself the Piru Bloods. Red is a natural association for the word *blood*; however, another factor was working in the language then. A familiar greeting among black men and women during the early to mid–1970s included the word *blood.* "How's it hanging, Blood? Say, Blood, did you see that? We'll see ya later, Blood." Consequently language played a role in the formation of the Blood family gang name.

The Crip family of gangs began to require its affiliates to dress in blue and prohibited the wearing of red. "Cuz" replaced "Blood" as a familiar greeting among Crip family members. Eventually this focus on not allowing any "respect" for rival gangs evolved into rules about not using the letter b in any written form. Exceptions are allowed for "disrespecting" a Blood gang. For a time it was popular for Crip gang members to wear British Knights tennis shoes. The emblem BK took on the meaning of Blood Killers. A favorite euphemism for rival Blood gang members is "slob." A common tactic to antagonize Blood members is, with graffiti, to identify the letters in the street name Piru as Pussies In Red Uniforms.

Blood gang members retaliate by calling Crip members names, such as "crabs," and they forbid the use of the letter c. This information is particularly interesting when one looks at gangsta rap recordings. One can tell the gang affiliation of many of these gangsta rap performers by looking at the spelling of words that begin with c, which a Blood member will spell with *k* or *s*. This form of disrespect tends to create a constant friction between the two groups, which is vital to the Bloods and the Crips to distinguish between their organizations. Silly as it may seem, this constant friction over colors and letters is the root conflict between the Bloods and the Crips. Nowadays individuals have personal vendettas to settle because of this assault or that drive–by. Fellow members being killed by rival gang bangers (members of a gang) is the fuel that keeps the conflict between these groups alive.

The Crips and the Bloods have become the epitome of gangs in America. When people talk about gangs, they are usually referring to the terrible situation in Los Angeles, where the gangs rule the streets. A result has been that the attention of the media, television, movies, music, etc., has focused on the Crips and the Bloods gangs. I believe some of this attention is warranted. I believe that the Crips and Bloods, or West Coast gang culture, has redefined our concept of street gangs in America. They were the first to evolve what I call the contemporary model of gang affiliation.

The old style, or traditional, gang was one with specific geographic limits. The center of this "turf" was relatively stable and confrontation was generally limited to the border fringes with rival gang members. (Think of a large box divided into four separate areas identified as A, B, C, and D.)

A member of gang A cannot travel outside his territory without the risk of confronting a rival gang. When the police arrive in territory A, gang A must lay

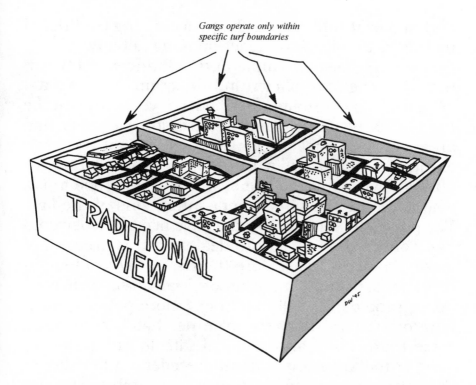

Gangs operate only within specific turf boundaries

TRADITIONAL VIEW

low and stay off the streets. Crime and gang activity is influenced by the presence of the police. This practice is often referred to as zero tolerance by police agencies.

Consider the result if the gangs were to organize as affiliates of each other. Although each gang acts individually, they all identify as friends those who share their colors and language. When the police show up in Rollin' 60's Crip territory, the gang leaves and conducts business with its affiliate gang, the Five–Deuce–Hoover Crips, to whom they give a percentage of the profit. This loose alliance builds relationships among the various gang family members and makes it difficult for the police, using traditional methods, to have an impact on gang activity.

When associations and alliances between friendly gangs are shown in a diagram, the diagram appears as a contemporary model of veins. Before the rise of this system of gang organization the police had an effective impact on gangs by the use of "zero tolerance," which is the saturation of a troubled neighborhood with police officers, who put everyone in jail who commits the most minor infractions of the law. The police, in some locations, have become frustrated and confused as to how to deal with this problem of loose alliances that, before the rise of the contemporary model of gang organization, was a relatively easy police problem. It will take time before police administrators realize that zero tolerance has become little more than a tool and is not, in itself, an answer to gang crime problems. The unprecedented mobility of the gang member has also created a problem for the

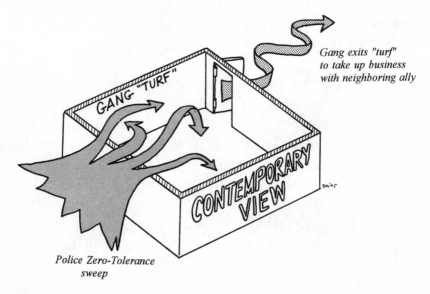

Gang exits "turf" to take up business with neighboring ally

GANG "TURF"

CONTEMPORARY VIEW

Police Zero-Tolerance sweep

community and has caused the gang life–style to grow in geometric proportion.

One fairly common practice among parents of minor gang members who are legitimately concerned about their children is to move them across the country to live with relatives. The theory is that if the child leaves the gang–infested area he will no longer be involved in the gang life–style. The theory seems like a good idea but it is flawed. A child interested in being in a gang will continue that interest in gang membership wherever he moves. The desire to be in a gang is much like catching a serious infection, such as pneumonia. Once you have pneumonia, changing your environment will not cure the illness. Furthermore, you are likely to spread the illness to others.

When a child who is involved or wants to be involved in gangs leaves one area and moves to another, he will attend school. The gang member who moves from Los Angeles, or anywhere else for that matter, brings with him his gang mentality. Sooner or later some kid in the new school will ask him where he is from and the answer will guarantee fifty new friends immediately. Everybody wants to know a "real" gang member. Instead of removing the gang member from the original gang and protecting him from further gang affiliation, the well–meaning parent has inadvertently elevated the gang member to gang *leader* in the new town or city.

Taken a step further, if a Crip gang member is threatened by a rival Blood gang or if either happens to be wanted by the police, the Crip or Blood gang member can move to another town or state that has both Crip and Blood families in it and survive quite nicely. The new arrival need not be familiar with the streets to commit crime. The local gang members will take him where he needs to go. The newly arrived "real" gang member has the added value of prestige, coming from a Los Angeles–based gang, and can therefore influence the actions of the newer gang. This mobility was, before the time of the Crips and Bloods, largely unheard of in gang circles.

The early 1970s brought "crack" cocaine, which was like gas to the flame for California gangs. Before crack, cocaine was a drug of the rich and famous. Small quantities of "nose candy" were sold at high prices. This cost prohibited many, including most gang members, from using or selling the drug. However, someone devised a way to "cut" (dilute) powdered cocaine and still achieve a good high by smoking it, instead of snorting the stuff.

In the process a small quantity of powdered cocaine is added to other substances and "cooked" until it reaches the consistency of cookie dough. The new substance dries into a hard cookielike state. When these "cookies" are broken they produce various sizes of "rocks," which are sold at reasonable rates, some for as little as five dollars.

Now cocaine was affordable to the average person on the street. The gangs who perfected this process had immediate and tremendous success. As their fortunes grew so did the risks from the police and rival gangs. The Crips and Bloods began recruiting younger and younger members, who, handled as juveniles, soon learned contempt for the law and the system. Within twenty years these street gangs have commanded the attention of every man, woman, and child in America.

As the sales force for this cocaine grew in the mid–1980s, the gangs were making a lot of money. They were recruiting members like never before. The new members were standing on every street corner, bus stop, and in every shopping center selling crack cocaine to anyone with five dollars. As in any business, a battle for the right to a sales market is brutal and without compassion for the enemy. Ultimately the price of crack began to fall, owing to a very broad distribution network. Most business people will tell you that when profits fall you must either seek new markets, change your product, or eliminate your competition. The Crips and Bloods have done all three.

The short rise to the top of the gang world by the Crip and Blood families of gangs is remarkable and therefore a likely target of media exploitation. Media exploitation of the Crips and the Bloods has added to their reputations. However, gangs were in America long before the Crips and Bloods. These other families of gangs, though not as popular among the media, have an increasing influence among our nation's youths.

The Folk Nation and the People Nation are two major gang families that originate from the Chicago/ Midwest area. Both gangs operate in their native Chicago area in much the same fashion as the Crips and the Bloods on the West Coast. The basic difference between these families of gang members and the Crips and Bloods is that colors mean nothing to the Folk or People nations. They identify more with tattoos and symbols than with a particular color.

The People and Folk nations are slightly more organized than other criminal street gangs. Their symbols and signs carry meanings that are written and given to prospective new members. The new prospects must memorize the information before being initiated into the gang. Additionally, both organizations expect their membership to possess some knowledge of the history of the family. Periodic tests are given by the older members of the various gangs that make up the Folk and People nations. Both nations, like the Crips and Bloods from Los Angeles, have a number of autonomous gangs that operate under the Folk or People nation banners.

All the Folk Nation gangs recognize the six–point Star of David as their main symbol. The points of the star represent love, life, loyalty, wisdom, knowledge, and understanding. The star represents the six sides of life: north, south, east, west, up, and down.

The trident, or three–pronged pitchfork, is another important symbol of the Folk Nation. It and the three-pointed crown stand for the three kings of the Folk Nation, who are credited with creating the Folk Nation in 1978. These "kings" are David, Hoover, and Shorty. The numerals 78 and 6 are also important symbols. The 78 represents the "Year of the New Teachings." The 6 is another reference to the six–point star. (Note the "Year of the New Teachings" coincides with the development of the contemporary model of

Folk Nation symbols

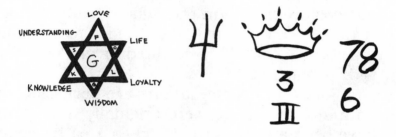

People Nation symbols

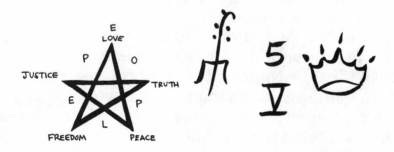

gang activity on the West Coast, which was discussed earlier in this chapter.)

Folk Nation gangs also assign significance to the right side of the body. If a Folk Nation member is standing in the typical "six–point stance" (legs together, arms crossed at the middle, shoulders broad), the right arm will cover the left arm. Most gang–related tattoos are found on the right side of the body. If a particular Folk Nation gang decides to use a hat for a symbol, it will likely be tilted or angled to the right side of the body.

The Folk and People nations are fairly new but their founding members were originally from gangs that have been a part of the Chicago area for generations. As the Crips and Bloods became infamous, the gangs in Chicago, who had relatives on the West Coast, learned about the contemporary model and forged alliances with other gangs. Kings David, Shorty, and Hoover organized the street gangs now known as Folk Nation.

The People Nation is the sworn enemy of the Folk Nation, organized in response to the organization of the Folk Nation. It is entirely unacceptable for a Folk Nation gang member to show any regard, at all, for a People Nation gang member. They are sworn to fight one another on sight and often do so with extreme diligence. The People Nation is, however, much like their sworn enemy. Whereas the Folk identify with the six–point star, the People identify with the five–point star.

The five points of the star represent love, truth, peace, freedom, and justice. They like to identify with the numeral 5 and the upside–down trident (pitchfork). Less is known about the People Nation because it does not write down as much information; therefore less information falls into the hands of the police. However, the basic distinction between these gangs is cosmetic.

The gangs remind me a lot of the Dr. Seuss story about those who had stars and those who didn't. In the story, those who had stars on their bellies felt superior to those who didn't. Someone found a way to put stars on the bellies of those who didn't have any and the groups could not tell each other apart. The first group then hired the same person who put stars on to take theirs off. So the circle goes with the Crips and Bloods, Folks and People.

There is, however, a substantial difference between these four families and the fifth gang family, which is Hispanic only. It is generally referred to as the Low Rider or pachuco gang. You should be aware that the Low Rider is a style of modified car. *Low Rider* is also a popular automobile magazine, and Low Rider car clubs exist that are not related to criminal activity.

There are also Low Rider street gangs that have taken everyday items and transformed them into gang symbols. Practically all street gangs engage in this practice. The Crip families of gangs use blue and the blue bandanna; Bloods use red and the red bandanna. The Folks use the Jewish Star of David; the People use the five–point star found in the American and Texas flags. Low Rider street gangs have adopted the Cholo man and the Catholic rosary, among others, as symbols for their brand of gang style.

Although the other four gang families have adopted membership from all ethnic and socioeconomic backgrounds, the Low Rider gangs seem intent on preserving a racially pure organization. Most Low Rider criminal street gangs are, in fact, racist. That is, the average Low Rider street gang considers its ethnic makeup pure and therefore superior to other gangs, including other Low Rider gangs of different ethnic makeup.

Many of these gangs distinguish between various Hispanic groups. Mexican Low Rider gangs will rarely admit any Hispanics other than Mexicans. Honduran gangs will accept only fellow Hondurans. Nicaraguans, Puerto Ricans, El Salvadorans, Guatemalans, and all the rest tend to allow only those who are of the gang's nationality to join. There is no pretense of brotherhood between various Low Rider gangs. Although some may band together to fight a common enemy, for example, the Black Disciples of the Folk Nation, the bond is temporary and short–lived.

The Low Rider gangs have a long and colorful history in the United States. Many gang members, particularly in the Los Angeles area, trace their gangs to the 1940s, before the era of the zoot suit. Low Rider gangs are the last to break with their traditional geographic turf–oriented style of gang life. Unlike that of the four other families of gangs, the Low Rider mentality is still based upon the *barrio*, or neighborhood.

Most Low Rider gang members consider themselves protectors of the barrio. They believe that they are preserving the heritage of their forefathers and that theirs is a sacred quest to become the epitome of the quintessential Hispanic male.

Unlike the other gang families, who have adopted females as full members, the Low Rider gangs still consider their women property or chattel. The female members in the Low Rider gangs seem willing to accept this role and often suffer extreme disadvantage as a result. Often these female members are left, literally, holding the bag of dope or weapons, and go to jail for their men. Or they become pregnant at an early age and end up trying to support themselves and their children in the barrio environment. The children grow up and complete the cycle as membership in the gang continues generation after generation.

Regardless of the nationality of the various Low Rider gangs, their costumes are strikingly similar: baggy work pants (of various colors, although khaki seems the most popular, depending on the gang) and a white muscle–type undershirt covered by a long–sleeved pendleton lumberjack shirt. The top three buttons must be buttoned; the others are un-buttoned. Some of these gang members convince their parents that this "pachuco" look is merely an expression of their Hispanic cultural heritage.

An extreme example of how this deception damages the child and the family occurred about four years ago in one of the neighborhoods that I worked. This neighborhood was infested with a Low Rider gang called the Lords of Alief. One of the leaders was a thirteen–year–old Hispanic boy whose father was active in local Hispanic politics. Our gang unit arrested this boy several times for carrying weapons (pistols), getting into fights, and stealing cars. We made several attempts to discuss this situation with the boy's father, who insisted that the police were picking on him because he was Hispanic.

The thirteen–year–old convinced his otherwise sane father that slicked–back hair in a net, a baggy pendleton shirt over the obligatory white muscle undershirt, khaki baggy work pants, and Stacy Adams pointed shoes were part of his Hispanic heritage. Granted, I am a white cop in Houston, Texas, and I haven't lived the Hispanic life, but I can read and I have traveled a little. I know of no Spanish–speaking country, anywhere in the world, where hair nets, pendletons, baggy khakis, and Stacy Adams shoes are part of the Hispanic culture.

These items are most definitely a large part of the Hispanic gang culture of east Los Angeles and other large cities across the United States. The boy's father, for the sake of Hispanic heritage, has taught his son that gang life is an acceptable way to express his heritage. His father is, in my mind, partly responsible for the current situation of his son. That thirteen–year–old is now seventeen and is waiting to face a charge of capital murder. (In Texas this offense is subject to the death penalty.)

The Crips, Bloods, People, Folks, and Low Riders are the basic five families of criminal street gangs in the United States of America. One analogy I like to use to clarify how the gang structure works is baseball. There are two professional baseball leagues in America, the National league and the American League. If you were to meet a person who told you that he was a professional baseball player, your next question would most likely be for whom does he play. The answer you are looking for is the name of his team. If you have a working knowledge of baseball you could determine much information if he gives his team name. If he were to tell you that he played for the American League, you would need more information. There are several teams in the American League. When pressed, he tells you that he plays for the Texas Rangers. Now you know a lot more about him.

The gang family is the same as the league in which the gang members play. Their "set," or individual gang name, is the team in the league. For example, there are many different Crip gangs, such as the Five–Deuce Hoovers, Rolling 60s, Rolling 20s, Grape Street Crips, Mixed Mafia, and the Playboy Mafia Crips. Conflicts and rivalries occur within each "league," or family, and rivalries are expected between "leagues." What this means is that not all Crip gangs get along, but no Crip gang gets along with any Blood gang. The same truth applies to the Folk and the People nations. The Low Riders, however, tend to believe that each team is its own league.

One interesting twist to these families is that as they have migrated across the country they have had to deal with one another. The West Coast gangs have spread east while the Midwest gangs have traveled west. Presently these gangs are slowly changing as the groups meld throughout the middle United States.

In Houston, Texas, for example, it is not un-common for a black member of a Folk Nation gang to hang out with a white Crip member. Both may get into a car driven by a Hispanic member of a Folk gang—very confusing situation for the unfortunate patrol officer who happens to stop them for a traffic violation. Likewise the purpose of this confusion shows in the gang member's response to questions at home and at school: "See, Mom, I ain't in no gang! I got all kinds of friends, black, white, and Hispanic" and "Oh, yeah, well, that car out there belongs to an-other friend who lost his keys so, ah, we had to hot–wire it. Honest."

4

ABOUT GIRL GANGS

No book of this sort could be complete without a discussion about female gang members. I am often asked about girls who become interested or involved in gangs. My response is that girls suffer the same problems and more that cause boys to get into gangs. Girls who become involved with gangs suffer from lower self–esteem, if that is possible, than their male counterparts.

The struggle for equality between sexes has not escaped the gang world. Girls have the same concern and fear about themselves and how they fit into their community as boys do—about self–image, which is, in many cases, more devastating to the girls than the boys. Our society sometimes demands that girls work harder at being attractive than boys. Girls are usually more concerned about fashion, physical appearance, and social position than many boys. Girls deal with all the stress that any boy might confront besides that brought about by social expectations of women. A result is that some young girls have low self–esteem and are, like the boys, subject to becoming interested in gangs.

Most common are the traditional girl gangs, which are predominantly populated by girls attracted, but not committed, to the gang culture. These gangs are support groups for the boy gang members and the girls are not as likely to be participants in crime, but they support the boys in their criminal activities. A member of such a gang might hide guns or drugs for her boyfriend or other members of his gang. She may provide money or safe haven for gang members wanted by the police or rival gangs.

A typical example is a group that calls itself the Las Wild Cholas (LWC). This group is closely associated with a Houston Low Rider gang called the Southwest Cholos (SWC). Very few members of this female gang are directly involved in crimes more serious than shoplifting. Their homes are, however, good places to start looking for felons, weapons, and narcotics hidden by members of the SWC.

Hispanic culture distinguishes between male and female social roles. Even the Spanish language distinguishes between gender of words. Typically a word that ends in the letter *o* is masculine and a word that ends in *a* is feminine. Hispanic males are expected to be leaders and to assume leadership in social and family relationships. Hispanic women are expected to be passive and supportive of their male leaders.

The Hispanic street gang magnifies these differences and creates an environment in which males must always show their "machismo" and cannot allow females to appear as their equal in any relationship. A result is that many Hispanic street gang members treat their affiliate girl gang members as property or chattel. Surprisingly Hispanic female gang members seem to acknowledge and accept this subservient role, at least publicly. They are not the only ones, however, to position themselves in this way.

Those I have interviewed reinforce my belief that traditional girl gang members seem to have an even lower self–image than their male counterparts. Evidence of this lowered status is demonstrated by differences in initiation rituals. The traditional girl gang initiation rituals, like those in boy gangs, are fairly standardized. The difference is that traditional girl gangs often give the perspective member a choice: violence or sex.

Girls recruited into gangs can either fight several of the members or have sex with multiple members of the affiliate male group. Many girls choose having multiple sex partners because they view this as less physically painful than being beaten by other members. Typically little or no concern is given the possibility of contacting sexually transmitted diseases or becoming pregnant by the recruited gang member or other members.

One group, the Lady Li'l Dogs, required new members to have sex with the five leaders of the male group, the Li'l Dogs. A result of the initiation was that many of them became pregnant. I used to joke that soon there would be a new gang in town called the Li'l Puppies. Humor is often used to disguise despair. The police, myself included, rely on humor to relieve the frustrations of difficult emotional situations. The prospect of thirteen- and fourteen–year–old mothers is definitely frustrating for any caring human being to consider.

The girls believed that, if they had sex with the boy gang members, they would become popular. They had hoped belonging to the Lady Li'l Dogs would gain them respect and that they would be cared for by their sister gang members and the members of the male Li'l Dogs. They were wrong. All they got was pregnant. The Li'l–Dogs and Lady Li'l–Dogs abandoned these girls because they were too busy to "party" with the gang.

Pregnancy introduced these girls to the myriad responsibilities and problems that come with parenthood, all of which were visited, unceremoniously, on them. None were prepared to be, or truly capable of being, mature mothers. Most will likely rely on their mothers, aunts, or other more mature women to help them raise their children. The others, unwilling or unable to seek the help of more mature females, likely will join the growing ranks of single young mothers who become dependent on social welfare.

The second type is what I call "new wave" gangs. I use the term "new wave" because the girls in them are riding a wave of feminism and are allowed to be full members of male-dominated gangs. Usually these gangs are one of the Crip, Blood, Folk, or People family of gangs.

Membership in this kind of gang is granted in the traditional way: members physically beat the new recruit. One difference is that sexual relations are not required or offered as an option to join. Unlike traditional girl gang members, who might choose violence over sex, the new wave member may endure a beating from either male or female members. This is an evolution, of sorts, in that the females in this kind of gang are on a more equal footing with their male counterparts. This equality carries with it the responsibility of full membership, which means that the girl members are not exempt from participating in the more violent activities of the gang.

New wave gang members often display aggressive male–like tendencies toward violence as a solution to life problems. They also may share a concept of "respect" and "disrespect" with an accompanying compulsion to protect their "respect" with violence. The shared view of violence as a means to obtain personal power and success allows the girls of a new wave gang to function as full members. Consequently many of these girls involve themselves with traditionally male-oriented types of crime: robbery, burglary, drug dealing, aggravated assault, and murder.

Increasing numbers of females in juvenile and adult detention facilities support the notion that females are becoming more involved in serious crime. Descriptions of females as suspects in serious crimes such as armed robbery are becoming more common. Girls are beginning to actively participate as full members of the gangs and are, therefore, willing to commit the same kinds of crimes committed by boys. Some are getting caught and are serving similar jail terms for offenses more commonly associated with boy gang members.

I have investigated several serious assaults committed by young women. Many of these assaults involve males showing disrespect toward a female member of an opposing gang. Instead of relying on the male members of her gang, as would be done by a more traditional female gang member, to protect her honor the girl gang member beat up the offending person. Later the girl gang member told me that she could not tolerate the loss of respect any more than a male gang member. In her eyes the assault was necessary to protect her status among her peers.

Unlike their male counterparts, the new wave members are also expected to perform as social companions and sex partners for male members. Some girls naturally select boyfriends in their own gang. There is the expectation of loyalty toward each other, as with any juvenile male–female relationship, and other gang members respect the two for as long as they are together.

Female gang members are also expected to bring male and female recruits into the gang. The females seek other females who might be interested in joining the gang in much the same way that male gang members attract new members. Male gang members rarely recruit females into the gang, but females routinely recruit males into the gang.

Typically a female gang member interested in a nongang member male will approach the boy and engage in playful light flirting. When the boy shows interest she explains that she dates only boys from gang X and that if he would like to date her he has to join gang X. Either he agrees to become involved in a street gang to date the girl of his dreams or he refuses, which is "disrespectful" to the girl. She may tell the boys in her gang that the boy offended her and they may target him as a victim. The boy that finds himself in this position is in a no-win situation. The gang benefits by having another method of recruiting new members or of identifying potential targets with which to enhance its image.

Some new wave gangs develop a sexual conquest mentality, like immature males whose mission is to bed as many girls as possible. These girl members are very popular among the male members for a time, but as her sexual reputation progresses she is reduced in stature to "freak" (a term reserved for girls who are easy to bed by anyone, in or outside the gang). The sexual double standard of promiscuity still exists, however; even among gang members the male who beds many is a playboy but the girl is, at best, a freak.

The third type of girl gang is the "hybrid" gangs. These groups are rare but their mere existence is alarming. The hybrid gangs are groups of girls who actively compete against boy gangs for the bragging rights to "rule" a neighborhood. Effectively these gangs are identical to the boy gangs except they are populated by girls.

Hybrid girl gangs seem to exist for the same purpose as the boy gangs and are the next step in the evolutionary progress of girls in gangs. They take on all the trappings and rituals of the male gangs and physically appear, except for obvious gender differences, like boy gangs. Hybrid gangs claim membership in one of the five families of gangs, dress as male gang members dress, walk the same walk, and talk the same talk as any male gang member.

Apparently, however, hybrid gangs are quicker to escalate to deadly violence than their male counterparts. Some attribute this to the fact that most members are physically smaller and weaker than their male opponents and therefore they depend more heavily on weapons as an equalizer. Others assert that girls are unencumbered by the social rules of combat experienced by most males in our society.

Most people have seen a fight between males, usually during their school days. Younger males fight by pushing and pulling or pinning their opponent to the ground. Older boys fight with fists and poke each other, generally above the waist and predominantly to the head or face. The male who intentionally strikes another in the genitalia may win the fight but will be thought of as a "cheater" by other males. Males tend, therefore, to stand toe to toe and box. These methods of combat have long been established as legitimate and fair ways for males to do battle with one another.

Females, on the other hand, have no such rules. Girls fights are often referred to as cat fights because of the clawing, scratching, pulling, and biting that occurs. Girl fights are rare in schools because girls are socially conditioned to settle disputes without violence and are viewed as less than feminine should they resort to violence.

I think that these fights are rare because they are more efficient than male fights. The only goal is to beat her opponent. Unencumbered by artificial rules of fair play or the possibility of raising their status, the girls are allowed to use whatever means are available to vanquish their enemy. The battle is therefore much more intense and personal between the combatants.

This social background taken to street gangs makes it clearer to me that girls attracted to hybrid gangs have no reason or desire to follow male-established rules of fair play or appropriate degrees of escalated violence. I think that most of these girls realize that they are, generally, physically smaller and weaker than male gang members and seek to obtain the advantage as quickly and efficiently as possible. Therefore they are likely to go from words to guns without much between.

Despite these differences boy and girl gang members, regardless of gang type, suffer from the same disease: low self–esteem. The cause of this disease is undefined boundaries and unfulfilled promises. Each in her own way is attempting, like her male counterparts, to fit into a social system that they just don't understand. Other than as sexual partners, girl gang members often believe that they are not welcome among their male counterparts and struggle even harder to belong and to gain the respect of their peers.

Girl gangs tell the same three lies to their members and respond to the same methods of firm, fair, and consistent discipline as do male gang members. Some girls simply choose to subordinate themselves completely to the male gang member; others seek equality but are willing to provide sexual favors for status, and a few seek to overthrow their male counterparts in their effort to fit into their society.

The problems and possible solutions discussed in this book apply equally to female and male gang members. Young women, girls, are losing their lives, both literally and figuratively, to gangs as surely as young men and boys are; however, to dwell on separating male from female gang members is, in my view, counterproductive to my purpose: to educate the reader about gangs. Similar distinctions have intentionally been limited or omitted regarding the ethnic and economic status of gang members because the problem affects everyone. The solution must include everyone as well.

5

THE LOOK I WANT TO KNOW BETTER

Do you remember the last time you were at a shopping mall? Do you remember a group of young people walking toward you, three or four or five abreast? As they got closer, it occurred to you that they were not going to walk around, but expected you, the adult, to get out of their way. Of course, you did move—there were so many of them and they looked dangerous. You shook your head sadly as they went by and wondered what is happening to our youths.

What you considered rude teenagers were, possibly, street gang members. They were convinced that you recognized them as a gang and that you afforded them the respect they deserved by showing the proper amount of fear. Gang members commonly mistake fear for respect. This scenario is becoming very normal in shopping malls, schools, and communities throughout the country. Many of these young people have the "look" I want to know better—the same "look" you need to know better.

What is this "look"? You know already: the extremely baggy pants, worn so low on the hips as to barely cover the buttocks—exposing one's underwear; the super–extra–large shirt, two–sizes–too–big shoes, hat on backward (or sideways or upside down); no–bones–in–the–body kind of walk that many youths believe cool or "fresh" or "hype." Many adults believe this is a passing fad and will go the way of poodle skirts and James Dean leather coats. Perhaps, then again perhaps not. After several years of observation I can unequivocally say that all gang members dress in the gang member fashion. However, not all who dress in this fashion are gang members. What is it about the "gangsta look" that attracts our young people?

The "gangsta look" is popular among our youths because rebellion is popular among young people. I rebelled when I was a teen and you probably did too. Perhaps your rebellion was more or less severe than the next person's but nevertheless you did rebel. Rebellion is at the core of the "gangsta look." The baggy clothing is a statement about the morals and values of the older generation. Just as the long–haired flower child look of the 1960s was repulsive to many older-generation members, so too is the gangsta look offensive to many adults today.

A gang member I deal with regularly told me about how he had tried to get a job at a local business. I will try to quote him accurately in the following passage. "Yo, Offisa Knox, I ben tryin' to gets me a job. I went to the store and said, 'Give me an app, I wants a job, cuz.' Then the man, he say how he wasn't hirin' right now. Two days later I seen this geek dude working there. He didn't hire me 'cause I'm black. See when yew is a brotha everybody be down on you, cuz. You can't git no whare." I asked my little gangster friend how he presented himself to the store owner and was told "like this, man" as he stretched his arms and did that cute little gangsta pirouette thing.

He had on a bold blue and black plaid long–sleeve shirt buttoned all the way to the throat. The shirt was so large that it could have covered three of him. A pair of extremely baggy black Dickies pants hung so low on his skinny hips that I was convinced that a hard wind would expose him to the world. A blue bandanna, carefully folded, starched, and ironed to razor sharpness, hung from his rear pants pocket, a pair of black and white "gangsta Nikes," and the appropriate amount of gold jewelry, patterned after various handguns, rifles, and shotguns, adorned his body. I stood looking at this picture of modern rebellion and rage and I told him he was wrong.

The store owner refused to hire him because he looked like a gang member; his skin pigment had nothing to do with it. Joe Businessman was probably relieved he didn't get robbed during the interview. I explained to this angry young man that appearances and communication skills are very important in the real world. I had to agree that it is not fair, nor is it necessarily right, but nevertheless it is a fact of life. I suggested that he change his appearance and speak in proper English sentences. He could have picked his job.

Two weeks later this young man was charged with aggravated robbery. He, like so many other young men and women, do not understand that rebellion is a part of growing up. He just couldn't accept that someone older than him might understand more than he does about what the world is all about. This is why he couldn't give up his gangster manner of dress or his gang jargon.

The baggy look speaks volumes to those interested in what our children are telling us. Baggy shirts and pants speak about low self–esteem. The child doesn't "fit" into society as he doesn't "fit" into his clothing. Naturally, when clothing is too big for the owner, it tends to hang off the wearer. Exaggerating this natural tendency heightens the visual perception of slovenliness. The outward appearance of slovenliness is most aggravating to us grown–ups. The child gets a response and therefore knows that someone is paying attention. The less the response, the more deviant the dress. Attitude, conduct, and social skills follow closely behind.

There is an advantage to this dress frequently commented on by law enforcement professionals. Every police officer knows that the age of the average felon remains fairly young, while the officer's age increases. Young, healthy, energetic felons have been harder for older, less healthy police officers to catch when they run—until baggy pants became vogue. Now even a portly twenty–year veteran can catch young felons with the best of them. It is very difficult to run while holding your pants up and quite impossible to jump fences simultaneously!

Benefits to law enforcement aside, there is no reason for a person to wear clothing that is two or three times too large for his body except to make a statement or conceal weapons. This gangsta look has become the uniform of the 1990s.

When your child comes home and tells you, "Mom, everyone is wearing the gangsta look," you need to know that there is some truth to that statement. Every child, teen, and young adult who perceives it cool to be *gangster* wants to wear the uniform of a gang member. Your child is telling you that he thinks to be a gangster is cool. He may not be actively considering gang membership, but if you allow him to dress the part, he will come to the attention of local gang members who will either recruit him or target him.

Those of us who allow our children to dress like gang members enable the gang member to proliferate. There are two reasons this situation benefits street gangs. First, the wearing of the gang uniform by nongang members allows potential new members to be identified and recruited. Second, because so many people wear the gangster look, it is difficult for school administrators, parents, and law enforcement officers to tell the difference. We all want to give kids the benefit of the doubt so we say nothing to them about their dress. We don't want to hurt their fragile egos. This allows the real gang member the freedom to move throughout the community in relative safety from the prying questions of authority figures.

Kids who think it is cool to look like a gang member, who dress the part, send signals to their peer group. If a child regularly dresses in various shades of blue or blue and black, for example, he may be targeted for recruitment by a local Crip or Folk Nation gang. Conversely, he also may be mistaken for a member of one of these gangs by a rival Blood or People Nation gang. If that happens, he gets assaulted and beaten up regularly. When the assault occurs it tends to reinforce the idea that membership in a gang is necessary for protection. If he is particularly unlucky, he may be shot by someone in a passing car, having been mistaken for a rival gang member. The message for the others who attend the school is the same. You need the gang to protect you from violence. The popularity of the gangster look does have a down side for the gang member. It has made it more difficult for the gang member to rely on clothing indicators as a visual clue about which person belongs to what gang. This confusion requires gang members to develop accessory indicators.

Typically gang members will choose symbols, tattoos, or jewelry that is easily explainable and will make these items stand for the ideals or ideology of the gang. Religious icons, such as rosary beads or the Jewish Star of David, have been and are being used by some gangs, besides the "look," to identify gang membership. Professional and college sports teams and personally designed hats are another method of identity. Traditional symbols, such as the colored bandanna, are also often used for identifiers.

I enjoy a conversation with some of what I call my "little gang–banger college wanna–bes." You know, the ones wearing those bright red, baggy, U.N.L.V. (University of Nevada–Las Vegas) basketball T–shirts. Or how about those Duke University jerseys? One of my all–time favorites was a kid wearing a black and blue Pennsylvania State University T–shirt. The conversation went something along these lines.

"So, K–money, you stayin' out of trouble lately?"

"Yeh."

"I thought you was gonna quit hangin' with them 60s [Crips]."

"Yeh, well I am. I'm not hangin' with them no more."

"Well, I see you're still dressin' like a 60s"

"Naw, man I just like Penn State, that's all."

"Oh, you gonna go there when you get out of high school?"

"Yeah, I'm thinkin' about it."

"Really? What state is it in?"

"Well...ah...I haven't really checked yet, you know."

The slogan or name on the shirt has nothing to do with why it is being worn by K–money. He wears it because it is a method of flaunting his gang colors while having a believable excuse for any passing authority figure who might want to give him a hard time. The same thing applies to bandannas. Often I have been told they are "sweat rags." Who starches, irons, and neatly folds "sweat rags"? It doesn't really matter what the color of the rag happens to be. If someone is taking the time to neatly iron, starch, and fold something, that something holds significance to the person. People, especially kids, do not waste that kind of time on a "sweat rag."

People who work with gang members regularly get requests from parents, school administrators, the news media, and others who want to know what specific gang uses which symbol, sign, or indicator. This specific information is important to the police department gang investigators, but, frankly, is not necessary for the general population. What is important for every adult, business owner, school official, and parent to know is how to identify which gang paraphernalia is gang related and therefore dangerous, and which is not.

Gang graffiti and the various signs and symbols of specific gangs tend to be fluid and require the constant attention of those interested in the subject to stay abreast of changes. The community can get bogged down attempting to classify which graffiti or symbol belongs with which gang, or the community can spend that energy more productively, focusing on solutions and preventative measures. I recommend that the person interested in gang activity look for patterns of dress and behavior. Leave it to the police gang unit to stay familiar with the specific gang graffiti and symbols of various gangs in your community. Consider the following scenario.

Six people arrive at a place all dressed similarly. All are wearing at least one blue item, which could be a hat, shirt, belt, pants, shoes, exposed underwear, or any other item of clothing or jewelry. None of the members of this group are wearing anything that contains red. Assume each got dressed independently of the others at six different locations. Now consider the statistical probability of six individuals dressing so similarly and arriving at the same location at the same time. Hardly a random occurrence, particularly when this group is noticed in the same location almost every day of the week.

Clearly, there is some organization at work with these people. However, only when these groups form does their gang membership become undeniable. The specific gang represented is important for the police to know because the members may be involved in some specific gang–related crimes, either as suspects or victims, in that area. However, it is enough for the average resident in the community to recognize that the group is a gang and that the gang is a threat to the community. When these people are alone, or in pairs, it is difficult to definitely identify an individual gang member. I recommend the "duck test" to identify individuals.

Simply stated, if you look like a duck, walk like a duck, quack like a duck, and hang out with other ducks, you will be hard pressed to convince me that you are a woodpecker! Despite their words to the contrary, gang members want people, particularly parents, to identify them. This is why most police officers and school administrators have little difficulty, with a moderate amount of information, getting gang members to admit to what gang they belong. Most gang members, once out of the closet, are only too happy to fill you in on initiation rituals and crime habits of rivals, and to try to persuade you that their gang is for protection only and is a "good gang."

The Hispanic male who tells you that he is a devout Catholic, which is why he must be allowed to wear his blue and white rosary beads around his neck at school, is pulling the wool over your eyes.

Chances are that child could not even tell you the name of the prayers represented by each bead (decades) on the rosary. If he could, he should also know that the rosary is not a piece of jewelry. The rosary is a religious icon, designed to be carried in a pocket and used for daily inspiration.

One of my favorite stories about a gang pulling the wool over the eyes of parents concerns the Disciple Queens, a female affiliation of the Black Disciples (Folk Nation). Several Disciple Queens had decided that their mothers would approve of their affiliation and the name of their gang if it were related to the church. These young women would leave their homes every day after school to go to a Disciple Queen meeting at another member's house. They would leave carrying a Bible, having convinced their mothers that this was a Bible study group.

The scam ended abruptly when several girls were arrested for possession of cocaine and weapons, which they had concealed in their Bibles for their boyfriends, the Black Disciples. The parents, particularly the mothers, of the girls were highly embarrassed and were concerned about what I thought of their parenting skills. I assured each of them that I was also a parent and realized that we all have good intentions but that sometimes we become distracted with the day– to–day business of life. A result is that we want to trust our kids until we can prove, beyond any doubt, they are not trustworthy.

The parents of these girls told me that they had a feeling that something wasn't right. One told me that she tried to attend one of these meetings with her daughter but was persuaded not to because her daughter told her that it would be embarrassing to the daughter. Another mother commented that she thought something was going on because this group was very secretive for a church group. Common sense (the duck test) was ignored by the parent. The young women were successful in getting into much trouble under the very noses of some otherwise good parents.

Another sign of probable gang membership is tattooing. How many Jewish people tattoo themselves with religious symbolism? Not many. Most Jewish people are adamantly opposed to the disfigurement of a tattoo. Either because of Talmud scripture or from the practice of Nazi Germany tattooing concentration camp detainees, Jewish people rarely have themselves tattooed. One of the common signs of Folk Nation gang members is the six–pointed Star of David tattoo. If the person is not Jewish, what other purpose might such a tattoo serve, except to identify a criminal street gang member? Again the duck test.

For centuries tattoos have been used to identify involvement with one group or another. There are many examples of various tribes across the world who tattoo their males, and females for that matter, with specific tattoos to identify to which clan or tribe the bearer belongs. Tattooing in modern America has always been considered a rebellious act performed usually in a person's youth. Tattoos can even identify a person's expression of mental condition. For example, heavy metal music fans tend to get tattoos dealing with death and the occult. Motorcycle enthusiasts often get tattoos related to the motorcycle outlaw mystique. Gang members' tattoos lean toward money, drugs, and firearms.

Some tattoos are self–inflicted or, particularly among the Hispanic gang youths, are done by a friend. A parent whose minor child displays a homemade tattoo should be, at least, alarmed, though I doubt they should be surprised. Usually the child interested in tattoos will make various kinds or styles of tattoos on his body with a pen or often will draw and copy letters, figures, symbols, or whatever is likely to be tattooed on book covers and school binders.

These indicators—clothing, bandannas, religious icons, and tattoos—help identify the individual gang member by others of his own gang and by rival gang members. They are also useful in getting recognition and some "respect" from school and community members. Kids interested in joining gangs are also interested in being recognized. Recognition is an important part of the gang attraction for some. Many kids believe that becoming recognized as a gang member will protect them from rival gang members or bullies. An additional benefit of being recognized by any group is that it lifts one's opinion about oneself. It feels good when someone notices you.

What gang members are after is an outward expression of self–worth. One of the things I have noticed among gang members is they do not feel they are worth anything. I mean that gang members do not value themselves as human beings. They estimate their internal worth by the monetary value of the clothes or jewelry that adorns their bodies. This craving for value in their lives is an important cause that is the underpinning for much of the behavior of gang members. The boasting, posturing, and demanding of "respect," the violence, and the rest are symptoms of youths seeking to discover what value they have in the system.

When people are successful, they feel good about themselves. Gang members want to feel good but have decided, for whatever reason, they cannot succeed within the system. They have, therefore, created a system in which they can succeed. One aspect of this system is the external image of self–worth, which is based on the importance of being "hype" or "cool." This external image of self–worth explains why gang members react violently to those who threaten their status and why many kids are prepared to fight and die for a Raiders jacket or a pair of expensive tennis shoes.

Normally persons at some point develop a sense that they are worth more than the value of their clothing or jewelry. Children develop this sense from stable home and social environments. Nowadays a stable home can be difficult to find. Television, movies, video games, and the nightly news reinforce the idea that life is fleeting and cheap. Sources of stability are more difficult to identify and consequently our children see value as a surface commodity.

If someone were to point a gun at you and demand that you give up your coat, would you give it up? You bet you would! Your car? You would surrender it as well. The money in your wallet? No problem, " take my wife's purse too while you're at it!" We recognize these things as replaceable and, when weighed against the loss of a life, relatively meaningless. What if, however, someone wanted to steal your soul? One might fight to keep that.

Consider what you might do to protect your property if you believed that your entire worth, in the world where you live, was represented by that Raiders jacket or those Air Jordan tennis shoes. Many of our so–called at risk youth are candidates for gang membership and have a distorted view of their own worth. Too many believe that their value to the community is based on the price or brand of clothing they wear. A child whose mother has sacrificed for six months to buy a Raiders jacket for Christmas is not likely to surrender his status at the mere presentation of a firearm. For the mother, it was an act of love; to the child it was a tremendous boost in personal status. Status worth dying for? I think not. However, it is not what I think that matters; it is what the kid with the jacket thinks that may determine if he lives or dies.

School is an important resource for determining whether your child is interested in getting into a criminal street gang or if gangs are interested in them. Your child's teachers, counselors, and assistant principal see your child, on average, more hours per day than the parent. When the child believes the parent is not interested in their school activities, he tries to draw the attention of someone who is interested. Normally these attention getters are fairly mild and limited to wisecracks in class. Some kids will perform for the other kids in the school. Occasionally the pranks, jokes, performances, and the like result in the school taking disciplinary action against the child. The parental response to this administrative discipline can and often does have a lasting effect on the future attitude and value system of the child.

The parents who, thinking they are displaying loyalty to the child, take the side of the child do a disservice to their own child, particularly faced with overwhelming evidence of misconduct or gang activity. Denial by a parent of the right of the school to require discipline or that the child is capable of misconduct at school is as damaging to the child as any outside influence might be. If a school principal, teacher, or counselor approaches you with their concerns about your child becoming involved in gang activity, you have a good school and you need to work with them and your child. It is easier for a teacher or other school official to label your child a troublemaker and blame poor behavior on bad parents. A school official who takes the time to call you and express these concerns is taking a big emotional risk on behalf of your child. You owe that school official and your child the benefit of at least considering the information you are given rationally and dispassionately. If the school official is wrong, no damage has been done; however, if correct, you will need help to save your kid.

Gang attire, tattooing (body graffiti), writing on the walls in the neighborhood and at school are all about the child wanting someone important to him to notice and care enough to say no. No; you can't dress like a thug. No; you can't deface property without some penalty. Yes; I will work with the teachers and the community to help you learn these lessons. I love you enough to show you where the boundaries are and how to succeed in the system.

6
GRAFFITI

Graffiti has been a part of the human condition since there have been people. Anthropologists study early graffiti wherever they can find it. Some call it "cave art." Early man had no language, we are told, and so he took to drawing his adventures on the cave wall, as a method of communication with others. The pictures have changed, the written word has been added, but the purpose of graffiti remains the same: communication.

There are several different types of graffiti. Unlike gang graffiti, not all types of graffiti are dangerous to the community, in a physical sense. It becomes an eyesore and is damaging in that it costs someone money to repaint, power wash, or sandblast. None of the graffiti types have ever raised the value of anyone's property.

I call "normal graffiti" the kind many of us have engaged in at one time or another. The "I love. . ." graffiti that adorns trees, telephone poles, and restaurant tables frequented by young lovers is relatively harmless. There is the "I was here" type graffiti, which you might see at famous places and tourist locations. There is also "poetry graffiti"—incredulous poems, filled with wit and vulgarity, found in the rest rooms of gas stations and truck stops.

"Hate graffiti" is a more serious kind, consisting of racist terminology, such as nigger, spic, gook, slope, camel jockey, sandnigger, and bubba white trash. Racist graffiti need not be limited to words to be effective. The German swastika and SS lightning bolts of the Third Reich still strike fear into the hearts of many Jewish people. The Ku Klux Klan symbols drawn on the walls of a black family's house or the drawing of a burning cross are enough to frighten many. It is common to find this graffiti mixed with the "poetry" kind.

Sometimes the racist or hate message is cleverly camouflaged in a short story or poem written on the wall in public rest rooms. Certainly these words and symbols frustrate those to whom they are directed but they rarely enrage any rational person to violence. Despite their annoyance factor and their disrespectful tone and costliness to eradicate, they do not pose an imminent threat to the physical safety of a community.

Some people attempt to explain gang graffiti as modern art and as expressions of the artists attempting to draw attention to the wrongs that society has committed against them. More believe that if the graffiti is left alone, the gangs will have an alternative to violence. A few believe that graffiti, though amateur, crude, and sometimes vulgar, contributes to the beauty of the community. These kindhearted persons are using their value system in applying that kind of logic. It is clear to me that such persons do not have a clue about what graffiti accomplishes for a street gang.

Just as a gang member's looks identify him as a member of a gang, graffiti identifies a neighborhood as the stronghold or target area of gangs. Attention to the way a neighborhood looks is as important as the manner and appearance of the residents in that neighborhood. Gang graffiti, unlike other kinds, presents a threat to the safety of the people who live where it exists.

Gang graffiti is an undeniable indication that criminal street gangs operate in your community. Its presence should be considered a wake–up call to the members of the community. Gang graffiti is not a signal that the community has failed or that its residence should give up dealing with crime issues. It is, however, a symptom of a much larger and potentially fatal illness. As for any illness, it is important to treat the symptoms while treating the disease. Graffiti is more like a virus than a cancer because it can, with community effort, be cured.

There are three reasons graffiti is important to a street gang: (1) it serves as a message board to broadcast threats and challenges to rival gang members; (2) it intimidates the neighborhood; and (3) most important, graffiti is a powerful recruiting tool.

Two distinct types of graffiti are generally associated with gangs. First, "real" gang graffiti is marking on walls, street signs, houses, streets, driveways, cars, clothes, or any other surface in which the gang logo, slogans, threats, or gang names appear. "Real" gang graffiti often marks, or claims, territory and declares superiority over rivals or enemies. Often this graffiti will include the "street names" of current gang members.

Second, "tagger" graffiti is art, compared with "real" gang graffiti, and uses traditional artistic methods in nontraditional ways to produce murals, self-portraits, still life, or any other subject of artistic interest. Often taggers merely write their "pen name" on a wall in a coded or stylized script to mark their passing by a spot. Unlike a consequence of "real" gang graffiti, a tagger artist's drawings are not necessarily inflammatory to the gang culture in the neighborhoods where its members coexist with other gang members. However, the mentality of the tagger is much like that of a "real" gang member. Therefore the artist can become violent when someone "violates" his "art" by painting over it or writing rival gang messages over it.

Gang members respond with violence to the messages on the walls. Taggers who become violent do so because someone has desecrated their artwork. Several taggers may form associations to "protect" their work. These associations become indistinguishable from the "real" gangs in the neighborhood, and violence is escalated between the taggers and the gangsters. To the police, the community, and the families of the victims, the distinction between "real gang violence" and "tagger violence" amounts to nit–picking, but to the two groups involved the differences are broad and profound.

To gang members, taggers are an annoyance because they tend to ignore the sanctity of the graffiti walls. The tagger looks on gang graffiti as lacking in artistic value and therefore the scribbling of the criminal element. The tagger seeks to cover this amateurish scrawling with "real art," namely, the tagger's idea of art. However, violent taggers are the exception and not the rule. Many taggers recognize the financial opportunity in selling their artistic talents to the gang world.

Occasionally taggers are hired by gang members to produce murals depicting their gang in action. Taggers are considered valuable assets to individual gangs because good–looking graffiti boosts the prestige of the gang (the better the graffiti, the more impressive the gang). Once taggers join a gang or a tagger association they cease to be taggers and become gang members.

As taggers become more involved in the gang, they use their talent to promote the agenda of the gang, and their art loses much of its artistic quality and refocuses on gang messages. The longer a tagger hangs out with the gang the more the gang infiltrates the mind of the tagger. Eventually he becomes like the rest of the gang, except that he is an artistically inclined gang member.

Gang graffiti, whether done by a tagger or by a real gang member, creates an atmosphere of failure for the community, which demoralizes the adult population, who ultimately surrender to the gangs by allowing the graffiti to remain, unchallenged. As the neighborhood continues to look more like gang turf, the gang members become increasingly bold in the placement of graffiti and may begin to place graffiti

on private homes as well. The capitulation of the adult population supports the self–sustaining myth believed by most gangs: the gang rules the hood. To the gang members, this is success. They have defeated the adults and command the respect—fear—of the neighborhood. Once the neighborhood gets the reputation of a gang stronghold, violence will follow.

Other gang members, driving through the neighborhood, notice the threats and boasts of the gang claiming the territory. Neighboring gangs may decide to test the mettle of this gang. For example, a passing carload of gang members sees a youth who is an apparent gang member walking through the neighborhood. The gang members stop and beat the stuffing out of him, who reports the incident to his gang. They drive to the rival neighborhood to retaliate. They find someone they believe is a gang member and beat him up, sometimes even hospitalize him. While in the hospital this gang member tells his friends who did this terrible and unjustified violence; his gang retaliates and the never–ending cycle of gang violence has begun.

Some gang members enjoy testing themselves and their fellow members in contests of "bravery." One way to increase one's respectability in the gang is to engage the enemy. The best way to do that is to go where there are gangs. A neighborhood that holds the promise, through graffiti, of having a gang to combat is the preferred target. The more graffiti exists in a community, the more likely that rival gangs will converge and engage in violent behavior, which will surely affect the lives of those who live in that neighborhood. An important effect of this gang violence is that it convinces children that their protection depends on belonging to the right gang.

Graffiti acts as a recruiting tool by advertising to the community the presence of the gang. The more a young person sees of a particular product, the more likely he will want to purchase the product. Spend thirty minutes in front of the television with a child on any Saturday morning and you will understand. Commercials for tennis shoes, toys, breakfast cereals, and the like bombard our kids with repetitive and catchy jingles and slogans. Take the child to a mall or grocery store and watch what they ask for. I'll bet they try to convince you that they cannot live without another box of Co–Co Puffs or another such product. The lesson is that repetition makes an impression.

Young people who become interested in gang life seek out contact with gang members whose graffiti adorns various walls in the neighborhood. Generally, they will align with the prevailing gang in the neighborhood, which is often the one whose graffiti adorns the most buildings. Nongang members who are interested in the gang life–style keep abreast of developments through the neighborhood graffiti. Any organization that advertises in as many locations as most neighborhood gangs advertise will grow—the purpose of advertising is to let perspective customers know of your existence.

Gang members can convince most recruits that they "rule" the neighborhood. They simply point to the nearest graffiti wall as evidence that the community accepts them and acknowledges them. The community tolerates the graffiti by not removing it and proves their point. The larger the gang, the more graffiti; the more graffiti, the larger the membership. Larger memberships to young people interested in gangs means greater safety.

The reality is quite different. The larger the gang, the greater the enemy pool; the larger the enemy pool, the greater the risk of conflict. More conflict increases the risk of deadly violence by members of the larger gangs. Membership in a large gang increases the risk to the individual members of that gang.

Community members in a neighborhood filled with graffiti are intimidated by youths who grow bolder each day. A feeling of dread overcomes a person entering a neighborhood filled with gang graffiti. Young men and women strolling casually in the middle of the street in roving bands, three or four abreast, daring you to run over them with your vehicle, causes most drivers to swerve around these moving roadblocks. This simple act of defiance by the youths is evidence, in their eyes, that the community fears and therefore respects them. As the intimidation grows, the deference shown to the youths in the street increases and encourages their raucous behavior. The emboldened gang members find recruiting new and younger members easier, and the gang ultimately will become entrenched in the neighborhood.

No doubt the average person would like to stop the car and tell the kids to get out of the street. A rational person, however, would consider the possibility that these young thugs are members of a local gang and could be armed. Therefore, discretion being the better part of valor, driving around the roving band of youths is probably the safest course.

The gang uses graffiti as a communications network. Graffiti unremoved by the community or rivals is a sign of a fairly stable gang environment. That is to say, the gang who put up the graffiti did so in an area generally agreed to be in the sole possession of that gang. When the graffiti expands to the edges of the gang's physical turf, other gangs dispute the claim to the area by marking out, writing over, or otherwise defacing the first gang's graffiti.

Equally important to communication is getting the message to the right readers. Codes are therefore a large part of the gang graffiti. The codes can exclude the uninformed and yet be widely known by gang members and others interested in gang activity. The fractured alphabets, upside-down and backward letters, number sequences, and the rest are as easy to read for the kids in the neighborhood as the local scandal sheet at the grocery store is for us adults.

Let's say that I am a member of the La Raza Folks. I write on my local wall that *La Raza Folks es primero en el barrio* (La Raza Folks is number one in the neighborhood.) Below this slogan I draw the six–pointed Star of David and a treble pitchfork over an upside–down five–pointed crown. This graffiti, left untouched, tells the community and the gang that no one else claims this as their territory and it is free for the gang to take as its own. However, the next day I drive by my wall and I notice that someone has come by during the night and drawn an X through the name of my gang. Additionally, the person placed the gang name *Mix Mafia Crips* over my drawing. Further, this audacious person has placed the numeral 187 above an upside–down and backward rendition of the word Folks. What does all of this mean?

The Mix Mafia Crips claim this area as their own and they have challenged the weaker La Raza gang to a war for the territory. The 187 is the California Penal Code citation for homicide and is gang language for their intent to kill all of the La Raza gang. I, being a good and longstanding member of the La Raza Street gang, report this situation to my gang and we go in search of the bodacious bunch that call themselves the Mix Mafia. We take them up on their challenge. The community rocks with fear as the sound of gunfire and shrieking tires rips through the neighborhood nights—all because of some scribbled lines on a wall!

To read and understand gang graffiti is an arduous task, but one well worth the effort by local law enforcement agencies. To communities, however, what is important is that they understand allowing graffiti to remain by property owners is tantamount to an invitation to violence. Gang graffiti must not be allowed to remain on a building longer than forty–eight hours; preferably it should be removed immediately when it is noticed.

Gangs sometimes return the next night or soon after their graffiti is covered and do it again, to test the resolve of the property owner. If the graffiti is removed soon after it appears, every time it appears, the gang will abandon its efforts and move to another location. In this way, the community can communicate to the gang that it is not welcome and will not be "respected."

Business owners sometimes have a period of no graffiti and then a different gang chooses the property to put up graffiti of their own. The process must begin again. Once the graffiti is noticed it should be removed within forty–eight hours. The second gang may do it again. Some business owners become angry because the costs of removal eat into the profits of the company. I sympathize with them; nevertheless it must be done.

Removing graffiti will become a chore like cutting the grass. The grass grows in the yard and every week it gets cut. It is a chore that few enjoy. The longer it is delayed, the more difficult the chore becomes. We might complain but every weekend we cut the grass. We do this because we want our property to look well kept and orderly. A business or public wall should not be any different.

Some business owners wait until graffiti completely covers a wall and then they paint over it. The logic is: Why paint over it right away? There will be more tomorrow. I'll just wait until it becomes so bad that I can't stand it anymore, then I'll paint it. The business owner who thinks this way is a dream come true to most gangs. After the wall becomes covered, the store owner politely repaints and provides a fresh canvas for the gang. The owner points to his freshly painted wall and says with conviction that there will be more graffiti on it by morning. And, of course, he is right.

The neighborhood gang mistakes the business owner's resignation to repeated vandalism by graffiti for acceptance of the gang's right to write on his walls. The owner inadvertently, through acquiescence, encourages gang activity around his store. Of course, working together from different frames of reference, the store owner and the gang members fulfill each other's expectations.

Gang members appreciate the owner letting their graffiti remain where people can see it. The gangsters proceed to fill up the available space with graffiti. The owner, wanting to save money, waits for the wall to get full and then repaints it. The gangsters also appreciate his cleaning of the slate. Now new and more impressive exploits of the gang can be communicated to the community. Again, applying "normal" values to the gang mind results in complete misunderstanding.

At every turn we try to apply our perspective to gang activity and every time we are at a loss to explain the behavior. Understanding the importance of graffiti as a marketing tool, community intimidation device, and communication network puts an uncomfortable spin on the whole graffiti issue. It suggests that these no–good, low–down gang members might have a brain with which to think. If that is so, merely putting them in jail may not be the answer.

7

EMPOWERMENT

How often have you heard lately how important it is for teenagers to control their lives? Some suggest that young people get into trouble because they lack a feeling of power that comes from control over their own destiny. A result is these young people strike out in violent and criminal ways to attract attention to this lack of control over their lives. I totally agree that many of our nation's youths are striking out in criminal and increasingly violent ways. I believe that young people are on a quest to discover answers to their life problems. I disagree, however, that the root cause of all this mayhem is a lack of power of the youths to control their lives.

The proponents of self–empowerment believe that gang members suffer from low self–esteem. They believe that the source of self–esteem is derived from the child's ability to control his environment. The theory is that if you control your environment, you control your destiny. Following this model, a child with low self–esteem needs greater amounts of re- sponsibility and freedom so that he feels more in control of his life; he then will begin to make appro- priate decisions that will raise his self–esteem. It is a pretty theory and sounds very nice but it is fundamentally flawed, in my opinion.

The proponents of this "empowerment" theory have correctly identified one of the symptoms that drives children toward gangs: low self–esteem. We can all agree that gang members possess abysmally low self–esteem; I disagree with the cause of that low self–esteem. My experience tells me that gang members are seeking boundaries that define what they can and cannot do.

The one common bond that exists in all gangs is external discipline. Every gang in this country has established rules and codes of conduct, which its members are expected to adhere to. Dress codes are an example. Many gangs tell their members either what they may wear or, more likely, what they may not wear. Punishment exists for the violation of these rules and codes of conduct, which is swift and certain and often physically painful. These punishments are viewed by the gang members as firm, fair, and consistent, equally applicable to all members of the gang, which suggests to me that gang members are not looking for individual empowerment but for someone to teach them how to succeed.

Rather than from needing more control over their lives, I believe their lack of self–esteem arises from having too much control over their lives and the lives of others around them. Think about it. Gang members routinely decide when and if they will attend school on any given day. They decide how they will cut their hair and what kinds of clothing they will wear. Many gang members decide whether to adorn their bodies with myriad tattoos. Most dictate to their parents when and if they will return after a night on the town. Some make decisions that affect the lives of those with whom they live.

The family of a gang member, by virtue of the gang member's autonomous authority, is at risk because of the gang member's decision to violate the law. There is always the risk when a gang member is in the house that the police will bust down the door to arrest him. The police are often more interested in their safety than in courtesy, and routinely run these kinds of arrest warrants with guns pointed toward those in the home. The police violating the sanctity of the home to search or arrest a gang member is a relatively minor risk for the family.

Because the gang member has decided to belong to a gang, his home can be identified as a target for other gang members. The idea that the home is a target implies that those who reside in the home are also targets. The biggest and most serious risk faced by family members of gang members is the danger of a drive–by shooting. Random bullets flying through the walls and rooms of a house can and do hit indiscriminate targets. How much more control does a gang member or, for that matter, anyone else need?

Gang members, regardless of age, are immature persons with a need, a craving, for adult leadership. The choices made by gang members are likely to be wrong choices made for the wrong reasons. They know it and so do we.

Like many other teenagers and young adults, gang members are living in a virtual reality world.

They are in effect living in their own movie. These gang members are the stars, writers, directors and producers of this movie. They believe they are in control of all the variables and are therefore in charge. For this reason many gang members have no fear. They have no fear of the school authority, no fear of the police, no fear of prison, of rival gang members, or of death. Any person who has no fear is a dangerous person indeed.

Normal children, with healthy levels of self–esteem, cannot make decisions until they have sufficient life experience on which to base a decision. This lack of life experience accounts for the reason many adolescents believe they are indestructible and that the world revolves around them. Combine this outlook with the no–fear outlook of most gang members, add a low self–esteem, and you have a recipe for poor decision making. Gang members cannot, on their own, see the risks to themselves, their families, or their neighbors inherent in the decisions they make.

If anyone needs to be empowered in this country, it is the parent and the community institutions. Respect for authority, sufficient to demand compliance with social rules of conduct, is the right of any civilized society. Social contracts, by which we all live, including gang societies, contain some demand for personal and social discipline. The first human beings that endeavored to live together had to establish rules of conduct to survive. Had they not done so, our planet would be populated by very strong, agile, and aggressive people who learned to use their muscles instead of their brains to survive. Only the very strong and agile could have survived.

The requirement that the rules of society be kept is necessary to ensure the maximum benefit for each member of the society. When the rules of conduct are followed, people can engage in trade. What you cannot make for yourself can be purchased or bargained for with skills or talents that you possess. As members of the community begin to specialize, they begin to have more free time to contemplate the problems of life and methods of dealing with those problems. Machines are invented to reduce the amount of physical work to produce food, goods, and services. Today's improvements in technology have resulted in a ton of free time for us all to contemplate the meaning of life.

Some Americans had enough free time, in 1776, to sit down and create a new form of government. During this creative process they established rules they thought should be obeyed by all. The rules and ideas were written in a document called the United States Constitution. Within the brief paragraphs of this document and the Bill of Rights, we Americans have established the rules of our society.

Little things such as life are more valuable than material things. One of my favorite rules is that we should not kill one another. How about this old favorite: a person's home is his sanctuary and it should be respected. Consider the novelty of a person's ability to express a differing opinion without fear of physical confrontation. All these things hold great value to most of us. Why don't gang members seem to hold them valuable as well?

The parent, the family, the community member all played a role in the abandonment of our nation's youths. We have left them with the inability to make sound decisions, lost in the vacuum of their meager life experiences. The American society, government, communities, schools, churches, parents, and the police will have to reassert themselves and commit to focusing on creating a sense of respect for the basic American rights of life, liberty, and the pursuit of happiness.

As parents, our responsibility is to raise strong, successful, and diligent members of our society. We must be allowed to teach our children discipline. Much of our inability to teach discipline to our children is because we are undisciplined ourselves. Government intervention in the management of discipline in community institutions such as schools also distracts us from teaching discipline to the child. Our elected officials, *we the people* placed in office, have created a situation where parents and teachers are afraid to expose themselves to civil and criminal liability for disciplining a child. Schools and parents cannot demand excellence unless they can also enforce common rules of decency and attention to the concerns of others—basic discipline. Discipline is not a dirty word and neither is it a naturally occurring phenomenon.

No human being is born with a sense of discipline. A parent or some other responsible adult must teach a child what is right and what is wrong. Consistent boundaries that remain intact help the child know the limits of his behavior. Understanding where the boundaries are is a very effective way of learning how to succeed within the rules. Over time the child will try the strength of these boundaries less and less frequently. Success within this kind of system leads to the development of a positive self–esteem.

When social boundaries are too flexible, it becomes difficult for the child to determine where the boundaries to deviant behavior are. The child then becomes confused as to where he fits into the structure of the system and must continue to assault the boundary limits. The purpose of these assaults is to try to determine where the line between right and wrong is. The child whose boundaries are forever shifting has no way to determine or measure success because there is no standard of conduct or behavior with which to compare his actions.

A child that experiences ineffective discipline becomes confused and often will engage in self–destructive and excessive behavior. His action is designed to get some kind of feedback from the parent. When the parent fails to respond to provocation and intentional disregard for his authority, the child becomes even more confused and begins to believe the parent does not care about him one way or another. An emotionally neglected child and a physically abused child share this sense of confusion about an internal sense of self–discipline.

Children who are beaten in the name of discipline are confused because the severity of the penalty does not fit the crime. They never have the opportunity to experience true external discipline and grow to have contempt for authority. Children in this situation will sometimes experiment with different kinds of excessive behavior. They hope to find a key that will identify what offense results in which punishment. During this experimentation many are attracted to the criminal street gang. The attraction? The rules are clearly stated and uniformly enforced.

Emotionally neglected children are very similar. They also engage in deviant behavior to get a response from their parents. Typically these kinds of parents are of the opinion that their children should be allowed to express themselves while they are young. The parents who feel this way take a very relaxed approach to external discipline and tend to allow their children to learn from mistakes. The children in such homes often misinterpret their parents' laissez–faire attitude as lack of concern. They begin to believe their parents do not care what they do or what happens to them. As a child's deviant behavior develops, no one seems to care enough to hold him accountable for his actions. So they continue to break the rules until they are arrested, imprisoned, or killed. This kind of child is also attracted to gangs because gangs care enough to tell them what the rules are and to enforce them.

The lack of effective external discipline or the use of physically brutal discipline will result in a child with lowered self–esteem and therefore one susceptible to many negative influences, among them criminal street gangs. Children crave firm, fair, and consistent discipline. This sort of discipline administered with care and love for the child creates stability. Parents, by their actions, must continually show their children that they can be trusted to frame their child's life.

What is wrong or right today must be wrong or right tomorrow. The child's safety and continued welfare depend on our leading them away from danger. Self–discipline is learned behavior—not something we are born with. We all learn to discipline ourselves because someone taught us where the boundaries were. When we traveled beyond those boundaries, someone brought us back around, swiftly and surely. Finally, we quit trying the boundaries and learned to stay within them.

When children are taught discipline by one or more parents, discipline becomes a habit that we know as self–discipline. Self–discipline results in more effective decision making, which leads to greater success within the system and outside the home; success outside the home results in confidence and a desire to continue that success. Sounds easy, doesn't it? Well, like this whole gang problem, it is easy to understand but extremely difficult to apply in reality.

The problem is that parents want to believe their kids. They want to build self–esteem by allowing certain freedoms and responsibilities to be experienced by their children. Equally important, however, is the safety of the child and the family. The conflict within most gang–member parents occurs long before the police get involved. Usually one or both parents see, but refuse to recognize, the signs of trouble. The child is going though a phase, etc. This critical time is the stage of the gang member's development when he is seeking to test the boundaries of parental authority. Parents who follow established standards against these attempts to breach these boundaries may have periods of rebellion but rarely end up with gang members for children.

Parents who allow their children to travel beyond established boundaries invite the destruction of the child and possibly the family itself. These children will seek out new boundaries to conquer. The parent who allows this to occur has lost control of his child and will find it twice as difficult to reestablish parental control. More often than not, the child will attempt to conquer social boundaries that will involve him with the police or with social care agencies. The conflict created in the family from such contacts further reduces the likelihood that the child can be reclaimed. Finally, the child becomes totally committed to the gang and views crime as a legitimate employment opportunity. Parents are not the only ones to blame for the present condition of our youths. There is plenty of blame to be shared with the community institutions.

Just like the family, the institutions of our society have given power to the individual offender and have placed us all at serious risk. The justice system is a mess. The perception among offenders is that there is no real punishment for committing a crime. Complicated formulas are used to determine how much time each convict should serve. In some states each day represents three days based on an eight–hour workday. Obeying the rules of the prison and not causing problems is considered good time.

There is extra credit for trustee status. And on and on. A result is that the prisoner does little of the time to which he was sentenced by a jury of his peers.

The juvenile systems are just as bad. They fail to account for the extreme violent and criminal behavior so common in the juvenile offender of today. Most systems were established to rehabilitate the errant youth who was a discipline problem—the truant, the petty thief, the runaway. These were the kinds of "crimes" most juvenile justice systems were designed to handle.

Today juvenile offenders are being handled at younger ages for more sophisticated types of crimes—burglary, robbery, sale and use of narcotics, major assaultive offenses, and murder. Both the penal and juvenile justice systems are failing to rehabilitate or to punish the criminal offender. The systems are the social last line of defense against anarchy and they are coming apart at an ever–increasing rate.

Schools, at the urging of a vocal liberal minority, have continually relaxed standards and have allowed minor children to have significant say about the policy of the school district. Remember when smoking was prohibited in any part of the school? Try approved smoking areas on for size. Remember when boys and girls had to follow a strict dress code? Remember when the school and the church were the focal points of a community? Corner convenience stores and fast–food parking lots seem to have taken their place. There is hope on the horizon, though. Now some school districts are trying to reclaim their campuses and have begun reestablishing stricter dress and conduct codes. Municipal governments are passing no-smoking ordinances for public buildings. Things are looking up.

We must take some power back from the child and reassert our authority over the lives of our children. We, as a society, must establish social boundaries of conduct, which must be enforced swiftly and surely and must also be administered firmly, fairly, and consistently.

We need to empower our other community institutions—the schools and churches—so that they can reinforce the values taught in the home. Schools need the power to hold all students to the same standard of conduct to facilitate learning. Most teachers will agree that in general conversation parents vocalize their support of the school engaging in discipline to maintain order and safety. The same teachers will likely tell you that some of those same parents intend for that authority to extend to other people's children, but not their own.

Schools presently must rely on the parent to establish credible authority over the child. That is as it should be, however; more parents need to listen to the school's side of an issue before entrenching themselves behind the child's explanation of the matter. A legitimate decision based on a clear understanding by the parent of both sides of the issue displays a sense of respect for authority and for justice, despite the outcome for the child. Whether you negotiate a lesser penalty, accept the school recommendation for punishment, or clear up a misunderstanding that results in a reversal by the school, you have displayed respect for the authority of the school, and your child understands that facts and truth win out over half truth and deception.

Schools can help the parents simply by establishing and strictly enforcing rules of conduct. One easy rule that is quickly enforceable is a dress code. Isn't it the responsibility of adults to teach the children how to succeed in society? What field of endeavor does not have some sort of dress requirement? Even narcotic officers and dope dealers dress according to a standard. Why can't we require our children to adhere to a standard of dress for school?

Many parents, after an initial battle with the idea, will agree that a dress code gives the parent an excuse to modify the way their children dress. "Honey, I just can't buy those really baggy pants and shirts you want because you can't wear them to school and we are shopping for school clothes today." See how that works? Instead of fighting a dress code, parents ought to be demanding one and that it be uniformly enforced. The ultimate dress code is the school uniform. Having had a child attend a public and a private school, I can tell you that it costs a lot less to buy uniforms than name–brand pants and shirts, and let's not even talk about shoes. Working together is the key between parents and schools. It should not be an adversarial relationship; you both want the same thing: a child to grow into a responsible adult.

Religious organizations are another source of self–discipline for a child. The practice of various religions can do nothing but help a child understand what his family and culture stand for, and should be encouraged, even mandated, by the child's parents. A family's religious beliefs are generally at the core of their concept of right and wrong. Most religions recognize the authority of the state and teach values beneficial to the survival of the individual in a social environment. Even atheists agree that people should respect the rights, property, and persons of others.

One purpose of government is to protect its members (society) from the influence of those who would violate the social contract by deviating from decent and responsible conduct and causing a person's safety to be threatened. I believe Americans have lost sight of this purpose of government; therefore a complete conceptual overhaul of the purpose of prison has to be undertaken. The time has come to reassess the value of punishment as a rehabilitative agent.

It seems to me that the recent episode of an American citizen being caned in Singapore brings this issue into focus. The American media and the population debated a long time over this issue. Some were glad to see a young American getting his comeuppance while others railed at the inhumanity of the situation. I do not think that anyone would wish a caning on anyone. So what was the attraction?

Many people believed that Singapore was doing what this country should do to curb crime and violence. I am not, however, suggesting that we establish caning as a punishment in America. Singapore residents experience and expect swift and sure consequences for violations of their social contract. This expectation happens to include severe physical punishment. The result? Very little crime in Singapore.

What I believe attracted many to the Singapore incident was the idea of swift, sure punishment administered firmly, fairly, and consistently. American interest in the Singapore incident is more about consistent expectations than about physically beating someone with a cane.

Let's talk about that. Our Constitution holds protections for our citizens. Among these are the right to due process of law, of protection from unreasonable search and seizure, and protection from cruel and unusual punishment, which rights are intended to protect the individual from the government. The same document also protects the rights of the individual to pursue happiness and to be secure in their person and their property, which rights were established to empower the government to protect people from criminals.

Every time a criminal steals, assaults, robs, pillages, or plunders, he is violating the civil rights of another person, just as surely as the rights of Rodney King were violated by some overzealous police. Once the state has met its obligation to provide due process of law, it should have the authority to punish a person for violating the rights of another. Punishment is, by definition, a painful experience. Pain comes in many shapes and forms, the most obvious of which is physical pain. A more devastating pain, however, is the loss of freedom.

Prison should be a place where social deviants at first lose all freedom. The resolve of the community not to tolerate criminal conduct should be made abundantly clear to the prisoner. There is no good reason why prisoners should have access to television sets, libraries, newspapers, telephones, etc. Likewise there is no reason a prisoner should not be expected to earn his way by working for the state, to offset the costs of housing and caring for him. The idea put simply: When you violate the rights of another you forfeit your own rights for a period of time established by a jury of your peers.

To protect the prisoner from cruel and unusual punishment, which total isolation from the rest of the world could be considered, access to television, newspapers, libraries, educational opportunities, and the like could be a privilege that could be earned. Once the prisoner accepts his lack of freedom as punishment, he will be ready to accept help in rehabilitating himself. At the point the prisoner realizes the value of the freedom he has lost he will be willing to relearn the social standards to which he will be held accountable on release from prison.

Changes should also be made in the judicial arena. The courts should reassess the value of plea bargaining. I often wonder who is getting the bargain. Inconsistent administration of punishment leads to contempt for those who operate the system and a total disrespect for the rule of law.

Take conviction of a first-time burglar, for example. Some of these cases are offered a two-year or three-year deferred adjudication, which means that when you complete your probation the record of your conviction is sealed or destroyed—erased for practical purposes. Other first-time burglars may get two or three years of regular probation; a third group goes to prison. The disparity of punishments results from plea bargaining. Criminals learn quickly that they can negotiate a better deal. They are given the power to decide their own punishment. Consequently no respect is given the prosecutor, the judge, or the law (social contract). Even those who receive very long prison sentences can beat the system by parole, early release, or some other innovative program designed to open more prison beds for the mass of youths cramming the criminal justice system.

Many of these youths are experienced criminals in their own right because of antiquated juvenile laws. Legislation needs to be enacted that removes investigative barriers from law enforcement organization pertaining to juvenile records. Laws such as denying the police the opportunity to maintain fingerprint and photographic records of juveniles allow some children to commit numerous and serious crimes without detection. A child who can commit any number of serious felonies without getting caught just might get the idea that he is not accountable for his actions. Criminal conduct becomes a habit that is very difficult to break.

The prohibition against using juvenile records in an adult court during the punishment phase of a trial should be lifted. Jurors need to know that this young offender is a career burglar who has now been caught for the first time as an adult. It should make a difference to the community. Although not 100 percent, past actions speak loudly about what actions can be expected from the defendant in the future, should he be left to his own devices. Honorable people have a habit and past history of acting honorably; there is a very good chance that an honorable person will act honorably in the future. Similarly, a dishonorable person will tend to continue in dishonorable pursuits.

I offer these suggestions to illustrate how the justice system, government, schools, churches, and other social institutions should be helping one another and parents. These groups and persons should be working together to resolve gang and youth violence issues. The key to success is offered by the gangs themselves: swift, sure punishment carried out firmly, fairly and consistently. When our society reassesses the appropriateness of these concepts, we will be turning the tide to a safer environment for ourselves and our children.

8

DENIAL

The biggest obstacle faced by any person, community, or government entity is denial. All the problems created in the community by youths who become attracted to gangs are simple to resolve compared with the problem of denial. Gang experts from California to Chicago repeat the same message to law enforcement officials in almost every seminar or class given for police officers who must deal with gangs: Quit denying the existence of gangs and accept their presence in the community. Only when denial ceases can action be taken and resources dedicated to deal with the real problems created by gangs. For some reason, despite all the expert advice, none of us want to admit that our city, school, or child is involved with gangs.

Denial of the gang problem by any community or person increases the potential of further gang activity and increases the probability that the gang problem will grow. Without a parent's denial, a child cannot dress like a gang member or hang out with other kids who want to become gang members. Denial by school officials allows gangs to promote themselves and recruit more members, thereby spreading the "disease" throughout the school. Without the denial of the community, gang members could not commit petty crimes or get away with any violence. When the community turns a collective blind eye to the activities of the gangs, the gangs can travel and organize without fear of being discovered. The gang becomes more bold as the community continues to ignore the issue. Crime increases and the community continues to try to ignore the gang issue until, at some point, the community must acknowledge the problem. By that time, however, the problem has usually grown past the capability of the community to effectively deal with the gangs.

Denial by city leaders prevents spending money and committing resources to deal with the problem. When there is no gang problem, there is no need to hire or train police to deal with it. Gang units require manpower, vehicles, computers, and other technological items, which cost taxpayer dollars. There are always other projects that could use those dollars, and because the gang issue is not real, in our city, we can defer the money to these other projects.

Denial by state and federal legislators leads to laws that encourage the conduct and reduce the accountability of gang members. A good example occurred with the 1993 Texas legislature. Texas had been experiencing a prison–overcrowding problem, so its legislators decided that decriminalization would effectively correct the problem. The state reduced the penalty range for auto theft, unauthorized use of a motor vehicle, and certain kinds of drug possession charges. Gang members like to steal cars and sell drugs. Now they can steal cars and sell drugs and face lighter penalties if they are caught in Texas.

Our system of law requires that persons be held accountable for their actions. Generally this is a good practice. The difficulty with not recognizing gangs is that we fail to recognize the importance of the presence of other gang members at the scene of a crime. When three people walk into a Stop-'n'-Rob convenience store and one of them robs the clerk, the other two, if they have not participated in any other way, cannot be charged with the crime. Failure to recognize the importance of the presence of other gang members at the crime means that some of the participants in the robbery go unpunished and the one who committed the crime cannot have his offense enhanced under organized crime statutes. A number of states do not yet recognize membership in a criminal street gang as constituting more than mere presence at the scene of a gang-related crime.

Because I am most familiar with the Texas penal code I will use it as an example. In Texas the state prosecutors must prove that a person, alleged to have participated in a crime, has committed some act in furtherance of the crime other than merely being present at the scene. That means that each person participating in a robbery, for example, has to do something to help the robber commit the crime. One could hold the weapon, another give the orders, and a third take the belongings from the victim. The problem with this scenario is that gangs often roam in packs and commit crimes as a group.

Imagine that you are walking down the street and are confronted by four gang members. You know they are gang members because of their distinctive dress.

They are carrying themselves in a hostile and menacing fashion and they look mean. One orders you to give up the wallet. You comply immediately. Why? You have not seen a weapon yet. There has been no explicit threat directed to you. Why did you give up the wallet?

You gave up the wallet because you knew these young men were together. Although not stated, the threat was very clear to you: If you did not give up the wallet, these four young thugs would beat the daylights out of you and steal your wallet. Only one of the thugs spoke to you; the other three remained silent and merely stood there. In a system that denies gang crime exists, this kind of crime will go unrecognized. The state denies the possibility that groups of people using their presence as intimidation is in fact an act in furtherance of the crime. The intimidation was the weapon in this case. You might not have surrendered your wallet unless you felt threatened by the presence of the four men.

When a person joins a gang, he realizes that crimes will be committed in his presence and he may be required to participate in some of these crimes if they are directed by a more senior gang member. A gang member must also make a physical gesture as a sign of commitment to the gang when he joins, usually as a "jump–in" ritual. The prospective candidate is physically beaten by several members of the gang. Taking the beating demonstrates the candidate's willingness to follow the rules of the gang and protect fellow gang members from the police.

Submitting to the beating is a requirement, a rule, of most gangs. The new member is given a story to tell his parents about the circumstances of the assault. When the police are called by the parent, the child must remain silent, decline to prosecute, or give false information to the police—evidence the new gang member is willing to protect the gang from the police or other authority figures.

All street gangs have a rule about backing up a fellow gang member. Usually backing up someone means that you, the new gang member, must get involved in an assaultive offense, up to and including murder. The gang will use the excuse that their rivals have committed a terrible wrong that cannot go unpunished. Further, gang members are expected to perform as surrogate family members and, at least on the surface, provide for the needs of one another, such as money, where gang-related robberies, burglaries, and thefts come into play.

A gang member's presence at the scene of a crime serves three purposes. First, the gang member who watches is a witness to the bravery of the acting gang members. As a witness he recounts the excitement and verifies the story told later to other members of the gang. Being there when the crime occurred enhances the status of the person who relates the story. Second, the presence of many gang members intimidates the victim and reduces the risks involved in committing the crime. The victim, for instance, might resist one or two attackers but would probably not resist four or six. Additionally, more people at the scene reduces the chance that the victim will be able to describe the one who committed the robbery. Third, the new gang member learns his gang craft by watching others commit the crimes he will later commit.

Denying the criminal intent inherent in street gangs limits the efforts to prosecute gang members under more stringent organized–crime conspiracy laws. Rarely will a prosecuting attorney accept charges on a gang member who was merely present but took no action during the crime. State and federal lawmakers must recognize and enact laws that will allow gang members to be held equally accountable for the actions of their fellow members who commit crimes in their presence.

Adult and juvenile laws need to allow for the prosecution of every gang member present during the commission of a crime. Additionally, juvenile laws must allow the police to maintain local files, records, and photographs of juveniles, of any age, who commit felony offenses. Parole, probation, good time, and fancy formulas designed to reduce overcrowding must be stopped for adult and juvenile correctional facilities. City and county officials must take equally bold action.

Let's face it: gangs are not the chamber of commerce thing to talk about. No mayor or county judge wants to admit that a gang problem exists in their area of responsibility. Gang problems do not promote the growth of business or industry in any city or county. When the mayor or county judge fails to get these companies and businesses to move into his city or county, opportunities for jobs are lost. Fear of public panic about the gang issue may, in the minds of these leaders, lead to businesses moving their operations to other communities resulting in a loss of jobs in the area. City and other government leaders are motivated, therefore, not to talk too loudly about a gang problem.

Denying a gang problem exists ensures that the city or county will experience the social decay it seeks to avoid. Residents of gang–infested areas begin to lose faith in the ability of their governmental leaders to deal effectively with the gang problem. People will begin to move to areas where they believe they will be more safe. As they leave, tax revenues begin to drop and trade begins to diminish; the town, city, or county begins to suffer and may die altogether—certainly not a very promising forecast.

Gangs in a neighborhood are like tooth decay. You can ignore a bad tooth for years but the tooth will continue to get worse. At some point it will become rotten to the core and begin to cause great pain. If you live with the pain, the tooth may become abscessed and ultimately you will have to spend perhaps thousands of dollars to correct the problem. The alternative is to take care of the problem early. The discomfort of having to get a tooth filled is substantially preferable to the pain and expense resulting from root canal therapy. There is the added benefit of restoring the tooth to health and keeping it longer. Similarly, the pain of spending money and resources to recognize and deal with gang members while the gangs are just forming is very small compared with the expense and resources needed to deal with an entrenched gang subculture.

School districts typically deny gang problems exist until the problem is so out of hand that no one can deny it. Think about how school officials view this problem. Who wants to send their children to a gang–infested school? This point is not lost on school administrators or school boards, who believe that when a school district admits to having a gang problem, parents will move out of the school system. When this happens, schools stand to lose tax revenue. The same descending scale that affects the general tax base is feared by most rational school boards and administrations. The bottom line is the same in their minds: our school district will lose revenue and prestige if we admit a problem exists. The flaw in this type of thinking is that it fails to account for the human ability to deal with adversity.

Consider the problem from the perspective of the parent. As the gang problem continues to grow in the school environment, the parents are hearing reports of "isolated acts of violence" on the evening news. Their children come home and tell them about the gang fight at school today. Eventually the children begin to complain to their parents that they are afraid to attend certain classes or school functions. Bus rides to and from school begin to be adventures in urban survival. The bus stops in some neighborhoods become like watering holes to predators. The prey (children) can always be found by the predator (gang members) at exactly the same time and place every school day.

Parents naturally become alarmed and attempt to communicate their fears to the school principal, who tells them that there are no gangs at this school. The principals usually are aware of the deceit but feel they can do nothing about the gang problem because there is an "unwritten school district policy" dictating that gang activity be denied to prevent general panic. Parents have three options at this point: (1) they can believe their child is lying; (2) they can believe the principal is unaware of the problems in the school and cannot, therefore, protect the child from these gang members; or (3) they can believe that the principal is intentionally lying to them. The third option implies that the administration is aware of the problem but is unable or unwilling to take measures to protect the child.

None of these options are positive for the school. They certainly do not lead the parent to have much confidence in the ability of the school to deal with these serious problems. Parents may decide to leave the school district and enroll their children in a "safer" school. The irony is that the school was trying to avoid this move by denying the gangs exist and it is likely their denial provoked the parents to move.

Consider what might happen if school administrators were more open. It is comforting to some degree to realize that the problems you have are not yours alone and that others have experienced them and survived. If a parent approaches a school principal about gangs, and the problem does exist, the principal should acknowledge it.

"Yes, we do have a gang problem here but we are working on solving it. Our teachers and administrative staff are receiving regular training in how to defuse or deal with gang situations and we have a strong disciplinary policy regarding gang activity. We are also working closely with the police to help solve crimes committed by gang members that attend this school so that they can help us remove them from our campus."

The parent can be satisfied that his child is being truthful, that the school district is aware of the problem, and that they are doing everything possible to protect the children. Instead of becoming provoked to leave the school district, the parent might become inspired to join the battle and help the school district rid itself of gangs. The actions and deportment of the school principal who acknowledges difficult problems and has the courage to face them often inspires parents to get more involved themselves because someone else cares enough to try.

While school officials are busy denying that gangs exist, the gangs are allowed to use the schools as a source of new membership and communication networks. Gang members brag to other students about how they cannot be controlled by the administration or the teachers. To gang members, adults who permit the wearing of gang colors to school and allow students to engage in all manner of gang activity on school property are weak or stupid. This position is supported, in the minds of other students, when gang members appear to commit major infractions of school rules with relative impunity. After all, what is a few days suspension to a tough guy gang member? The result is that many of the students view the gang member as exciting or cool and therefore worthy of imitation.

All the while, gang members are finding and identifying potential recruits—students who, like themselves, do not seem to fit into the mainstream of campus life. When a student begins to imitate the clothing and characteristics of a gang member, he is noticed by one or more gangs, who will seek to recruit him.

Everyone who has ever attended an American middle or high school can appreciate the effectiveness of the local "grapevine" information superhighway. Like all other grapevine communication networks the information is not likely accurate. Kids use this network throughout their school life and many believe the information is accurate. The fact is that the battles and experiences reported by or attributed to gang members are often larger than life. The stories become more interesting as time passes and as they are embellished by more and more storytellers. The inflated stories continue to grow and ultimately make it back to the originating gang, whose members bask in the glory of these expanded adventures. Rival gang members, not to be outdone, either start rumors or act so as to establish their group as the subject of this school yard gossip machine. Gang members sometimes get caught up in believing their own publicity and will commit a more heinous crime than that attributed to their enemy. When two or more members of rival gangs confront one another, conflict is unavoidable. One group must establish itself as the more aggressive or dominant gang.

All this activity occurs under the very noses of the teachers, principals, and administrators, who are too busy denying a gang problem exists to notice what has happened to the school. The students, meanwhile, soon become more interested in the latest gang rumors than in what teachers say in the classroom.

Upscale communities are also deep into denial that continues to promote gang activity. The more prestigious the neighborhood, the deeper the denial. Gang members suffer more from low self–esteem than lack of money. Many wealthy children suffer from low self–esteem, as do middle– and lower–income children. All are subject to becoming attracted to gangs. The only difference is that the wealthy gang member has parents who can afford to post his bond and can hire a more expensive attorney.

Members of the community wield the real power to deal with a gang problem. A community is, after all, a collection of those who live and work in an area. From this pool of community members come the witnesses to the crimes committed by local gang members, who can testify in court and hold criminal gang members accountable for their actions. Within this pool of community members are business owners who could provide job opportunities for some of the local youths. There are artists, musicians, political leaders, and even athletes who could spend some of their time sharing their knowledge and skills with the community youths.

Legal and educational reform are two important ingredients that can have an impact on the growth of gangs in this country. Adult community members elect and serve as elected officials on school boards and governmental bodies. The community should elect people willing to change the legal system to protect the community from those who would destroy it. They ought to elect school board members willing to help and support administrators trying to reestablish discipline in the classrooms and hallways of their schools. We all know this is true but it is very difficult to accomplish.

The difficulty lies in the practical side of life. Most community members are too afraid of retaliation to step forward if they see a crime committed. Gang members are very scary, individually and in groups. They depend on intimidation to hold entire neighborhoods at bay while they plunder and pillage at will.

The irony of this fearful denial is that the witness who chooses not to be part of the solution today will very likely be the victim tomorrow. The rationalization that I will mind my own business and not get involved creates a situation whereby a felon can remain undetected in your neighborhood. The felon may get around to victimizing the witness to a previous crime. The witness, now the victim, longs for someone who saw the crime committed against him to come forward and help put the thug away this time. It doesn't happen, however, because the witness in this case is also too afraid to stand up to the criminal. The cycle of crime and violence continues, and the neighborhood, the community, is paralyzed by fear of gangs.

Neighborhood fear of gangs promotes gang activity by allowing the members of the gang to roam throughout the neighborhood without fear of being challenged. The youths who live in the neighborhood see that gang members are feared by the adults and are given a wide berth. To the young people interested in feeling important, this situation seems like a made–to–order prescription. Again the gang grows.

The ultimate power within the community is the parent, whose responsibility it is to teach his child the skills necessary to survive in the social environment. When a parent denies that a son or daughter has begun to affiliate with a gang, he sentences his child to a lifetime of failure. Parenting is a tough job. Developing the skill to discipline without damaging the fragile self–esteem of a young human being is a formidable task indeed.

Some people do not distinguish between discipline and abuse. Children should not have to suffer the physical or emotional pain that abusive parents force upon them. Equally damaging, in my opinion, however, is the home without discipline, which will also produce children who have a distorted picture of reality and suffer incredibly low self–esteem. My experience with gang members and other young offenders tells me that there is little discernible difference between low self–esteem caused by physical or psychological abuse and that caused by the parent who chooses not to discipline his children at all. Both child-rearing practices tend to give the child the impression that he is worthless.

The child in the physically abusive home may feel hated by the parent. He may come to believe that he is worthless and deserving of this contempt because even his parents have no use for him. The child who receives no discipline at all may have similar feelings, for different reasons. He may come to believe that his parents do not care what happens to him because no matter what he does it seems to be fine with his parents. He begins to believe that they are worthless. If your parents don't care what happens to you, who else will care? If they don't care, why should I?

Discipline is not about beating a child into submission. Discipline is the setting of limits and holding the child accountable for his actions. Administered firmly, fairly, and consistently, discipline can encourage and develop self–esteem and self–discipline. With this process all human beings, since the beginning of time, have learned the requirements of social survival. Discipline can take place only when the parent and the child understand where and what the boundaries are and what will happen if the child crosses those boundaries.

When parents do teach discipline in the home, the child gains a more accurate picture of reality and therefore a better opportunity for success. Parents who have firmly held to specific principles and codes of conduct create a confident child who understands the social rules. The external use of discipline by the parent incorporates the values and rules of conduct into the psyche of the child. As the child negotiates the social environment successfully, less and less external discipline is required by the parent. Knowledge of the boundaries has given the child the ability to discipline himself and avoid conflicting with social expectations. As the child grows and continues to make appropriate decisions, his esteem rises with his self–discipline.

When the child violates a rule of conduct and is not disciplined, he becomes confused. Was the conduct appropriate or not? The rule says the action is not appropriate, yet the parent made no effort to discipline the child. The lesson learned is that a particular rule does not apply to the child.

When the child repeats the behavior and is soundly punished, he begins to have doubts about the information he is receiving from the parent. The lack of consistency creates an environment of mistrust and may result in a very rebellious child, one constantly trying to determine when behavior is appropriate and when it is not. Add brutality to the mix and unfair discipline and the mistrust of the parent can lead to outright violence directed toward the parent and later toward society. The lowered self–esteem caused by a lack of discipline or by brutality disguised as discipline creates a situation where the child must fail.

The lack of consistent standards resulting from no discipline or brutality makes it very difficult for the child to compare his decisions with a socially acceptable standard. When there are no firm standards, whatever decisions the child makes can only be considered correct. Because the child thinks there are no standards and that whatever he does is correct, he is destined to fail in the larger community. The social failure and the inability to understand why they are failing create a lowered self–esteem.

A common mistake of many parents of gang members who deny their children are involved in gang activity is coming to the defense of the child, regardless of the facts. This parent will take the side of the child despite overwhelming and compelling evidence against the child. He believes that the teacher, school, the police, and the world in general are out to get his child. I have always been amazed at some of the questions asked by parents on their arrival at the police station to retrieve their errant children. My favorite question is: "What did you [police] do to my son that made him act crazy enough to get arrested?"

A child must be taught the rules and expectations of the community in which he will live. A parent who automatically assumes the child's behavior is the fault of someone else teaches the child that he is not responsible for his behavior. A parent who denies clear evidence that his child is involved in a gang encourages the child to continue to make poor decisions and teaches him to totally disregard the social contract to which he will ultimately be held to account. Children with parents like these have a very difficult time learning that society will hold them accountable through social sanctions.

A parent who protects his child from the consequences of his actions teaches him that none of society's rules apply; thus the child learns contempt for the authority of the school, police, and courts. The kind of parent I have described undermines the ability of the school and the community to enforce rules. A result is that his child becomes a threat to the community. The community will protect itself from such threats at the expense of his child.

9
THE CURE

It has taken the United States of America well over two hundred years to get into the condition it finds itself in today. There are no quick fixes or magical cures. American morals are overweight and out of shape. We must change our collective diet and embark on a moral fitness program if we are to correct the problems of today's young people.

American society was once a melting pot for world cultures. People used to come to America and became Americans. The heat has cooled and the pot is now congealing into separate clumps of various ethnic backgrounds. Today there are African Americans, Hispanic Americans, Irish Americans, Indian Americans, native Americans...the list is endless.

Specialized treatment for immigrants has resulted in a desire among other groups to receive specialized treatment. In some cities, street signs and business signs are displayed in two or more languages. Our educational system spends millions of dollars teaching students in their native language. These things are all quite convenient for the immigrant but they promote separatism within the community. Consequently various ethnic and minority groups compete for the education dollar. Each group seeks dominance in trying to become the prevailing "empowered" group. The only ones who lose are the children.

Children of immigrants become confused when their parents' morality and the comparative immorality of the American culture collide about what is right and what is wrong. Should they follow the standards of their parents or should they try to conform to the standards of the American culture? The immigrant children are jealous of the apparent financial independence of their American–born counterparts. It seems the American kids have no difficulty in purchasing or acquiring the latest style of shoes, clothes, and electronic devices.

American kids, however, may become jealous of the attention given the immigrant families, particularly by the power base of the community, such as the school district that recognizes the contribution of one immigrant group and not others. The city council that erects street signs in English and one Asian language, while ignoring the Spanish language barrier, contributes to the sense that the power base of the community supports these groups more than the mainstream of the U.S. population. Conflict between groups then becomes inevitable. Some of this conflict is manifested in the formation of street gangs, which are very separatist. The common street gang seeks to separate its membership from the rest of the world and lay claim to the right to "rule" the neighborhood.

One's heritage is an important part of who and what one becomes in life. I am not suggesting that people who come to America should forget their native heritage. What I mean to say is that we should work toward an American culture. The tapestry of the various immigrant cultures should be valued. However, the common interests of all these groups should be melded into one collective culture, which we call American. If there is no American culture, where do children of mixed ethnicity or race belong?

Should I research and become more Scottish because my heritage derives from Scotland on my father's side? Or should I learn the ways of a Frenchman because my mother's side was French? What shall I teach my son? His ancestry is now Scottish, French, and German, because his mother is of German descent. What about *his* son or daughter? You can see how the problem compounds with each generation.

It is more practical and much easier for a parent to teach a child about his family heritage than to require society to teach all cultures equally. We need to recognize, as a society, that American culture is more important in America than any other culture.

Our Constitution lists certain inalienable rights that can be neither amended nor abridged. Certain truths are held to be self–evident; chief among these are that all men (and women) are created equal. We have built the strongest nation the world has ever known on these principles. Now is the time to turn back and refocus on them sanely and sensibly.

Three areas of our American system need correcting: the family, the community and the law. Laws pertaining to general welfare of the community must be changed as must prison facilities used to enforce the law, both of which are short–term responses to crime. Corrections have to be made to reestablish the credibility of the law.

Our society must commit itself to reinforcing common values, such as those that pertain to life, liberty, and the pursuit of happiness. The nuclear family structure must be returned to a highly re-garded and honored place in our society. American families need to participate more in the lives of their children.

What follows are some ways in which positive change in the structure of the family, the commu-nity's perception of right and wrong, and the struc-ture of the law can be made. Some may consider these ideas controversial but they are founded on a simple theory that promises broken cause contempt but promises kept create respect.

The Family

I am obliged to mention the role of parents in these suggestions for change, because it is the most im-portant role. This subject is exceedingly touchy and one that I approach with the greatest of care. Let me preface my comments about the family with this statement: I believe that families will continue as they have in the past. I do not think it likely that the role of parents will change because of this book.

Problem parents are not likely to read this book or take an active interest in the lives of their chil-dren—those who physically or psychologically abuse their children, ignore their kids, or are just too tired to deal with them are not likely to be interested in the contents of this book. Parents simply not aware of the dangers their children are in when they emulate the gang look will benefit from this book. These parents will have the greatest impact in reducing the threat of gang violence in the neighborhood.

The absolute cure for crime can be illustrated with an equilateral triangle. The base of the triangle is the family. The left side is the law enforcement/judiciary/penal system. The right side is the community itself—the people, churches, schools, and the like. When the three elements of the triangle depend on each other, they can help the youths avoid serious trouble, in theory. No community that I am aware of has ever been able to rely on the base of that triangle—the family.

We must come to grips, as a nation, with the fact that we will not be able to get the families of gang members to join the struggle. We should continue to try to recruit the parents of gang members and try to get them more involved in the lives of their children. We must also realize, however, that we cannot count on great success working with parents. Understanding the reality of the situation dictates that we attempt to succeed through social training of our youths.

Supporting the school's authority to set standards and establish rules is a good start. Supporting laws that promote social accountability and institutions that enforce the social standards, prisons, and youth facilities are vital. Finally, we must understand that leadership by example is what our children need and expect. We, as parents, teachers, and responsible adults, must live our lives responsibly and thoughtfully.

The mother of a fourteen–year-old gang member once said that she had done all that she could for her child. She said that her solution was to turn the problem over to God, who was going to have to turn her son around. Her position was that she had taught her son the difference between right and wrong and that God would now have to turn him back on the road she taught him to travel. This woman's comments reminded me of a story I heard when I was young.

The story is about a God–fearing man caught in a terrible flood. Two men in a small rowboat were trying to rescue people and came upon a man standing on the roof of his home in knee–deep water. The man was obviously deep in prayer. The men in the boat called out to him and offered to take him to safety. He refused. He told his would–be rescuers that he was a godly man and had faith in the Lord that the waters would subside soon. The men in the boat left.

Several hours later a second boat came by and those in the boat saw that the water had risen to just below the man's chin. They told the man the river was still rising and wasn't supposed to crest until the water reached another ten feet. He was firm in his conviction and said that he was devout and had faith that God would not let him drown. Again he refused rescue and the boat left.

A few minutes later a helicopter rescue unit saw the man on the roof struggling to keep his nose above the water. They lowered a rope and told him to grab onto it and they would pull him to safety. He again refused. Above the noise of the helicopter they heard him yelling something about God not forsaking him because he had great faith in him. The man drowned.

When his soul arrived in heaven the man was ticked off. He told St. Peter that he wanted an immediate audience with God and that he wanted an explanation why God had allowed him to drown. After all, he was a devout and faithful man and had many years left that he had been looking forward to serving God with. After his little tirade, a booming voice reverberated through heaven. God explained the situation to the man, reminding him that he sent two boats and a helicopter to rescue him but his help had been refused.

The moral of the story is that we must use the tools and resources we are provided to extract ourselves from danger. We must never give up on our youths. If we do we will all lose. Hard work and grim determination will reduce and maybe even eradicate gangs from our neighborhoods. We must do the work. We cannot depend on divine intervention, for like the man in the story we probably cannot recognize it when offered.

We are in a war for the lives of our children. The battles and the war will be won by one parent, street, community, town, county, and state at a time. Some battles will be hard fought and costly. If we are going to turn the tide on this epidemic of gang and youth violence, however, we will have to fight and win. Those of us who join in battle for the hearts and minds of our nation's youth must never waiver or surrender.

The Community

Why do human beings live in social settings? Human beings are not fast enough to catch wild game. If we could catch it, we are not strong enough to kill it and eat it. We are, frankly, physically defenseless against anything larger than a house cat. We do possess a brain, however. That brain has shared information with other human beings over the years and ideas have been born—weapons for protection and hunting, farming tools and skills, shared labor resulting in enough to share with all. These are some of the reasons we began to live in communities. Individual skills began to increase. Some excelled at manufacturing; others were good at providing raw materials. I hate to kill and skin deer, but I like to make and sharpen spear points, so I'll trade spear points for venison. My family gets fed and I don't have to lug a 150–pound deer for a mile and a half across the prairie.

Human beings live in communities for protection from predators, real or imagined, to improve our ability to succeed, and to benefit from the skills and knowledge of others. There are, however, certain drawbacks. Among these are human predators.

Because some human beings were predatory, communities had to establish rules of conduct. The community elders or chiefs began settling disputes between community members. When members were shown to be incorrigible they were banned from the community or summarily executed, depending on the rule violated. Over the centuries these common rules took on the effect of law. They became known, in English–speaking countries, as common law.

The communities that make up the social fabric in this country also are important in the future of our American cultural morality, perhaps stronger and more important than corrections in law, which will be discussed later. Communities set the social expectations and guidelines on which we base our system of justice. Community expectations are ultimately what we are required to follow in order to live within the community peacefully and productively.

American community standards have eroded over time, allowing those who prey on the weakness of others to prosper. A result is increased crime and a heavier burden on the social systems designed to deal with crime. The only method of combating further erosion is to undertake the difficult task of re-organizing collective community standards. Simply speaking, national and local community standards need to be raised.

I am constantly amazed by many of the gang members with whom I have had contact. They almost always have some sense of the bigger picture. They know that they are feared in the community, and derive their sense of power from that fear. They know the community doesn't like them but they consider the community weak because, generally, the community tolerates much activity within the neighborhoods. The gangs themselves do not tolerate any other gang and do not understand how a group could tolerate them—unless it is weak and unable to respond. If so, the neighborhood and the community, create an opportunity for the gang members to commit more violence, and the residents of the community become targets of the violence.

A criminal street gang depends on the community ignoring their actions. When the gang is ignored it can and does grow. As the gang grows it affects the neighborhood more and always negatively. Graffiti increases, violence increases, fear increases, and perceived safety levels diminish, which results in lowered property value. Then others not interested in the condition of the neighborhood move in. They will be the undesirables: prostitutes, drug addicts, thieves, robbers, burglars, and more gang members. Neighborhoods and communities must band together to have an impact on gangs and crime.

When was the last time you could name at least one person who lived in every house on your street? There was a time when neighbors knew one another and what children belonged to which family. This familiarity was a source of concern to me as I was growing up. I could not smoke a cigarette within two blocks of my home, because someone would call my mom and tell her about it. Nowadays neighborhoods do not seem as close-knit, particularly where there are a lot of young families.

The age of the residents does seem significant. Older, well–established neighborhood residents tend to know more of their neighbors and owners of various properties, because they were present "in the old days." Younger residents tend to be preoccupied with their careers and raising their children and are seldom interested in the lives of their neighbors. Many are also concerned about civil litigation and find it easier to simply stay out of other people's business. A result is that younger families tend to be cut off from the world around their own homes.

I have a neighbor who locked her keys in her car with the ignition running. She called a friend from across town to help her. It never occurred to her to come next door and ask one of her neighbors for help. I asked her about this and she explained that she didn't want to bother me. I think this anecdote speaks volumes about what is going on in our communities.

We are so concerned that we might bother someone that we will suffer alone. Yet most people like to be needed. The "bother" that we are so concerned about is an opportunity to do what we all want to do anyway: help our neighbors. Of course, if we let a neighbor help us we have to speak to them occasionally. We run the risk of getting to know each other, and the next thing you know we'll be telling each other about vacation plans. We may have to learn to rely on each other to make sure our homes looked lived in enough to keep burglars away. Of course, there may be a problem of having to reciprocate when the neighbors leave town on *their* vacation.

Our neighbor may just prevent the burglary of our residence, because he knows we are not in town and no one should be rummaging through our garage. By the time the police arrive, the burglar may have found a way into the house and gets caught red–handed. More important, our neighbor may see our child becoming involved with local gang members before we are aware of a problem. The neighbor may be the one person who can alert us to our child's attraction to the gang. He can report a child hanging out with known neighborhood gang members while the parents are at work. Information about your home becoming the afternoon hangout for the local ruffians is important for you. Surprisingly, many neighbors presume that a parent is aware of his child's attraction to gangs and that the parent supports the activity. The proof of that support is that the gang members are allowed to hang out at the home. Although the primary person responsible for the education and welfare of the child is the parent, the community also shares in the burden of raising our children. Our ability to intervene, before it becomes too late, depends on knowing what problems our children face. Without information from several sources, including the neighbors, we cannot make legitimate decisions about our children's activities. The members of the community, therefore, have an obligation to inform a parent when a child has ventured beyond the boundaries of community standards. When the parent fails to restrict or discipline the child, the community has an obligation to take corrective action against the child for the child's benefit and for the safety of the community.

This change in community thought must occur one city street at a time. Over time, however, entire neighborhoods can begin to regain control. Neighborhood parks can be restored and kept up. The community and the children in the community can be enlisted to remove trash and debris, paint over graffiti, and take pride in their neighborhoods.

Apartment residents and home owners can pressure businesses in the community to ensure that they keep graffiti off their walls. Residents of subdivisions can and must insist that city government create ordinances that require business and private property owners to remove graffiti promptly. Finally, residents of school districts need to empower their school principals and officials to make policy decisions intended to make gang activity difficult.

The community is more than a group of people who live in a geographic area. Schools, churches, community organizations such as the YMCA and the YWCA, the Boy Scouts of America, little league baseball, football, and soccer, among many others, are also part of the community and should be tapped as resources. Our children will rise to the level of expectation to which adults hold them accountable.

Let's start with the school. A child's first experience in dealing with the real world occurs in school. As the child grows he learns what the world expects of him. Schools must raise the level of expectations enough to challenge the brightest student but not so high to cause the lowest student to lose hope of success. Generally, elementary schools are very good at this concept, but children develop at different rates; skill differences become more apparent as children grow older.

By the time a child enters middle school or junior high, it is quite clear that some of them need more supervision than others. Middle schools are ill equipped to deal with gang members who have learned to succeed through failure. They are not prepared for the student who can and does succeed academically when he is removed from his regularly assigned school and placed in a detention environment only to return to academic failure upon return to his regularly assigned school.

School officials and administrators tend to focus on correcting the many to account for the few. Why should 90–plus percent of the school population not be allowed to carry backpacks to school when perhaps only 3 or 4 percent of the students are likely to carry a gun to school? Most school administrators say that they must protect the 90 percent from violence and therefore they must restrict the entire population from some activity to protect them from those who might abuse the privilege. I see this issue much differently from how I see a dress code issue.

A dress code for any school is vital to the teaching process. The dress code establishes that the school is not like being at the mall or at a convenience store or standing on the street corner. Effectively, a dress code teaches the student how to dress and function in a work environment. After all, the goal of education is to make our children marketable in the workplace, is it not?

Precedent for dress codes exists in all facets of the work world. Dress codes teach self-discipline and respect for the work environment. The banning of backpacks or the purchasing of metal detection equipment is, however, a different matter.

Banning backpacks or purchasing and installing metal detectors at school entrances tends to detract from the school environment and lends credibility to the claim of the gangs: they rule the school. These actions tend to be viewed by most students as punishment that they feel is not justified. Other measures need to be taken that take into account that most of the student population is not involved with crime. Here the community and the school administration need to work together.

One of the many things I have noticed about gang members is that they tend to perform acceptably while they are in a discipline–oriented school environment. An independent school district in Houston, Texas, is a good example and one with which I am familiar. It has a school called the I.S.C. (Individualized Study Center), whose population derives from all the middle and high schools in the district. The students who attend this school are considered extreme discipline problems and would normally be serving lengthy suspensions for serious infractions of school policy. The principal is a very capable woman whom I admire for her strength of character and stern will.

She and I have noted that on many occasions students known to be hardcore gang members will perform academically well until about two weeks before returning to their regular school. During those two weeks these students become hard to deal with, argumentative, and verbally and sometimes physically abusive toward other students and teachers. It occurred to us that the gangsters did not want to return to their regular school. They wanted to remain in the I.S.C.

As we looked at their academic performance, a pattern started to develop. The gangster kids, on arriving at the I.S.C., quickly conformed to the school rules. They completed their class work and, for the most part, their homework in a timely manner. Their grades began to improve, in some cases to above average. These kids were beginning to succeed and they were enjoying it. The sheltered environment of the I.S.C. protected them with "having to do the work" so that they could "get out" and back into their regular school. Returning to the regular school was not all that attractive to them; they really wanted to continue their academic success. When they returned to their regular school environment they knew they would also return to their gang-member friends—the ones who recognize failure as success. They knew their old friends would rebuke them if they continued to succeed in regular classes. Their solution was to begin acting out in I.S.C. classes, hoping to be forced to stay in the program.

I have also noticed this phenomenon among other "correctional" programs. One of the best examples is the prison boot camp, which will be discussed later. The kids or young adults involved in these programs readily accept and excel in a structured military environment; many of them will attempt to stay by disobeying orders or by committing a minor infraction. The problem with prison boot camp is that it teaches more than self–discipline. Gang members often come out of these camps with a clear understanding of the value and potential benefit of having persons in their gangs respond to authority without question. Nevertheless, the actions of gang members in these environments is profound evidence that tells us how to fix their problems. I often wonder when we will begin to listen.

The gangster kids are not quite ready for the freedom of middle and high school. For whatever reason, they need someone to look over their shoulder and demand that they perform. What they need is a school dramatically oriented toward externally imposed discipline of the student, which happens to be diametrically opposite the goals of most middle and secondary educators. Their goal is to promote more individual thought and responsibility, and therefore the curriculum is structured to promote internal, or self, discipline.

Instead of punishing the good students by forcing them to live within more structured and externally disciplined parameters, we should send the students who need the discipline to an alternative middle or high school. That notion ought to raise a few eyebrows! There is controversy over the idea of separating students in this way. We don't want to "label" the kids, so we strive to let them remain in the mainstream classroom environment.

The problem is that in allowing the kids who need more external discipline to remain in a mainstream class, we are doing them a great injustice. These kids need the external discipline to get the education that they need to survive but aren't getting it in the mainstream classroom. They also are disrupting the mainstream classrooms and schools with their violent acts and disrespectful antics, which denies the mainstream kids an opportunity to learn and succeed at an accelerated rate. The social concept that everyone learns equally is outdated and needs to be adjusted.

School administrators, community leaders, and parents need to recognize that some kids need closer supervision and external discipline to achieve in school. Achievement in school will result in an increased self–esteem and desire at some point to exercise self–control for legitimate success in the community. When kids succeed they have no need for a gang to support their failure as success.

My vision of such a school system would be that one alternative facility could be used as a middle and high school. It should be staffed with "battle–hardened"—experienced—teachers and assistant principals, who have a firm, fair, and consistent approach to classroom discipline and education. The teachers should be motivated by the challenge of teaching kids who need a firm hand to guide them. The principal, assistant principals, and teachers should decide collectively about what activities will constitute what level of discipline in the classroom and school. The principal must be prepared to support the disciplinary decisions of the teachers.

This school would begin the year with no students. All students would at first be sent to their original schools, where they would have an opportunity to prove, through their actions, that they can garner enough self–discipline to remain on the regular campus. As the year progresses, the principals of the mainstream schools would send those students whom they identify as needing additional classroom supervision or external discipline. This alternative school would include most gang members besides other youths who may be causing difficulty.

The students, once assigned to this school, would remain for the rest of the school year. No student could be expelled or suspended unless he were remanded to the custody of the state juvenile authorities by order of a court, or he is an adult sentenced to an adult prison. Keep in mind that to a gang member failure is success. If a child can get kicked out of the bad kids' school, his reputation will grow and he will be lost to crime. Those that would ordinarily be suspended or expelled would be assigned to one– or two–person classrooms for the period of suspension or expulsion. This practice would prevent students from intentionally committing acts that are likely to get them expelled or suspended.

My experience with gang members tells me that some of these students will continue in criminal and gang activity at school and in the community. Because the school I have described concentrates on the "bad apples," it is appropriate to outfit it with metal detectors and to prohibit backpacks, etc. The refusal of the system to kick troublesome students out of school develops an environment of forced acceptance of academic goals, which in turn creates an excuse for those who begin to perform academically to have their academic success tolerated by their gang or peer group.

The excuse is that they have to perform to earn the right to get back into the regular school. At first they will want to return to the regular school to continue their gang activity. What will likely happen is that the gang member will learn to have confidence in his or her academic skills, which will lead to a better self–esteem and the child no longer needing the gang. At some point the gang member will recognize the lies inherent in the gang life–style and will abandon it.

Some educators might argue that gang members could intentionally commit acts that will place them at this school. I agree that this scenario is likely. Hardcore gang members want to recruit new members. The pool of potential new members would be much more concentrated at the discipline school than in the much larger general population. A few may want to prove themselves worthy of gang membership by being sent to the discipline school. However they get there is fine because only those that need the discipline will apply, as it were. The gang recruiters and those interested in gangs would otherwise be contaminating the general population of students. The kids who intentionally commit acts to get themselves assigned to the discipline school are probably in need of that discipline. We should welcome them.

This long–term disciplinary school could contribute to reduced disciplinary activity in the regular schools. Expelling students to a disciplinary school should motivate all but the most incorrigible students from actions that might get them expelled to the disciplinary school. The students considered mainstream will continue to view expulsion and suspension as negative and undesirable consequences to an action. The student who intentionally violates a rule to get suspended for a few days, to get out of school, will not be able to accomplish his goal; therefore he may not commit the act.

Internal expulsion (being sent to the "discipline school") will also motivate the mainstream kids to behave, once it becomes common knowledge that expulsion does not mean you don't have to go to school.

The key to success with gang members is prohibiting them from failing. The gangsters get the discipline and the special attention they crave. The mainstream kids can enjoy middle and high school years and can attend schools that encourage and promote independent thought and self–discipline. The inability of a gang member to get kicked out of school, except by committing a criminal act that results in placing him in a prison or juvenile facility, will force him to succeed. Once the gang member succeeds, the lies told by the gang show through, self–esteem grows, and independence is possible.

The school is not the only place where progress can be made in getting gang members and those interested in becoming gang members to rethink their position. Churches, parks, and other community–based programs, the YMCA and YWCA, and the Boy and Girl Scouts of America can and should be encouraged in the community approach to solving or having an impact on gang problems.

One of my pet peeves when listening to politicians and community leaders is what I call the "let's store them on the basketball court" speeches. During the speech or interview, the person says something to the effect that "what we need are more basketball courts for the youths to play on" or "Our community needs more green spaces and parks where the children can play" or "What we really need is more playground equipment!" As if all that were required to make a child well–adjusted is to provide him with a basketball court, a park, or some playground equipment. These are things. Children do not need things. Children, of all ages, need responsible adults to praise them, encourage them, and teach them discipline.

A basketball court, a park, and more playground equipment do nothing for a child except relieve temporary boredom. The real benefit of basketball is in the discipline required to learn to play it well. The park is a place to be with family and friends. Playground equipment is for developing muscle and coordination. All of these facilities must be supervised by responsible adults. Without supervision the basketball court and the park become hangout locations, and playground equipment simply rusts into oblivion.

The boxing clubs, baseball leagues, basketball leagues, tennis matches, and the wide world of sports activities cannot function without appropriate leadership. Precisely because these activities have adult leadership is why they reach many kids who would otherwise turn to gangs to find discipline and a sense of success.

Despite the proliferation of sports clubs and organizations, many gang members are not impressed enough to become involved. Many gang members are not interested in sports. The usual approach to youth gang intervention has been based on sports activities, which are naturally discipline–oriented. However, in our zeal to convert the gang member, we have forgotten that not everyone is attracted to sports. Some enjoy performing on stage. Some like music, others like to write. A few are interested in business. We are going to have to face the reality that all gangster kids cannot be lured from gangs by sports.

Community resources such as Junior Achievement or local businesses starting apprentice programs might be positive outlets for some. Neighborhood theaters could be formed and produce outdoor plays for the neighborhood. Music, of all kinds, could be encouraged as long as an adult with musical experience supervises the practices. Photography, sculpture, and painting would be good for some of the taggers, or gang artists. Imagination is the limit to these possibilities.

The reality is that all these opportunities cost more than money. They cost time and energy. Everyone is just too busy today to volunteer in the afternoons or on weekends to help the kid down the street stay out of a gang. How do we get these kinds of community activities going?

Businesses that can afford to hire a few kids part–time need to do so. Instead of waiting for the "right" kid to come along and present himself in a way that inspires one to hire him, go into the neighborhood and find a kid that doesn't look like he would ever get a job. Offer it to him with the condition that he come prepared to learn a skill and be willing to conform to the dress code. If he doesn't want the job, go find another. Keep doing that until you have hired all you can hire.

Why don't more people who possess a skill or talent share it with the youths? Because frankly we are scared of things we don't understand. So are the gangsters. Take a couple of friends into your neighborhood park, for moral support if nothing else. If you are an artist, set up your easel and start painting. You'll have an audience before long. Teach them what you know, encourage their attempts. If you can, help them obtain materials.

Taking back a neighborhood park from the criminal element doesn't mean that you have to conduct a military campaign. It is simply neighbors refusing to abandon the park to the criminals. Using the park for positive purposes will bring positive results. Of course, the occasional friendly visit of the local police officer isn't a bad idea either, but the focus should be the neighbors. Although it is commendable that some people are willing to volunteer in areas of the community outside their own, this volunteering is less effective than that by a person from the same community.

Outside volunteers are good for hospitals or tutoring programs at schools and that sort of thing. What I am writing about is having someone from the community where the gang members live reaching out and helping them succeed. It takes a person more frightened of what the neighborhood might become than what might become of him to have a lasting and meaningful impact on a kid interested in gang life. Just remember that kids and dogs can see right through the slickest huckster or charlatan.

Honesty, conviction, a clear view of reality and the willingness to talk about it are all required of any person who wants to volunteer to work with gang members. They are a tough audience. They will try your patience and your resolve. When you get one to respond you will have accomplished a great rescue. The really cool thing about gang members is that where one leads, more will follow.

The Law

Our present system of justice in America has focused on the rights of the accused, a legitimate focus. The framers of our Constitution were concerned about government invading the lives of persons and falsely accusing them of crime, without due process of law. We have, as a nation, acted as if the Constitution of the United States existed for the sole purpose of protecting those accused of crime from the terrible menace of government. We have lost sight of the purpose of government and law.

Our government is charged with the responsibility of providing as safe an environment as possible in which all can pursue individual interests. Our government is charged with the task of protecting our nation from foreign and internal threats to national interests. One guarantee often ignored is the constitutional one that every citizen shall remain secure in his property and in his person. This guarantee is often abused by defense attorneys and others who argue their clients were improperly accused because their right to security was violated by an improper search or arrest warrant. The same constitutional right is among the favorite appeals to various appellate courts in America. What happened to the right of the private citizen to be secure in his property and in his person and to be protected from the *criminal* who improperly seized his property?

In considering the violation of civil rights, most consider only the police or the government. Anyone, however, can violate the constitutional rights of a person. Anyone who breaks into a residence, robs someone at gunpoint, sells drugs, or commits any offense against another is violating someone's civil right to be secure in his property or person. The rights guaranteed in the U.S. Constitution, in fact, are the basis for all criminal law in this country. We have forgotten the broader issue of justice.

Over the past fifty or so years Americans have concerned themselves with cruel and unusual punishment. We have looked for more humane ways to hold felons in custody. We are striving to make the death penalty a humane process, which certainly strains the fabric of credibility with me. How do you humanely kill another person? It is an oxymoron.

Criminals are adult children who have never learned to accept responsibility for their actions. The crimes they commit are always committed by someone else (they were framed), or they were forced to commit them (couldn't find a job). My favorite excuse is that they just couldn't help themselves, which implies that the person has no self–control. These people feel that an internal force, beyond their control, compels them to commit crime. My experience tells me that most crime in America is committed because the offender believes he can get away with it, or that the proceeds are worth the risk of getting caught.

Another factor is education. Most prison inmates do not possess a high school education, which makes it difficult for them to understand the confusing and complicated formulas that determine when a prisoner has completed his sentence. All they know is the jury sentenced them to twenty years and they served twenty months. In their minds the sentence (promise) of the jury and the court is laughable and worthy of contempt. They believe that they have beaten the system.

The exact situation was made clear to me during the sentencing portion of a trial in a federal court. A gang member was on trial for felonious possession of a firearm. The maximum penalty for this offense was ten years in a federal prison. He was sentenced to five years. When the judge finished reading the sentence, the gang member turned to his lawyer and asked, "How long do I have to do?" His lawyer told him he had to serve all five years. The gang member said, "Yeah, well, what about good time and parole?" The lawyer told him about the difference between the state and federal prison systems, that there is no good time or parole in the federal system. Further, the lawyer explained that his sentencing time would not start until he reached the prison to which he was assigned. In other words, he did not get credit for the year he spent in the county jail pending trial in federal court.

The gang member was already on parole from the state system from a sentence of about twenty years. He was not concerned with that, because he was out in the street. He was, we suspected, still involved in his gang business of selling dope and committing home–invasion robberies. His parole meant nothing to him. It occurred to me that the only thing this gang member knew was that he was going to prison for five full years. The fact that he could not negotiate or reduce his time in any way made that five years worse, to him, than having to spend the next twenty years on parole.

The federally convicted gang member responded to a firm sentence that was not negotiable; his response told me that we have made serious mistakes in using a rehabilitative approach, which has given us early release and "good time," with prison inmates without first getting their attention through punishment.

America must come to grips with punishment as a rehabilitative agent. No rehabilitation can occur unless one of two conditions takes place. One, the person being rehabilitated must want to be rehabilitated, or, two, the person will want rehabilitation because he will be made uncomfortable if he does not. You and I modify our behavior on this basis all the time. We break laws or rules if we believe that the punishment or pain will not come or will be negligible.

Driving is a good example. How many of us don't exceed the speed limit on the interstate when there is no police officer around? Not many! How many of us automatically slow down, whether we're speeding or not, when we see a police car? Most of us! I do that and I am a police officer. The point is that the pain of getting a ticket tends to make us modify our behavior, at least temporarily. The same applies to other crimes. For substantial rehabilitation to occur we must get the attention of the prison inmate.

Inmates are not required to contribute, through work, toward their own room and board. They are in "time out" while we provide for their every need. Our nation's prison inmates have high school G.E.D. courses, college courses, technical schools, and skilled labor training available to them at no cost. Why then is our repeat offender rate so high? Clearly, we are failing to rehabilitate our prison population. We should not be at all surprised. The value of these rehabilitative privileges is lost to the inmate because he does not have to work to obtain it. The inmates do not recognize them as valuable and why should they? It costs them nothing.

Many privileges that prison inmates have they consider rights: television, access to newspapers and magazines, movies, weight–training equipment, books, and law libraries. Inmates may file civil suits and appeals at no cost. They receive free legal counsel as well—free to them; the cost is paid by you and me in tax dollars. These items and services cost a lot of money in the free world. One must have substantial financial backing to enjoy a health club, newspaper and magazine subscriptions, movie theaters, a color television, etc. Have you checked on the cost of competent legal advice lately? It is expensive. Court costs are on the increase as well.

Prison is certainly not a pleasant place, but neither is it so bad that the thought of going back would modify a burglar's desire to break into your house and steal your possessions. What I suggest is that the focus of prison be punishment, with rehabilitation a secondary goal. That is to say, when criminals are held to account for their criminality, they have been punished. Once they are punished, it is possible to rehabilitate those who want rehabilitation. I propose that society accept the reality of crime and start expecting criminals to be punished first and rehabilitated later.

Some readers will jump to the conclusion that I am advocating physical brutality at this point. I am not. I believe that physical brutality is less likely to inspire compliance to the rules. A measured and precise punishment would more likely result in compliance to a rule or law. Punishment, like discipline, comes in many shapes and forms. The most devastating punishment I can think of is having another person in charge of your daily regime. To lose one's freedom of choice in any matter, much less in matters as individual as eating and sleeping patterns, is and should be considered punishment. Many do not understand that it is possible to punish a person and not violate constitutionally protected rights against cruel or unusual punishment.

Punishment is not brutality. The forfeit of freedom for a specified time is punishment. Forfeiting freedom makes it more valuable to the person being punished. Privilege is the reward of freedom, which is why the removal of freedom is a punishment.

Prison inmates ought to be reduced to appropriate food, reasonable health care, and shelter. The reduction to basic subsistence should adequately point out the value of freedom and rights enjoyed by citizens. The removal of those rights will help the inmate realize that the prison experience is punishment for violating the rights of another. The maintenance of the inmate at this subsistence level will be counterproductive unless the inmate has some hope of redemption. For this reason, inmates should be allowed and encouraged to earn a living while in prison.

Prisoners will learn to value their privileges when they have to earn them. The lessons in vocational classes or college courses will be remembered if the inmate has to pay tuition. Education that costs something is more valuable to the person who must pay for it. The precedent for this environment already exists; it is called the real world. I do not think it cruel or unusual to expect those receiving a benefit to pay for it. If payment is not forthcoming, the service or product should be denied.

Convicts should be allowed to *earn* the privilege of using exercise equipment, watching television, purchasing newspapers and magazines, or visiting the library. Those who help reduce the costs of operating the prison would enjoy these and other privileges. Inmates who work and stay out of trouble, who indicate that they are interested in rehabilitation, should be allowed the privilege of enrolling in trade school or college courses, for which they would pay tuition.

Most Americans earn their way and pay for the privileges that they experience. Many in the real world would jump at the opportunity to learn a new skill or receive a college education, but they simply can't afford the tuition. Generally, these people must work harder to achieve their goals. Why can't we make those who disregard our laws and our Constitution do the same?

Granted, our prisons are overcrowded and something needs to be done about that. However, what is being done needs to be changed. Prison officials and politicians have created complicated formulas that allow for so–called good time. Good time accrues when a prisoner does what he is supposed to do and stays out of trouble. This prisoner gains credit of about three days for each day served. The theory is that eight hours is a workday. Because the inmate stays in jail twenty–four hours per day, he should get credit for three eight–hour workdays. They get credit for time served while they sleep because we (society) keep the poor felons locked up twenty–four hours per day! We need to keep in mind that the inmate made the choice to sign up for this "job" when he committed the crimes that landed him in prison.

The formulas used in prison systems around the country are designed to equalize the need for additional bed space with the public's desire to spend no new tax dollars on confinement. Place on top of this issue the heavy weight of federal guidelines, and there exists a recipe for social disaster. I am most familiar with the Texas prison system so I will use that as my example.

There was a time not long ago when the Texas Department of Corrections was self–sufficient. That is to say, it cost the taxpayers nothing except the salaries of the guards and support personnel to operate the prison facilities. During that time, inmate labor was used to produce the required products for use in the prison system. Some overstocked items were sold to the public at a profit, which was used to purchase and update farm equipment and supplies. As the years progressed, the liberal slant of the country began to take its toll. More restrictions were placed on the prison as to what could be built, manufactured, grown, made, or sold by prisoners. At the same time, more requirements were imposed by the court systems to provide inmates with minimal space, requiring the prison system to provide televisions, newspapers, magazines, and the like to inmates. Federal courts stepped in to regulate the number of inmates that could be housed in the state prison system, and now we have the current broken system to deal with.

We have a population that is tired of crime and demands that lawmakers require more time and stiffer penalties. Meanwhile the federal caps caused the Texas prison system to allow fewer inmates to be transferred from the various county jails. The jails soon became more overcrowded than the prisons. County government sues the state government for the costs to the county taxpayers to house prisoners in the county jail. Lawyers get involved, and the next thing you see is a bunch of thugs being released from the county jail on the 10:00 p.m. newscast.

We don't need to send people to prison forever to make an impact on crime. We don't need to violate their civil right against cruel or unusual punishment. The solution to crime problems are being screamed at us by our young people: firm, fair, and consistent discipline. Pick a standard and apply it universally. Hold everyone accountable to the same standard and be consistent with discipline when the standard is not followed.

We, the voting public, need to let our lawmakers know that we want to be safe in our homes, communities, and schools, even if that means taking a different perspective on crime and criminals. I have given this subject much thought and I have looked to the gang member to give me advice about what influences him. A detailed yet simple plan results that could have some significant impact on crime in America.

I know that gang members respond to discipline; evidence can be obtained by interviewing any boot camp counselor or administrator, who will report great success with some of the most hardcore gang members. The reason: the military environment is, in many ways, a parallel of the gang life from which they come. They understand, almost intuitively, the need to obey the commands of a superior.

What they learn in boot camp is not necessarily what was intended. Many boot camp graduates return to the gang with renewed respect for "rank" within the gang. Some even teach their gang the more important lessons they learned while at boot camp—physical fitness, immediate response to directives of command, and the mental condition to follow direction without questioning the authority for those actions. In short, a criminal street gang member is the last person that should be assigned to a penal boot camp for rehabilitation. He needs something different from a military–style boot camp.

Gang members understand the importance of punishment as a rehabilitative agent. Every gang, regardless of location or size, has a rule about what will befall a member who violates the rules of the gang. Not being bound by law or the U.S. Constitution, most gangs resort to physical violence as punishment. The individual gang member, however, routinely accepts this punishment. Usually the gang member being punished modifies his behavior and reaffirms his desire to continue with the gang.

Most gang members I deal with also recognize the importance of continuity. Consistency is a vital part of their internal disciplinary process. The rules are spelled out, corrective action for violation of the rules is clear, and discipline comes swiftly after the perceived violation.

One of the first things we must do is not make promises we are not prepared to carry out. For example, we should not be promising sentences of twenty, thirty, or forty years or life in prison unless that is what we really intend, understanding that the state will be responsible for the convicted felon for that time. When a jury promises a convicted felon that he will be confined in prison for twenty years as a reward for his crime, what can we expect that felon to think about a system that lets him out after twenty to twenty–four months? The jury, the law, and the disciplinary process is made a mockery. The criminal loses respect for the system, the law, and the citizens who are "dumb enough" to abide by that law. The empty threat of twenty years in prison is, in many ways, worse than not sending the criminal to jail at all.

Overcrowded jails and prisons are problems. We cannot continue to stockpile American youths behind bars, so we must reach them. Giving a felon a sentence (promise) that will be kept is the quickest and most cost–efficient way to accomplish this task. The process begins with an overhaul of the existing statutes and a review of the average amount of time spent for the various offenses. Let's say that someone in Texas is convicted of burglary of a habitation for the first time. Research tells us that the average prison time served by first-time burglars is two years. Our example burglar is sentenced to two years in prison. No parole and no good time. Two full years are then served by the burglar.

The prison–overcrowding problem presently demands that the first–time burglar who was sentenced to twenty years has to be released in two, according to complicated mathematical equations, to make room for the next felon coming into the system. Soon enough people realize that first-time burglars spend only about two years in prison. To pretend otherwise is foolish. Let's sentence (promise) felons to prison terms that we, as a society, are prepared to keep. That way the first–time burglar knows exactly what he faces if convicted. When he hears a jury sentence him to two years, he'll know that he will be two years older when he sees a public street again.

Consistency is lacking within the court systems of America. A first-time felon may receive six months probation in court A while the same offense may result in a sentence of sixty years in prison from court B. Narrowing the parameters of punishment would make sentences more consistent among the courts. Consistency would take the guesswork out of the discipline for the defendant and the complainant (the people of the state). Consistency would lend credibility to the system. Credibility would result in respect by the law abiding citizen and by the law violator.

Prison wardens have difficulty with this proposal because they say that they need leverage to motivate prisoners to follow the rules and remain peaceful. I agree. However, at present they are using carrots. I believe they need to use sticks.

All states have judicial districts that serve those who live in these districts. Crimes that occur inside prisons or on prison property are prosecuted in the jurisdiction where the prison facility is located. I think it more efficient to establish a *prison* judicial district. The prison courts could handle administrative and criminal matters that occur on prison property. The purpose would be to identify recidivists (repeat offenders) while they are still in prison and prevent their release into the community. Laws should be made that would permit the administrators of penal institutions, through these prison courts, to extend the sentence of a prisoner for violations of prison rules. Extensions should not exceed a six–month period per incident and must be ordered by the prison system district court.

An example of this action might be that an inmate routinely refuses the orders of a guard. The prison officials act by removing privileges in an effort to get the inmate to comply with orders. Ultimately the inmate returns to the subsistence level and continues to refuse to follow orders. The warden or his designee could then petition the prison court for an extension of the inmate's sentence, up to six months. If the prison court, after a hearing of the circumstances, agrees, the prisoner's sentence could be extended. The inmate would remain in the subsistence level until he indicated that he was willing to abide by the rules. He would then be allowed to begin accumulating privileges again.

The violation of a state law while confined in the prison system would result in extending a prison term by the amount of time the violation would ordinarily be subject to. Any additional sentence imposed by a prison district court would have to be served as a consecutive sentence. Presently American courts can assign sentences as consecutive or concurrent. A consecutive sentence must be served after an existing sentence has been completed. A concurrent sentence is served at the same time as an existing sentence. Concurrent sentences are, in my opinion, a cruel hoax perpetrated on the community to give the impression that a person has been severely sentenced to more than one prison term.

The Cure

This hard–line approach to prison misconduct has two purposes. First, inmates will understand that the law means what it says and they can expect to extend their stay by violating rules or laws. Second, it will be possible to identify recidivists earlier and keep them off the streets longer. The inmate who chooses to rehabilitate can serve his original sentence, learn a trade, get an education, develop some effective life skills, and reenter the outside world. The inmate who does not follow the rules can stay in prison until he wants to learn.

If an inmate refuses to follow the rules in prison, he is not likely to follow the rules outside prison. Reviewing an inmate's discipline history within the institution is common in parole systems. Parole boards routinely consider discipline to determine who would be likely parole candidates. The only difference is that in the system I describe there is no parole. You either do your time, follow the rules, and get out or you stay until you submit to following the rules.

Probation can also be an effective tool for rehabilitation. The problem with probation is that it is so overused by the courts that it carries no weight in the minds of those who receive it. A result is that thousands of probationers have never seen their probation officer and have never reported regularly. Using probation to reduce prison overcrowding is not a sound practice. In effect, probation is considered a victory by the criminal.

This victory is largely because of an overburdened probation system that cannot keep up with the staggering number of persons placed on probation by the courts. (The courts use the plea–bargaining system to relieve caseloads, and probation is definitely an incentive to plead guilty, especially if you *are* guilty.) Probation departments have no control over how many probationers are assigned by the different courts, and a result is a dramatically overwhelmed system. Many probation officers have hundreds of probationers on their caseload. It is unreasonable to expect one person to keep up with hundreds of probationers each month. Therefore it is easy to violate probation and return to criminal habits. No one will be the wiser until the violator is rearrested for another crime.

Plea bargainings are a distasteful practice that I, unwillingly, agree must continue to be a part of our criminal justice system. Unfortunately our current judicial and penal system cannot afford to provide a jury trial for every person accused of a crime. We therefore have to provide an incentive for those guilty of a crime to admit their guilt, which will save court time and tax dollars. The only incentive I know is a plea-bargaining system. Plea bargaining must be limited, however, to offenders who can be considered for probation. The carrot in that system must be probation.

As much as I hate to admit it, some offenders should be allowed the opportunity for probation. However, probation should be dramatically different from what it is today. All probation should be supervised, and the county should be prepared to pay a probation department to hire enough probation officers for supervision of the probationers. Realistically, no probation officer should have more than twenty probationers to supervise. In the likely event that the probation office has no openings, the person sentenced would not be allowed on probation; he would have to go to prison until an opening occurs in the probation department for him to fill.

All probationers should be required to report in person at least once per week, and each probation officer must visit the probationer at random times and locations at least once per month. Probation should be used as a punishment for offenders who the court has determined are likely to accept the punishment and are willing to be rehabilitated. A probationer should be dealt with harshly if he violates the terms of probation. A missed meeting, failure to maintain a job, unwillingness to serve community hours, whatever—the violation ought to result in immediate arrest of the violator and he should be immediately transported to prison to begin serving his term. The term should begin anew without credit for time already served on probation.

Changes in how we think about our roles in and responsibilities to the community are where the answers lie to many questions plaguing our nation. Questioning the wisdom of separatism is a first step on a very long road to recovery. Recognizing that we all benefit from a collective standard of discipline and that freedom can exist only where the standards are strictly and jealously guarded is the next step. Realizing that we all have an interest and a role in raising all of our nation's youths, whether we like it or not, is the third step on a very long journey.

MESSENGERS
OF LIGHT

*The Angels' Guide
to Spiritual Growth*

Books by Terry Lynn Taylor

**The Alchemy of Prayer:
Rekindling Our Inner Life**

**Messengers of Light:
The Angels' Guide to Spiritual Growth**

**Guardians of Hope:
The Angels' Guide to Personal Growth**

**Answers From the Angels:
A Book of Angel Letters**

**Creating With the Angels:
An Angel-Guided Journey Into Creativity**

MESSENGERS OF LIGHT

The Angels' Guide to Spiritual Growth

Terry Lynn Taylor

H J Kramer Inc
Tiburon, California

Published by H J Kramer Inc.
P.O. Box 1082
Tiburon, CA 94920

Editor: Nancy Grimley Carleton
Illustrations: Marty Noble
Cover Art: Adolphe-William Bouguereau,
   La Vierde aux Anges (detail)
Cover Design: Spectra Media
Composition: Classic Typography
Book Production: Schuettge & Carleton
Bouguereau Painting:
   Courtesy of Musée du Petit-Palace, Paris,
   Giraudon/Art Resource, New York

Manufactured in the United States of America
20 19 18 17 16 15 14 13 12

Library of Congress Cataloging-in-Publication Data

Taylor, Terry Lynn, 1955–
   Messengers of light: the angels' guide to spiritual
growth/by Terry Lynn Taylor.
      p.   cm.
   Includes bibliographical references.
   ISBN 0–915811–51–0 : $12.00
   1. Angels.   I. Title.
BL477.T39   1989   89–92333
291.2'15—dc20   CIP

Angels can fly because they take themselves lightly.

G.K. Chesterton

To Our Readers

The books we publish are our contribution to an emerging world based on cooperation rather than on competition, on affirmation of the human spirit rather than on self-doubt, and on the certainty that all humanity is connected. Our goal is to touch as many lives as possible with a message of hope for a better world.

Hal and Linda Kramer, Publishers

Contents

Foreword

When I first met Terry Taylor and heard about all of her remarkable angel experiences, I was a bit envious. I wanted an angel experience, too.

Every night before I went to bed, I'd send out a mental prayer fax requesting my very own bona fide angel experience. "Okay, highest angel. If you're really there, prove it. I want to meet an angel. ASAP. Thanks, hon."

I figured it was all right to be blunt because, as Terry assured me, angels appreciate a no-nonsense approach to things. They also have a great sense of humor, which I hoped they weren't indulging at my expense as the weeks passed and the only remotely heavenly visitation I received was a house call from two effervescent Jehovah's Witnesses. I dispensed of these hefty ladies quickly enough, although the guilty thought did occur to me that they might very well have been angels in disguise and I'd really screwed up.

"Don't worry about it," Terry would laugh. "You'll have an angel experience one of these days. Just be patient."

Several weeks later, I was sitting in a coffee shop in Silverlake, writing away, when a round, jolly, bearded young man in a loud Hawaiian shirt waved to me from another table.

"You look like the kind of person who'd like to see something wonderful that I just bought!" he trilled.

"Sure," I replied.

He trotted over to my table with a big bag, from which he produced the most beautiful carved stone cherub head I'd ever seen.

"Oh!" I breathed. "I've been wanting one of these for at least a year!"

"Would you like it?" he smiled.

"Would I! I mean . . ." I looked at him keenly. "How much is it?"

"I'll sell it to you for twelve dollars."

I knew that this was a fabulous bargain because I'd just been to Bullock's, where tacky-looking terra-cotta cherubs were going for thirty-five bucks.

"It's a deal!" I grabbed the cherub. "Who are you?"

My new friend shrugged and plopped himself down at my table. "Eat, eat!" he admonished me. "Never let the food get cold."

I found out that his name was Chris L'Esperance, that he was an artist, and that he had a collection of some 150 cherubs and angels. Which was when it hit me like a celestial brick.

"Are you an angel?" I inquired.

Chris roared with big, booming laughter. "Maybe. Are you?"

"Not that I know of. But you have all the qualifications of an angel according to my friend Terry Taylor, who's writing a book on them. You're happy and friendly and you like to laugh and you just brought me a mysterious angelic gift."

Chris looked at me intently. "Is there anything else you need?"

"Yeah," I said. "About five thousand dollars, before April 15th."

"Taxes?"

"Uh huh."

"When is April 15th?"

"Two weeks. Never mind, I know it's ridiculous. I can't think of a single way five thousand dollars is going to come into my life between now and then."

He was silent for a moment.

"You'll have the money," he pronounced presently. "Not in two weeks. But in three. You're going to have a lot of money. A lot of money."

Something about the way he said that gave me a tingly feeling.

I don't know why, but I just knew that he wasn't your average, everyday Los Angeles cornflake.

I raced home to call Terry. "I met an angel!" I babbled, as soon as she answered. "Wait till you see this cherub he sold me. And he says I'm going to have my tax money in three weeks."

Terry just laughed her wonderful, tinkly laugh. "That's great," she said. "But just remember that angels can be off by a few weeks, or even months. Time isn't one of their strong points."

"If he's off by years, what'll I tell the IRS?"

"Oh, he's probably pretty much on target. Don't worry."

Three days later, I was sitting in my agent's home when the phone rang. He excused himself and came back about five minutes later.

"How would you like a check for eight thousand dollars?" he asked.

I got that tingly feeling again.

"How?"

"That was an editor. They've got a book project, and they're looking for a writer. You'd be great."

Well, to make a long story short, I got the job and a check for over eight thousand dollars five weeks later.

"That angel was only two weeks off," I told Terry when I took her out to dinner to celebrate.

"That's not bad. They can really go out in left field sometimes. But that's usually only when they're having fun with you, like when you ask for something really stupid. This one knew you needed the money."

Anyway, there are such things as angels, and they do come into your life when you call on them, and even when you don't. And Terry Taylor will show you how to get in touch with them, how to spot them, how to utilize them, and, most importantly, how to learn to love life the way they do. Angels, you see, are not just the winged beings of Judeo-Christian heavyosity who reside within the dusty halls of biblical lore. Nor are they dead people sprouting feathers. Not in Terry's book, anyway. As she so convincingly explains, angels walk the earth just as you and I do, and in fact could very well be you and I, for each and every one of us has angel potential just waiting to be unleashed. Terry has encountered angels in the form of gas station attendants, drifters, waitresses, you name it. (I myself met an angel posing as a counter girl at one of L.A.'s most obnoxious MacDonald's.) And once you begin to be able to sniff out angels yourself, life suddenly becomes a never-ending adventure, in which those you meet are no longer faceless strangers but rather possible harbingers of joy.

Through Terry, I soon became adept at making contact with the heavenly kingdom. I learned about angel mail, a technique whereby you can send letters to the angels of various people whose aid you're seeking or whose annoyance you'd like to obliterate once and for all. I learned about angel conferences, in which you can summon as many angels as you like for a board meeting to discuss and resolve the agenda of your life. I learned about angel satchels, convenient forms of baggage that are smaller and lighter than a breadbox, in which you can place people or situations who are bothering you and let the angels take care of the air freight. Most of all, I learned how to give up the things in life that distressed me, surrendering them to the care of the cosmos, and to actually believe that I could have anything that I wanted out of life.

Well, almost anything. The angels never gave me the marriage that I thought I wanted, with the man I thought I wanted. This really bothered me. "So what's with this angel mail?" I said crossly to Terry one day, six months after I had sent a letter to my dearly beloved's highest angel asking for us to get back together. "It's been six months and I haven't heard a thing from the angels. Their postal system must be worse than Italy's."

"Just trust," Terry assured me. "If they're not getting you something, it's for a good reason."

I'll say. On a worthiness scale of one to ten, this man turned out to be a minus six. He eventually made my life so miserable that I was seriously considering joining the Jesuits. And a year after I'd used angel mail, the man I'd truly waited for all my life just happened along.

"You see?" said Terry. "You just mailed the letter to the wrong person, that's all. It took the angels a year to track down the right address."

So, I'm a convert to angelology. And after you read Terry's book, chances are you will be, too. I hope so, because once you let the angels take care of everything that once drove you crazy, you'll find yourself on the road to true happiness. So pack all your troubles in the old angel satchel and smile, smile, smile. The angels are here.

Mary Beth Crain

Preface

The purpose of this book is to expand your awareness of angels. This book is not about whether or not you believe angels exist (this is not up for debate); it is about knowing and noticing the ways of angels so you can incorporate angel help into your everyday life.

There are many popular positive-thinking and self-help books around; *Messengers of Light* is *not* another positive-thinking book. Angels are the missing link in the chain of self-help titles. These ever-helpful messengers of divine providence have thus far been neglected in the context of self-help, self-development, and self-reliance programs that expect people to do everything by and for themselves. Angels are heaven-sent agents who are always available to help you create heaven in your life. This book will help you expand and develop your awareness of angels so you can obtain unseen help with your spiritual growth and happiness.

If you listen, you will hear angels in the lyrics of songs. You may even see angels in faces, paintings, windows, or the sky. You may feel them touch you gently on the shoulder. You may find yourself reading about them in the newspaper or hearing about them on the evening news. And you may notice their jasmine or rose scent in the strangest places. Looking for angels will bring them to you.

About the Structure of This Book

Messengers of Light is divided into five parts, sequentially designed so that the information introduced in each part will be useful in the following parts.

The chapters are kept short for several reasons. For one, angels are light and playful. They do not want information about their ways to overwhelm anyone. Also, the philosophy behind this book is not to give pat answers, but to encourage you, the reader, to come up with creative questions to answer and problems to solve for yourself, in your own special way, with your own special awareness of how angels can assist you. Short chapters also enable you to skip around the book and read whatever appeals to you in the moment.

Part One covers the nature and origin of angels in a "light" manner. Angels have been around for a long time and have taken various forms in almost all of the world's religions and cultures. This section discusses angels in terms of their own realm, which is heaven.

Part Two introduces the angels you will be reading about throughout the book, and gives examples and definitions of the various "halos" angels wear. This section will explore the roles angels play and their special activities.

Part Three is the method section; in it, you will discover ways to attract the angels described in Part Two, and ways to get their attention focused on you for achieving favorable consequences and joyful living.

Part Four is about leading a more angelic life. This section gives a few ideas and practices meant to help you incorporate your higher self into your everyday life.

Part Five offers a potpourri of noteworthy angel propaganda. It includes descriptions of other people's experiences with angels, and it also lists other books and miscellaneous information on angels.

Keeping an angel journal will be helpful as you read the book, for writing down thoughts about angels and for putting into practice the methods recommended in the various chapters. See the introduction to Part Three for more on keeping an angel journal.

How I Came to Write This Book

You may wonder, before or after reading this book, where I got my information and why I decided to write a book on angels.

For as long as I can remember, I always knew that angels existed and I always thought they were a good idea. My philosophy was: Why question something that makes so much sense to me? So, instead of trying to disprove the existence of angels, I collected positive information about them and stored it in "the back of my mind" as an ongoing research project. As a teenager, I tended to be a bit reckless, and I had a friend who also had this tendency. I remember that each time we had a close call, we would comment that our guardian angels were probably fed up with working overtime. We also discovered that our guardians could do other special things besides saving us all the time. We figured out that if we asked them they would help us get things we wanted. When I look back at the silly things we asked for, I see how truly patient and loving they were with us, and that is the beauty of it. All human requests, regardless of importance, will be considered by angels and brought to pass if they are for the highest loving good for all concerned (or, at the least, if they aren't exactly harmful).

Approximately five years ago, my research project gained momentum with the help of my close friend and spiritual witness Shannon. Together, we began looking in earnest for books and various other sources on angels and their ways. We started searching out people who we thought either were angels or had had experiences with angels. Whenever we met someone, we would ask, "Have you ever seen an angel?" We started noticing and sharing the synchronistic events the angels gave us. Most of all, we discovered how fun and light life can be when angels are around in full force.

When I started out with the idea for a book about angels, initially I was going to try to attribute all mystical, metaphysical, and psychic experiences to angels. I was going to include all the extraterrestrials and channeled entities I'd been told about under the banner of angels. I was also going to try not to talk about God in the book for fear of turning off some readers. Well, when I actually started writing about angels, I was led in a different direction. I found that the experiences people had with extraterrestrials just didn't fit the experiences that I and others have had with angels. In fact, they were very different at the core.

Because these are subjective experiences and the theories about them are so elusive in nature, I won't go into the details. I will point out a major difference I found in the stories about extraterrestrials or "disembodied spirits" versus those about angels. The major difference is that in all the nonangel situations, there was a great deal of *interference* (positive and/or negative) in the life of the person who was receiving the messages or experience, and the messages came in the form of "words," often including very verbose details. In contrast, the angel experiences consisted of joyful feelings, strong intuition, inspiration, and a sense of "permissionary" noninterference. Words as such were not used by the angels; rather, the "communications" were interpreted into words only later by the person to describe what was meant and how they felt. In every case, the angel experience left the person with a sense of well-being and deep peace.

I also found it awkward to talk about angels without mentioning God. It seemed silly when I tried to think of angels flying randomly in circles—just happening to do something nice once in a while, without some sort of leader or higher being in charge, or without an ultimate purpose. So, when I do mention God in the book, I mean to represent the love that is the angels' raison d'être—the love that they play with to maintain love in the universe.

My information has come from various sources: experiences, literature, and the people I know. The main source I used for the book was my strongest intuitions regarding angels, which came from a synthesis of all the outside information I've taken in and all the inside information I have from a deep sense of knowing. And, of course, I asked the angels to inspire me at all times. I don't feel I have "channeled" angels in the traditional sense, because angels speak to us in feelings and guide us by inspiration. Most of all, angels give me the feeling that I'm not alone in the universe, and that I am loved. I have tried to remain true to myself and to the angels. I wrote this book to share information that has made my life fun, happy, meaningful, exciting, successful, loving, easy to take, and less serious!

Here are some of the main messages angels have for us: Life is really not serious, and humor and levity equal creativity. Life can be beautiful, like the colors of heaven. Humans need to incorporate celestial play and joy into their lives. We can trust the loving ways of angels and in turn learn to trust and love ourselves.

Angels make life happier and easier. Use this book as a guidebook to the realm of the angels. Discover ways to create angel awareness and to attract angels into your life. If you do, the angels will share with you their antistress, antigravity, and antiaging secrets.

Acknowledgments

Writing this book was fun. When people found out I was writing a book on angels, they all had something positive to say and often positive help to offer. The angels brought many new friends into my life in the last couple of years, and brought me closer to those I already had. There are many people I would like to thank for their help and inspiration in making this book a reality.

First of all, I would like to thank Francis Jeffrey. I told him lightly (after buying a book about angels that didn't cover the subject matter I wanted) that I was going to write a book about angels. I wasn't really serious at the time, but he convinced me that I could do it. He assisted in the writing, contributed many new ideas, and helped me clarify my own ideas. He also wrote a wonderful essay for the Angel Forum in Part Five.

After realizing that I could, should, and must write this book, I tried to bring my long-time friend and spiritual sister Shannon Boomer in on the project. She convinced me that I could write the book by myself, but that she would help. Much of this book came from experiences we have had together and from long conversations about angels over the past five years — so in many ways she did write this with me and I owe her many thanks.

Next, I would like to thank another long-time friend, Linda Hayden. Immediately after I told her about my idea for an angel book, Linda began gathering information for me. She also became my foremost cheerleader and was always there to encourage me with this project during all my human ups and downs. Linda knows the true meaning of beauty and its healing effects, so being around her meant the angels were at work with their magic. When I think of my friends Linda and Shannon, I know I am truly blessed.

When I told my family about the book, my father said ironically, "Well, we sure know you've been surrounded by angels in this house." The thing is, it's true. I am always surrounded by angels in their house. You see, my mother (Nancy) and my father (Gordon) are very much like angels and just don't know it. Their unconditional and unfaltering love has brought me through many difficult times and many changes. I would like to thank them for once again helping me through a change — writing this book. I also want to thank my sister Kathy, her husband Steve, and their children Elizabeth, Jessica, and Nicholas for providing some humor and fun for the book. I especially want to thank Elizabeth for the poem she contributed to the Angel Forum and Jessica for her funny comments on angels, which I used in various places. Thanks also to my brothers, Tim and Kevin, for their help and inspiration.

The first positive response I had from the publishing world came from Dan Joy, senior editor at J.P. Tarcher, Inc. Dan came over one evening and spent several hours helping me get the proposal in shape, and he had a lot to do with helping me find the right publisher. I thank him for all his valuable support.

The angels truly knew where to look when they wanted to find the right publisher. Hal and Linda Kramer are publishers with a vision to make the world a better and happier place to be. There could be no better publishers for this book, and I want to thank them for their insight and for their help along the way. Not all writers can call up their publishers directly, whenever necessary, and receive just what they need. I consider myself very blessed to know them.

Hal and Linda knew just where to find the right editor. Nancy

Grimley Carleton came in at the end of the process and truly polished my work. I want to thank her for the long hours she spent making sure I said what I wanted to say. Also, I am very honored that she found the time to contribute a delightful piece for the Angel Forum. Thanks also to Uma Ergil, Hal and Linda's angelic assistant.

Other help from the publishing world came from the positive feedback I received from Steve Bucher of Lowertown Books (Minneapolis) and from Philip di Franco of Di Franco Productions. I thank them both for their time and their happy-go-lucky dispositions.

I wish to thank Laura Huxley for spending an afternoon talking with me about the book and for her helpful advice about the writing of books in general.

I also wish to thank Dr. Linda Zwingeberg Fickes for kindly allowing me to excerpt her article "Healing With Angels" for the Angel Forum.

I owe many thanks to my friends: to Violet and Derek Budgell for their cheerleading and the wonderful angel gifts they gave me for inspiration (and to Violet for being the essence of charm); to Deirdre Briggs for her supportive and generous nature and for bringing me books and information on angels; to Laura and Dean Larson for their encouragement, for the angel theme Christmas party, and for promoting angelic beauty through Laura's art and Dean's photography; and to Diane Piazzi for fourteen years of humor, laughter, and friendship. Many thanks to Mary Beth Crain for her lighthearted foreword and Angel Forum piece.

The community of people I lived with while writing this book provided helpful encouragement, and never a dull moment. I would like to thank John C. Lilly, Lisa Lyon-Lilly, Barbara Clarke-Lilly, Nina Lilly, Charles Lilly, Frankie Lee Slater, Rudy Vogt, and Chicharra, for always being there with encouragement, humor, excitement, and friendship.

Other friends who helped in important ways were George and

Jackie Koopman, Jai Italiander, Jeannie St. Peter, Larry Raithaus, Joe D. Goldstrich, Michael Siegel, Michael Shields, Patricia Le Dell, and Leticia Boyle. Thank you to Kathy Faulstich for letting me overhear her angel story, and to her mother, Katherine Portland, for a lifetime of encouragement and inspiration.

Special thanks to all who participated in the Angel Forum whom I haven't yet mentioned: Suzanna Soloman, Carol Kramer and Karyn Martin-Kuri, Daniel Kaufman, Kutira Decosterd and Moonjay, Filomena, and Gideon Boomer.

I would like to thank Wesley Van Linda of Narada Productions and Kathy Tyler and Joy Drake of InnerLinks for help with the section on their ANGEL® cards.

And I thank all the angels I've ever known.

Part One

The Nature and Origin of Angels

Chapter 1

Angels Now and Historically

Most of us have seen paintings of angels who look like beautiful humans with wings and flowing attire. Angels are usually depicted with halos, auras of white light that encircle their heads. When we read about angels, they are usually described in the same way, but sometimes they are said to appear as dazzling, almost blinding, white light.

How did artists and ancient scribes come to the conclusion that angels have wings and halos? Early books of the Old Testament did not depict angels this way; they were described as ordinary humans dressed in white goatskins (symbolizing purity, light, and holiness), or as wingless youths. Wings and halos showed up in Christian art around the time of the Roman emperor Constantine (A.D. 312), who converted from Roman paganism to Christianity after seeing a cross in the sky before a major battle. Before that, the Greek pantheon included winged gods such as Hermes and Eros, who, in addition to their other functions, carried messages between the gods of Olympus and the

2

lesser gods of earth. The word *angel* comes from the Greek word *angelos*, meaning messenger. Because angels functioned as God's messengers, eventually they were thought of as having wings, like the winged gods Hermes and Eros. Wings symbolize the quickness with which angels travel carrying God's messages. The halo or aura of white light symbolizes their origin or home, which is heaven.

The pictorial image of wings and halos provided believers with a focus and an icon to adore. Soon, art was thriving with winged angels, and poetry and drama followed suit.

So, historically, angels were thought of as messengers between God and humanity. Messages we receive from God through angels are meant to bring us closer to achieving heaven on earth. As a species, we haven't really changed that much. For most of us, picturing angels with wings and halos is still the easiest way to visualize them. This is fine, because angels can appear in any form our imagination will accept.

Angels in one form or another exist in almost all of the world's great religions. They are mentioned in recorded history as far back as three thousand years before Christ. Because this book is about the present, about how angels can help us right *now*, I am not going to involve you in a detailed history of ideas about angels. Entire books have been written on this subject. I will mention just a few highlights of this story.

The ancient cultures of Egypt, Babylon, Persia, and India all acknowledged winged angels (sometimes called "gods"); it is likely that these traditions influenced the Greeks and Romans, who began painting wings on angels in the West. The Yoga Sutras of Patanjali, an Indian meditation teacher roughly contemporary with Plato, told how one could contact "celestial beings" by meditating on the light inside one's own head; these beings of light make the connection between the human and the divine realms. (I know a meditation devotee who is continuously in touch with the angelic realm, and she is enwraped in a cloud of angels wherever she goes.)

An especially significant development in angel history came from Persia, where Zoroaster (also known as Zarathushtra, ca. 628–551 B.C.) wrote in great detail in his Avesta about his encounters with a number of angels, and said that angels are extensions and projections of God toward humanity—not separate beings standing between God and humanity. (God is portrayed by Zarathushtra as presiding over a court of angels—oversized humanlike figures, both male and female, who reflect God's radiance.)

The idea that angels are expressions or extensions of God, rather than independent beings, was emphasized by the Gnostics, contemporaries of Jesus, who warned against accepting angels as intermediaries between humans and God—in effect, as "God's brokers."

There seems to be renewed interest these days in the three orders of angels with three choirs in each: The highest order consists of seraphim, cherubim, and thrones; the second order consists of dominions, virtues, and powers; and the third consists of principalities, archangels, and angels. Again, a number of books and essays interpret these concepts, and I will list some of these in the Annotated Bibliography in Part Five. The orders of angels are worth reading about if you are highly interested in how angels have participated in history and in the philosophical viewpoints concerning their existence.

Angels today are not really different from angels when they were first discovered. Angels have always been thought of as the main connection for humans between heaven and earth; although the concepts of God and heaven have varied, angels have consistently helped humans with our spiritual growth and happiness.

Chapter 2

What on Earth Is an Angel?

Close your eyes and see what comes to mind when you think of angels. Do you see a picture of any specific person? Does a specific incident come to mind? Do you experience a feeling of warmth and lightness passing over you as you imagine angels? Now, think about heaven. What colors do you see? Do you imagine beauty, peace, joy, and happiness? Do you think of heaven as a realm different from the one we live in here on earth?

There are many ways to interpret heaven, and many ways to interpret who and what angels are. The many interpretations come from the fact that we are all unique beings with unique experiences of life. To establish some common ground for the sake of this book, let us consider heaven as a realm or plane separate from the realm we live in on earth. Heaven is the realm of joy, lightness, happiness, unconditional love, laughter, and beauty. Let us consider that angels exist in heaven as separate beings of the highest divine power in the universe. They are beings of light who send information and loving thoughts through our higher self to inspire and guide us. These angelic beings have all the properties of light—speed, brightness, and the power to heal and to obliterate darkness.

Because we are unique beings, the way we experience and picture angels will vary accordingly. The angels discussed in this book simply want the highest good for all concerned, so you may picture them however you like. These angels want to help you connect your highest self with heaven, so you can be happier here on earth. Angels sense that the natural state of life is one of joy, happiness, laughter, and beauty, the qualities of heaven, the angels' own realm.

An angel is a guardian and messenger from heaven. Heaven is where miracles originate, where love exists as pure, unconditional healing energy, and where humans are regarded as a protected species having free will. An angel can bring the heaven realm to humans on earth if we want it and are willing to accept it. This book describes the various ways angels can inspire us to be happier and more creative beings—without taking away our free will. Angels do not control us, and they do not learn our lessons for us. They do, however, know our inner nature and can step in and protect us when they know we truly want it. They also have the ability to inspire us and send us messages that help us with our everyday life.

One way to think of angels is as coaches in the game of life. Coaches don't themselves play the game they are coaching, but they are still very important to the players. Coaches don't necessarily have to be able to play the game well; they just need to understand human nature. An angel can be our private coach by reminding us to include fun and happiness in our life game. Angels can coach us in bringing love, beauty, and peace into our lives. Angels cannot understand why more humans don't join in the divine cosmic dance of the universe. Angels and children get along well, because children can readily play and have fun— and they do it with joy, singing, screaming, and laughing. Angel coaches teach fun and merriment.

Most people do not take angels seriously. This is fine with

the angels, because they are free from the seriousness of our realm. They see most humans as being consumed with seriousness. Angels teach us that nothing is truly serious. We human beings can perform feats of amazing creativity when our minds are freed of the weight of seriousness. We can heal ourselves from disease (mental and physical), and we can turn our lives around by changing the way we think. Angels recognize the great number of higher possibilities with which human beings are blessed. They are assigned to teach humans the way of lightness, so that "human potential" can become "human reality."

Being human is something angels envy at times. Angels admire the human ability to enter deeply into the passion of love — to have strong convictions from the heart. They envy our freedom of choice, or free will. Free will gives us humans tremendous creative power. We have the power to create timeless gifts of art, literature, music, and great thinking to inspire the human race, even long after we are gone.

We have been given freedom of choice, meaning we can choose any spiritual or nonspiritual path we desire. Our free will gives us those little "ups and downs" we experience along the path we have chosen. Human beings are influenced by many cycles, including our natural biorhythms, the seasons of the year, energy waves, astrological movements, and so forth. It is natural to have some days that are good and some that are not so good. Our choices can help shift the low-energy days in a lighter, more energetic direction. Since we have free will, we can choose to transform or transcend the low points in our lives. At the least, we can understand that some low points are a natural part of life, and we can learn not to be distraught by them.

Sanaya Roman explains, "You choose the range of intensity of your emotions. Some of you have chosen a very broad range, from immense pain to great joy. Some of you have chosen narrower ranges, preferring to work with subtle levels, such as moderate joy to moderate unhappiness. Because you live in a polarity, for each positive emotion you have you will also have its opposite.

Emotional calm comes from finding the balance point, bringing all your emotions into harmony with your Higher Self." Angels want to teach us emotional balance, so that we can have the peak experiences of freedom and joy on their credit and not have to pay with the low opposite of human despair.

Angels work (play) behind the scenes to inspire in humans our inborn gifts of talent and genius. They also work (play) around the clock in their timeless dimension to synchronize human life. Their main function is to keep you from feeling unimportant in this vast sea of humanity. In the heavenly scheme of life, you have a special position; the angels around you are in charge of the research and development concerning your spiritual quests on the road to unconditional happiness (truly the road less traveled).

Chapter 3

Angels and
Our Physical Senses

Most of us do not see angels as physical objects. Some have seen angels as fields of dazzling light, too bright to stare at for long. If you do see an angel, the angel will probably take the form you are most willing to accept. Most of us have seen pictures of angels with wings and halos. If you want to imagine angels as beautiful humans with wings, this is fine; if an angel is destined to appear to you, he or she will probably oblige you by taking such a form. Angels have appeared to people throughout history, but this is rare and generally surrounds a "big event."

To get to know angels, it helps if you can transcend the "seeing is believing" paradigm and adopt an open mind and a stance of "knowing by intuition." Reality is much more than just what we see. And it is much more than what we hear. Consider for a moment the field of electromagnetic energy that surrounds us; we know this field exists, but we cannot see or hear it with our usual physical senses. We need some kind of receiver. For example, radio and television signals are silent and invisible to us until we turn on a radio or a television set, but these signals exist around us all the time. We see physical objects through their reflection of a narrow band of the frequencies called "visible light," but we see only the rays of light that actually enter the pupils of our eyes, not the entire three-dimensional field of electromagnetic "light" energy that surrounds us.

Candace Pert is one of the scientists who discovered endorphins. Endorphins are natural opiates found in our brains that act as filtering mechanisms. Endorphins are used to filter selectively the incoming information from every sense (sight, hearing, smell, taste, touch, and pain), blocking some of it from percolating up to higher levels of consciousness. Candace Pert states, "Each organism has evolved so as to be able to detect the electromagnetic energy that will be most useful for its survival. Each has its own *window on reality*." Aldous Huxley spoke of the nervous system and the brain being a "reducing valve," or filter, that enables us to experience only a fraction of reality.

If environmental information is filtered selectively by every sense, and if there are happenings around us that are not registered in our usual waking consciousness, then consider this: Part of the reality that we filter out is angelic activity. Angels are very busy, and they exist in many places at once; if we could see them readily, we would experience chaos, and we might all go crazy. When saints and mystics hear voices and see visions, other people get frightened and tend to label them "insane."

Legend has it that in ancient times angels, fairies, elves, brownies, and various other magical creatures were easy to see and talk to (perhaps this is the origin of folklore and fairy tales). Anyway, humans became so preoccupied with the magic of this realm that they were not paying attention to the physical world. So for growth and survival reasons humans for the most part had to "turn off" the ability to see and hear these magical creatures. I have talked to several people who do "see" angels, but they don't like to talk or boast about it, because it is very personal to them and of a sacred nature.

When we "hear" angels, we may hear a beautiful chorus of voices singing in the distance. I have heard about cases of angels embellishing the music a person is listening to with their singing (if they like it). Or you may "hear" sweet tingling bells or chimes at subtle times when angels are around you.

Angels sometimes leave a fragrant scent around for us to smell, in places where we can't figure out where the scent is coming from. Two floral scents they especially like are rose and jasmine.

Some people know angels are with them because at strategic times they feel a hand touch gently upon their shoulder or feel a presence so strong and calming it compels them to look around for someone who isn't there.

Don't worry if you are not able to have magical, imagistic, or physical sensations regarding angels. Angels are not here to interfere with our growth, and some of us get carried away with magical thinking and mystical experiences. The most important attitude to cultivate in attracting angels is one of optimistic, unconditional love and happiness. Angels surround the truly happy and loving person, encouraging more love and happiness. Whether you can experience them readily with your physical senses is unimportant. What matters is finding a way to know angels for yourself, and steering clear of the "seeing is believing" nonsense we have all heard at one time or another.

Angels are like thoughts. We cannot see our thoughts, but we know they exist. We can have as many thoughts as we want; there is no limit. Imagine for a moment a source field where thoughts become form. Think of a positive loving thought as a blessing. Imagine how it travels as a healing beam of light to whomever the thought was about. See it reach the person and lighten up his/her heart and mind. Now that person has a light heart and sends out blessings to those around. The original blessing has created a chain reaction of happiness that reaches out to more and more people. Now imagine what a negative thought can do. I won't describe each link in this chain, but I'm sure your imagination will help you see the damage negative thoughts can do.

Thoughts are powerful and real even though we don't see them—and so are angels. All of us have our "own window on reality," so we experience angels in our own way. There is, however, a common denominator: Angels don't hurt us; they help us. Any messages, experiences, happening, thoughts, and feelings that interfere with or limit our well-being and separate us further from our highest self do not originate from angels. Angels exist in a realm of positive, loving energy and pink love light. When we have peak experiences of joy and love, we have connected with the angels. Angels don't *have* peak experiences; they *are* peak experiences. (Angels don't experience the ups and downs we humans do.) Angels serve as models of the joyful and happy thoughts that we can share.

Chapter 4

God as the Origin of Angels

To know and understand the ways of angels, you must realize that God is their boss. Angels work for God in various capacities to maintain the loving order of the universe. God is the origin, and angels are God's first creation. Don't let the word "God" scare you or turn you off. If necessary, whenever you see God mentioned in this book, substitute a term that makes you feel more comfortable, such as "the Universe," "Mother Nature," "the Great Spirit," or whatever name puts you in touch with a higher power. Just keep in mind that angels belong to a loving higher order, which they work and play to maintain. Also, please keep in mind that God and the angels have an outrageous sense of humor.

The bottom line is that God is love, and that we are loved unconditionally by God. We are always free; God does not love us because of what we do or how much *we* love God. God loves us up-front, and whenever we want this love it is consistently available. Because there are no fixed guidelines or rules to follow for receiving unconditional love, we sometimes become perplexed and want to know how we're doing. We humans are

13

always looking for signs of approval or disapproval. We want clear boundaries to tell us how far we can go and what line we cannot cross over. We seem to want uniforms to wear, rules to follow, and outlines of our fate and destiny to fulfill.

There are no rules or formulas for finding good favor and love from God. God's love *has* to be unconditional because God gave us free will. If we didn't have free will, we would probably be sent to earth with a set of instructions and rules describing what we are supposed to do in this lifetime, and what our main purpose is supposed to be. But because we have free will we can step over any boundary, break any rule, and take off any uniforms. So where does that leave us? Loved and basically free. Our freedom is what makes us truly great, but it can also get us into trouble and cause us to miss joyful opportunities.

Some human beings spend their whole lives trying to figure out what kinds of actions will please God. They can't stand the idea that it is so easy, that God loves us no matter what we do. God loves us even when we don't love ourselves. God's message is love and forgiveness—to love and forgive ourselves, and to treat ourselves kindly.

Why are we even here? I certainly can't answer that question for you. Maybe life is all a big joke and we are let in on the punch line when we die and then spend eternity laughing hysterically. One thing I do know is that if we use our free will to make ourselves happy life is much easier, much more creative, and much more humorous. In short, it is much more fun. Free will accounts for the ups and downs of life. The ups and downs are just part of the game; ideally, the downs will help you appreciate and take advantage of the ups. Because angels don't have ups and downs in their realm, they can help bring you up faster when you've gotten down.

El Shaddai is a name for God that means "the God who is more than enough," the God who is much more than we could even desire. God wants us to be happy, and angels are God's emissaries to help us create happiness on earth. If we can learn ways to trust the abundance of a God who is more than enough, then we will have more than enough, even enough to give away, which will bring us even more.

This talk about God is *not* meant to offer you yet another belief system or cosmology; it is meant to let you know that angels come from the realm of heaven, where a pure source of unconditional love (which I have called God) exists for all of us. Unconditional love is our source of healing, happiness, and bliss; it is the ultimate freedom. Angels want us to find pure unconditional love for ourselves — to find God in ourselves — so that we will be free to create our lives as gifts that continue to give throughout time.

Don Gilmore, author of *Angels, Angels, Everywhere*, defines angels as "forms, images, or expressions through which the essences and energy forces of God can be transmitted. An Angel is a form through which a specific essence or energy force can be transmitted for a *specific purpose*." In Part Two of this book, you will learn about angels in terms of the various spiritual essences and energy forces of God they adopt. I use the term "halo" to represent the various forms and images angels transmit from God for specific purposes in our lives.

Part Two

Halos
Angels Wear

About Part Two:

Classifications of Angels

Angels of divine providence act in a variety of ways. Part Two will expose you to the busy angelic realm. You will learn about the many "halos" (or "hats") angels wear, which denote the specific essence, energy force, or spiritual expression they represent from God and heaven. A halo is a band of light that encircles an angel's head; this circle of light constantly connects the angel with heaven. Halos also provide a system of classification. In Part Two, I will describe angels in terms of certain classifications symbolized by their halos. Each chapter (big halo) has several subsections (small halos) that describe more specialized classifications of angel vocations.

Chapter 5 in Part Two is about our personal angels, who are integrated with our higher self. These angels stay around us all the time to inspire, guide, and protect. Our personal angels watch over the many spiritual paths available to us, and they act as guides and teachers to accelerate our spiritual growth. They stay nearby, cheering us on and awakening our creativity to its highest potential. Angels are always in close contact with our higher self. The higher self exists in a realm separate from our physical reality. In this realm, the higher self can remain in continuous contact with angels (if we want this and are open to it). This is why it is sometimes so effective to communicate by asking our guardian angel to speak to the guardian angel of someone else concerning our deepest and highest desires.

Chapter 6 is about angels of the moment. Angels of the moment come to us at those times when we need extra help. They help heal us when we are sick; they rescue us when we are lost, in trouble, or in danger; they provide coincidental events that remind us of the divine providence and order in the universe; they transform grave situations so that seriousness leaves and humor prevails; and they sometimes engineer miracles.

Chapter 7 introduces angels who embellish human life. These angels "make life worth living," so to speak. They provide us with unconditional happiness, fun, and mirth. They also help out with romance and wealth. And they help us extinguish worries that plague our lives.

Chapter 8 concerns angel psychologists. Angel psychologists help us understand and analyze ourselves by acting as brain program editors. Wearing this professional halo, they bring an awareness of internal behavior patterns, so that we can take advantage of the freedom to change our behavior if we so desire. Angels help us become the best we can be. Angels are also the beings behind the mythological gods and goddesses of ancient Greece, Rome, and India. These archetypal angels help us understand ourselves because they represent the original models for human personality.

Nature has en entire hierarchy of angels collectively known as the devic kingdom. Chapter 9 gives a quick overview of this devic kingdom, of the angels and lesser beings who are in charge of flora and fauna.

Chapter 10 tells you how to design your own flock of angels. You can name these angels and call upon them for help with any situation that arises. This will prove helpful if you need angelic assistance for a specific area in your life that is not included in the angels' job descriptions elsewhere in Part Two.

Remember, angels are like thoughts; you can have as many as you want for help and guidance. After reading Part Two, think about how angels work in your life. Then, read Part Three to learn how you can employ as many angels as you want using the methods for attracting angels into your life.

Chapter 5

Personal Angels

Guardian Angels

For He will give His Angels [especial] charge concerning you,
To guard you in all your ways.

Psalms 91:11

A guardian angel is assigned to each person on earth. Each human being, regardless of belief, status, shape, or size has the privilege of a guardian angel. Your guardian angel is with you all the time, wherever you go, whatever you do. It has been said that when God looks at you God sees two—you and your guardian angel. When French farmers traveled a road alone and would meet up with another single traveler, they would greet one another by saying, "Good day to you and your companion" ("companion" meaning "guardian angel"). Your guardian angel has been with you throughout time and was there when you decided to come into this world as the special human you are today. Your guardian angel remembers and keeps track of the high goals you set for yourself, the high aspirations you have stored deep in your unconscious mind.

My first memory of my guardian angel goes back to when I was three years old. I was playing in an off-limits area in our backyard with one of my teddy bears. Somehow, the teddy bear fell down a ravine. I stood looking at it for a minute, trying to decide whether to forget it or go and get it. I decided to go and get it, because it was the smallest bear in my collection and therefore important. I took one step toward the ravine and heard a voice say, "No, don't go down there; leave the teddy bear and go back up to the house." I remember feeling as if there were a barrier between me and the ravine. Considering that I wasn't supposed to be there in the first place, I left and went back up to the house with only the memory of my teddy bear. I remember thinking that he would make friends with some little animals and everything would be okay.

You may remember a time in your life when you were reckless and could have been seriously hurt, and it seemed like an invisible force pulled you to safety. Maybe you don't have a story like this but have heard one or read one somewhere. Guardian angels are known to most of us who drive cars, especially on the freeway. Many times, I've experienced that cars that were heading for an accident with me were lifted or pushed out of the way at just the right moment to avoid a collision.

When people sustain serious physical injuries and someone comes at just the right time to save their lives, the rescuer usually came because something told him or her to get there quick. The injured person's guardian angel went to the other person's guardian angel and relayed the emergency message. Basically, guardian angels are known for protecting and guarding us in all our activities on earth.

Why not explore ways to get to know your personal guardian angel? There are many ways your guardian angel can help you, beyond saving you from car accidents and bodily harm. Develop an intimate relationship with your guardian angel. You can ask your guardian angel for knowledge and insight about confusing situations in your life. You can also ask him or her to speak to the guardian angels of any people in your life concerning the involvements you have with them. Pay attention to your intuition; it will become more brilliant when you are in harmony with your guardian angel, for it is through the inner knowing of intuition that you will receive messages from your guardian angel to warn and guide you. Have you ever stopped yourself from doing something because you suddenly had a strong sense it would be a mistake, only to find out later that, if you had followed through, it would have been disastrous?

Be creative with your guardian angel. In private, be like a child who has an invisible friend and confidant — guardian angels enjoy this. Children have been known to see and talk to their guardian angels. This usually happens before children can communicate exactly what they see, but some of us can remember far enough back in our lives to a time when we spoke with and saw our guardian angels. If you have children, study their behavior when they are alone. Many children have invisible friends they talk to wherever they are, and babies sometimes seem to stare at someone who isn't there. When babies giggle and grin while sleeping, some say that they are playing with the angels. It is also fun to ask children what they think angels are and to have them draw an angel.

In Catholic grade school, children are taught about their guardian angels in first grade. They are taught that their guardian angels are faithful friends who help them while they are on earth by giving them messages of what God wants them to do, and who guard them from evil. Teachers may even encourage the children to move over in their seats to make room for their guardian angels. The Guardian Angel Prayer (see the end of this section) is recited each day. A friend of mine who is in her sixties remembers her teacher telling the children in her class that if they didn't finish their rosary prayers for some reason they didn't need to worry because their guardian angels would finish it for them.

At certain times in children's development, their guardian angels call in assistants. Extra help is usually needed during the "terrible twos," when children need to explore their boundaries. After things have settled down (depending on the child), extra help is usually not needed until a child becomes a teenager and starts driving. At this point, some teenagers could use an army of guardian angels, but suffice it to say that most teenagers have at least two guardian angels working overtime to protect them during this generally reckless period. Help may not be needed as much during the twenties, when people learn that they are not indestructible. Later in life, extra help will vary according to need.

Many human beings suffer through life, and they may regress in their evolution because they are deeply unhappy about something. Unconsciously, they seem to be trying to kill themselves with the choices they make and the way they react to life. Unhappy humans are frustrating to the guardian angels who watch over them. Angels are certainly not going to participate in unhappiness, so there is nothing for them to do except wait for that one instant when the person chooses to stop suffering and a transformation can take place. We have free will, so if we want to suffer, or if we think that is what we are supposed to do, it is our choice.

Sometimes it seems that our guardian angels have taken a vacation. Something awful happens that we cannot believe God or our guardian angel would allow. One of the great mysteries of life is why bad things happen to good people, and why good things happen to bad people. We can speculate and come up with explanations such as karma, lessons we must learn, and so forth, but some of the injustice that happens on this earth can never be explained satisfactorily. Our guardian angels never really go on vacation, but the more positive and "optimystic" we are the easier we are to protect and nurture. So fill the moment with the trust, hope, and faith that your guardian angel will always take care of you. Don't worry about tomorrow or about the misfortune of others. Be grateful you are who you are right now, and give thanks to your guardian angel.

Always keep in mind that you have a guardian angel, who is the same today, yesterday, and tomorrow. Your guardian angel wants to remind you that at this very moment you are alive, and that whether or not you are happy about this fact it is true. Your biological and mental "machine" is running on some level of efficiency, and your guardian angel wants to keep you from feeling like a victim. Your guardian angel is looking out for you, waiting for your next step; whether it is from misery to normalcy, from normalcy to feeling good, or from feeling good to total happiness and delight, your guardian angel wants to guide you toward the next higher step. Your guardian angel is always by your side, to remind you of the important and special part you play on this crowded planet.

Reciting the Guardian Angel Prayer from the Catholic tradition can help you focus on your guardian angel's presence.

Angel of God, my guardian dear,
To whom His love commits me here;
Ever this day [or night], be at my side,
To light and guard, to rule and guide.

Messengers

The New Testament was first written in Greek, and the word for angel comes from the Greek word for messenger, *angelos*. The Old Testament was first written in Hebrew, and the Hebrew word for angel is *malakh*, which also means messenger. In both the New and Old Testaments, there are many stories of angels appearing to humans with messages. These messages usually concerned major events, for example, announcing the birth of the messiah. We don't hear of angels appearing that much anymore, but they are still relaying messages to us. Because we don't always see and hear them physically, we have to be especially creative and perceptive to receive our messages.

Angels have ways of relaying messages we don't expect. Have you ever found yourself sitting for hours at a desk racking your brain for the answer to a question or problem? Just as you've decided to stop your pondering, a dove flies onto your windowsill. Noticing this dove gives you a sense of warmth and peace, and you find yourself walking toward the window. Then, as you look out the window, a truck goes by with words written on it that give you the answer you spent so much time trying to force out of your brain. As soon as you were able to release the struggle, the message came to you effortlessly.

Pay attention to the subtleties in life. Angels have many ways of reaching you, but often you miss them. For example, a child, in a moment of spontaneity, may blurt out a statement for which only you know the meaning. While thumbing through a book, a page may fall open with a clear message in the print. Headlines in the newspaper, taken out of context, might contain your message. Angels with messages often appear to us in dreams. Angels are very creative in the ways they communicate with us; we have to be just as creative when we listen for our messages.

Messages from heaven are always for the highest good of all concerned. If you receive messages or impressions that *seem* positive, but don't *feel* positive, ask yourself, "Does this message resonate with unconditional love?" Usually, a very clear yes or no answer will come to you. Messages from heaven never urge force or domination in situations, and they are usually (but not always) general rather than specific. Detailed instructions, such as "Walk to the corner, buy some cigarettes, smoke one, then call your neighbor and tell him off," are clearly not messages from heaven. Heavenly messages are often along the lines of "Don't worry. . . . Be creative. . . . Everything is all right. . . . All is well. . . . Trust. . . . "

Angels inspire us through mystical insight and sudden brilliant, or even bizarre, ideas. Some of us experience angels as inner spiritual forces that guide the higher self by instilling noble thoughts and ideals into our consciousness. All angels are messengers of some sort, regardless of the specific roles they play. Angels who are couriers of God have important news to carry. These messengers will keep at you until you receive their news, so remember to relax, release, and let your intuition guide you.

Spiritual Guides

When the pupil is ready, the teacher appears.

Spiritual guides come in and out of our lives according to need. They usually represent the essence of a particular culture, race, or religion, or they can represent a career or avenue of life. They are teachers.

When a new guide comes to you, you may find yourself with a voracious urge to know all there is to know about a particular culture or religion previously foreign to you. You start buying books, artifacts, incense, music, or clothes that will teach you the essence of this new interest and its spiritual offerings. Soon, people come into your life who are also studying the same essence in their own spiritual quests. Whether this process happens suddenly or subtly, it offers an opportunity for growth in a new direction.

Through meditation or other means, you may be able to see your guides. Basically, all you need to do is notice where your interests lie and listen to messages from within. When you discover your guide or guides, you can accelerate the pace of the lessons you are learning, as you explore the many possibilities for growth and for guidance.

For example, if one of your spiritual guides is a Native American, you may have visions that put you in touch with Mother Earth, which may bring you greater respect for the planet, which in turn may drive you to take action in some way.

If your guide is a Zen Buddhist, your lesson may concern losing your ego for a while, developing intuition, and learning to be. You may even change jobs to something more basic and less mental in order to learn new ways of being.

It may be that one of your guides represents a personality from the past, such as Florence Nightingale. In this case, your guide may portend a time of service and attention to health and nourishment.

If your guide is Celtic, you may find yourself fascinated with fairy faiths, Arthurian legends, kings and queens, harps, and mystics.

Spiritual guides teach us about spiritual values that are unfamiliar to us. Recognizing our guides through the subtle or dramatic shifts we make in our lives will help us understand our inner goals or a particular spiritual quest. Our guides never really leave us, but they may fade so that other guides can come to us when there are new lessons to learn. Spiritual guides are angels of basic teachings; they give us new insight and new creativity to bring us into harmony with our higher self.

Muses

Creativity comes from the spiritual realm, the collective consciousness. And the mind is in a different realm than the molecules of the brain. The brain is a receiver, not a source.

Candace Pert

Muses are creativity ministers who inspire our talents and gifts. We are all capable of creativity of some kind, but often we need to understand that the wellspring of creativity may rest in a world we don't see. Regardless of where our talents lie, there are muses ready to inspire us far beyond the limits we place on our humanness. There are no limits to creativity when we are inspired by angels. Creativity goes beyond talent to genius when humans develop their ability to listen to inspiration.

In Greek mythology, there are nine muses, the daughters of Mnemosyne (Memory), who were part of Apollo's retinue. These nine daughters were the goddesses of inspiration: Clio of history, Melpomene of tragedy, Urania of astronomy, Thalia of comedy, Terpsichore of dance, Calliope of epic poetry, Erato of love verse, Euterpe of lyric poems or music, and Polyhymnia of sacred or religious music.

You may notice that there are three muses directly representing poetry, and many past and contemporary poets acknowledge muses as the source of their inspiration. William Blake, an angel artist and poet once said, "I am not ashamed, to tell you what ought to be told — that I am under the direction of messengers from heaven, daily and nightly." Blake attributed all artistic genius to angels.

In Rome, it was customary to thank the genius of the house — the *lares* — at every meal; some homes even set a place for this angel. The *lares* was the spirit of the family's founder and the source of the family's creativity; genius was a part of everyday life. The word *genius* comes from the name for an ancient Roman male's guardian spirit. Juno is the name for the female's guardian spirit. At ancient birthday celebrations, the Romans honored the genius spirits, recognizing them as the source of the individual's imagination.

To muse means to meditate and reflect for creative inspiration. Whenever you need creative insight, muse away. Get in touch with your own creativity ministers, special angels who can speak to you with inspiration for your particular talent in this lifetime. Whether your gift is solving mathematical problems, painting a masterpiece, or composing great music and literature, learn to listen to your inner guidance to transform talent into genius. Please note that the existence of creative muses does not mean that we can't take credit for our artistic and creative achievements. We are the ones clever enough to expand our consciousness to allow their input, and we are the ones who do the actual work. So give yourself credit for being the genius you are.

Cheerleaders

Several years ago, I found myself wanting to make a major change in my life. While I knew this change would make my life happier, I wasn't sure how the people closest to me would react. I knew that many of them would not support my decision. My decision was leading to painful feelings of guilt, until I discovered my personal cheering section.

Coming out of a meditative state, I got the image of tiny cheerleaders cheering my life on, no matter what I chose to do, even if it was a choice no one else supported. These cheerleaders were cheering, "We like who you are" and "You deserve to be happy; go for it." I then had the courage to go ahead with my deepest desire, and in time everything worked out for the highest good of all concerned.

You, too, have an angelic cheering section for your higher self. These angels cheer with little voices, "Don't give up. . . . We like who you are. . . . Everything's going to be okay. . . . We are proud of you." There are some angels who cheer almost everything you do. Their main purpose and function is to support your decisions unconditionally without advice. This is nice when you want to make an eccentric or drastic change and other people seem to be holding you back.

Of course, you won't hear your cheerleaders' voices if you are about to do something unkind or destructive. Below the levels of goodness, the cheerleaders are silent.

Quite often, our deepest desires are difficult to follow because we judge ourselves and our position too harshly. We listen to the advice of others, instead of to our inner self. To know and follow our deepest aspirations will bring us luck. Sometimes, this may require taking a risk or two, so, if you venture out on the road of your convictions and find yourself feeling alone, remember that your cheering section and your guardian angel are there with you and that loneliness is only temporary. Listen closely; your cheering section is sending words of encouragement: "Go, team, go! Take the ball and run. . . . Don't look back!"

Copilots

As copilots, angels fly second in command on your life voyage. If you ever need them to take over, they are ready and capable. In fact, if you become disorganized, it is a good idea to let your copilot fly for a while. The pieces of your life that are scattered all around will fall into order, and you can relax and get some rest or play while you are guided back on track.

Copilots act as your invisible secretaries, arranging and ordering your days so that you don't have to make extra trips, reminding you about appointments and deadlines you are about to miss in your confusion. Take advantage of your personal secretary and give out some dictation. Dictate what time you want to get up in the morning, and how you want your days to pass. (See Chapter 20 in Part Three on the bedtime angel review.) Be specific, set deadlines, and ask your copilot to clear out confusion. Be creative and personal with your copilot angel and find new ways to accomplish your tasks so that you'll have plenty of time to create an enjoyable life.

Soul Angels

Many people ask, "Do we become angels when we die, so that we can watch over those we love?" There is a wide range of answers in the various books that address the subject of death and "near-death experiences." Some support this theory, and others don't. Some say that angels are beings created completely separate from humans.

Some people who have had a near-death experience, or who have done a guided imagery exercise of their own death, say that when they left their body deceased relatives and loved ones were there as angels to guide them into the other realm. A lot of the angel books I've read relate stories about deceased loved ones relaying important messages back to earth. These stories are very detailed and interesting and the messages usually save a life or something similarly dramatic.

According to one Tibetan Buddhist idea, each of us is a composite of aspects drawn from bygone and living personages who have influenced us in some way. Upon death, the composite disassembles and is distributed into the universe, especially to loved ones and those we have influenced. This process would leave the spirit free of its humanness in the other realm, and would benefit humans left behind. If you have loved ones who have died, remember this idea and claim a part of their composite that you could use in your own life. If you are drawn to a personality from the past, say, for example, to Thomas Jefferson, decide what it is that attracts you and take this facet into you to embellish your own composite.

Because there are so many theories concerning this subject, I will leave it to you to decide. Whatever else you do, take the love you have deep in your soul for the loved one who has crossed over and ask that this love continue to grow and transform, ask that this love watch over you. Every once in a while, I feel a blast of love coming to me from someone I have loved who has died. This is a very special feeling and is very close to the feelings I receive from my contact with angels, and very often this feeling gives me insight and inspiration. Unconditional love has no limits; it can pass back and forth through time and space in an instant. Allow yourself to experience this process directly.

Chapter 6

Angels of the Moment

Healers

There is more than enough evidence to support the theory that what goes on in our minds profoundly affects what goes on in our bodies. Healing the body can begin with healing the mind, supplying the mind with what it needs to be healthy and happy. Eliminating negative beliefs that detract from health and replacing them with positive healing thoughts also helps the body heal. (See Chapter 8 on brain program editors.) Today, many people are healing themselves by changing the way they think, by changing their attitude toward themselves and toward life.

It is interesting to note the *Oxford American Dictionary*'s definition of "to heal." These are some of the phrases used: to make whole or sound; to bring to an end or conclusion conflicts between people and groups; to settle and reconcile; to free from evil, cleanse and purify; to form healthy flesh again — to unite after being cut or broken. So, in essence, healing involves repairing and making whole after a separation or break in one's life. Healing is the act of cleaning up messes left over from the past.

Angels can serve as healing agents in many ways. They can help us heal ourselves by channeling healing rays from God. They can help us settle our conflicts with other humans. They can relay messages of forgiveness and reconciliation to others in our lives if we are willing to forgive and forget. Even if the people in question are no longer alive, angels can reach them.

You can ask healing angels for insight into what thought patterns are blocking integration. Ask them to release learned pain and transmute it. All the methods and practices mentioned in this book can be used for healing with angels. Basically, all angels are healers as well as messengers. So all healing practitioners can call upon angels for extra guidance and love.

Since angels are responsible in part for arranging coincidences, they can arrange for you to find the right doctor or healer for your particular condition. They can also rearrange your cells on a microscopic level, with the help of your own imagination. Visualize angels programming your immune system with healing messages and charging it up with energy.

When people get so sick that they are no longer in control of their own healing energy, or if something terrible happens and they end up in a coma before it is their time to die, healing angels are sent down from God to take charge. These healing angels purify the atmosphere around those who are gravely ill and unconscious. In doing this, they provide a barrier against unwanted and sickening influences. Inside the barrier, they purge the atmosphere of negativity, providing pure, clean, comfortable energy. Then the healing rays of love have direct access to the one who is ill and suffering. If you know anyone in such a state, help the angels by visualizing a healing force of angels around the person.

Healing angels do not compete with or feel prejudice against hospitals and medical doctors. Each hospital, whether it likes it or not, has its own guardian angel. Nurses have been known to see angels around humans who are recovering from grave illnesses, and doctors are often guided by divine insight. When healers recognize the role of healing angels, these healers can be more powerfully effective in what they do.

Balance of the body/mind and the spirit is the basis for healing. This is a simple concept, but it can be difficult to put into practice. So bring in the healing angels to help you.

Some books on healing are listed in Part Five. Incorporate angels into whatever you read on healing. Use your imagination, and you will discover the many ways angels can help with the healing process. Also, see Linda Zwingeberg Fickes's article in the Angel Forum.

Rescuers

Angels of the moment rescue us in various ways. If we are in grave danger of being physically injured, they will do whatever they can to help us (as long as we are not resistant). Angels of the moment sometimes appear as humans. Or they may come in full angel regalia to rescue someone from the throes of death. Occasionally, we become our higher self (or our guardian angel) and act as an angel of the moment. At these times, we may not even be aware of what we are doing or of the resounding effect we have on a situation.

I once overhead a telephone conversation at a Thanksgiving dinner celebration in which a close friend of the family was telling her sister about an angel of the moment. This friend was going through a crisis; her husband was in the hospital suffering from a stroke. To add to the stress of the situation, her husband had to be moved to a hospital in the next state (where we live). This woman was staying with her mother, and each day she was driving the freeway, which she had never done before, to be with her husband.

For a while, she wasn't aware of her husband's true condition. One day when she was feeling quite vulnerable and had driven to the hospital without her mother along for support, the doctors informed her that her husband was dying from cancer in its advanced stages. After hearing this news, the woman was left alone in a sterile, cold hallway, feeling lost and helpless. Suddenly, a beautiful young man in his twenties appeared and said, "You look like you could use a cup of coffee." She said, "Boy, could I." She went with him and had cofee. He made her feel better and even told her she reminded him of his mother, which did wonders for her (she is one of the most effective and loving mothers I know). He said he was one of a group of volunteers at the hospital and would make sure her husband was fed and looked in on when she wasn't there. After her cup of coffee with this exceptional young man, the woman felt a sense of peace and strength, which enabled her to make the drive home without falling apart. Then I heard her tell her sister that the young man just disappeared and she never saw him again. She ended by saying to her sister, "I think he was some kind of angel."

Yes, he was an angel of the moment. Was he a "real" angel who manifested in the body of a young man, or was it simply the young man's higher self being utilized in this situation? Well, whoever he was, he was a rescuer, and he gave this friend a sense of peace and well-being of the sort only angels are capable of transmitting.

Synchronism Agents

Have you ever thought that there was something more to coincidence than just random chance? Psychologist Carl Jung and physicist Wolfgang Pauli thought so, and they termed this "something more" synchronicity. Synchronicity involves the peculiar interdependent relationship of two events whose connection is apparent to the observer but whose relationship cannot be explained by the principles of causality. Such contemporaneous events seem to influence each other in ways for which we do not yet have a scientific explanation.

Jung explored the relationship between objective "chance" events and the subjective "psychic" state of the observer of these events. One of Jung's theories is that the inner and outer words are mysteriously connected, so that something happening in the outside world affects what is happening inside the inner world, or vice versa. Most theories of psychic power say that mind exerts influence over matter, or that the mind can sense or predict events that are distant in time or space.

Another possible explanation of the "something more" could be that events happening right now are part of a larger pattern that was set up earlier, or that events are being controlled by an agency in the cosmos that arranges coincidences. Such an agency might involve angels in "cosmic coincidence control."

My own view is that angels are the agents of synchronicity. Not only do angels arrange helpful coincidences, they can also use this power to send us messages. One way they communicate with us is through "synchronisms." A synchronism is a coincidence for which you recognize that strange "something more." Synchronisms are difficult to describe; they need to be experienced and explored personally.

The first step in developing your capacity to experience synchronisms is to attune your awareness of events and symbols that have meaning to you. Obviously, I have an interest in angels, and many of my synchronisms involve songs with the word *angel* in them. There is a music store that I've gone to five or six times and each time they are playing a different type of music, and each time I've heard at least one song with the word *angel* in the lyrics. Many times I have turned my radio on to find that a song with *angel* in the title is playing or that a phrase about angels is being sung at that very moment.

One way to explore synchronicity is through ANGEL® card readings (see Chapter 14), through tossing the *I Ching*, or even through tarot readings. These systems are not meant to tell the future but to make visible what is happening in the present, reflecting our state of mind and the current path we are traveling. Don't ask the same questions over and over; once is enough. (As an old saying goes, the master speaks but once.) Use tools like these as means for gaining insight only, not as a crutch for making decisions. Synchronicity can help us become more aware of what is going on in our unconscious mind.

Synchronisms are personal, and it is up to you to figure out the "something more"—the meaning. This is tricky, because how do we really know what these events mean? Be careful not to get too excited over the details of synchronisms. Don't get to the place where you are making important decisions based on deeper meanings you have read into a particular situation. Basically, I use synchronisms as an indication that I am on the right track, in the right place, for the right lesson, at the right time. The mere appearance of a compelling synchronism may itself be the message, telling you that you are playing a part in a larger pattern controlled by unseen influences.

Synchronisms are also fun, and they make life more interesting and humorous. Explore your own psychic abilities and define your own synchronistic events however you choose; there are no rules.

Humor Transformers

Many people these days are talking about transformation. Transformation means making a great change. When we ask for spiritual transformation (either consciously or unconsciously), we will get it, and we may be surprised with what this entails. When we strive for the ultimate spiritual change in our lives, tests and lessons will follow us wherever we go. The ride along the road of spiritual transformation is not always smooth, so it is important to take along your sense of humor.

The angels of transformation teach one lesson—humor. They teach us that nothing is serious and that laughing at our human selves is freedom. They teach us to laugh instead of complain. Finding humor in life is not that easy; it is much easier to be serious. Every day, we are plagued by seriousness; just turn on the evening news, and I guarantee you will soon find yourself worrying about your safety, your security, your health, your future—the list goes on and on.

Spiritual transformation is a personal choice each step of the way. Angels won't do it for us; *we* have to do our own spiritual "work." That is, only we can look inside ourselves and become aware of what we want to transform. But the angels can help us by pointing out the humor in any situation. To find the humor in a seemingly humorless situation, such as being stuck in a spiritual dilemma, stop and ask, "Okay, angels, what's so funny about this one?" We must choose a way out of every dilemma, so choose humor and call upon the humor transformers for assistance to see how funny the dilemma really is.

If you catch yourself complaining, transform your complaints into laughter. Humans are funny, especially when we complain; complaining is actually endearing if it is done with a sense of humor. It is truly amazing how many trivial things we take seriously each day; it's hilarious! What really *is* serious? What have those awful people done to you this time? Have you almost starved to death lately, or have you been threatened with jail for not paying the rent? Well, if so, try laughing; some people may think that you're a comedian out of work and buy you dinner. Then they'll find out you're about to become homeless and since you're so funny and they haven't been laughing enough lately they'll ask you to move into their place.

Do you remember the times as a child when you would be crying because of something that seemed so dreadfully serious and then all of a sudden the desire to cry would leave and you'd want to laugh but you knew that that would blow it with your parents, but you couldn't help it and burst out laughing anyway? The humor transformers are ready to restore the divine humor that will bring you into a state of grace. So when you lose your desire to be serious, let yourself *burst out laughing*; the state of grace happens in an instant.

Miracle Engineers

According to the *Oxford American Dictionary*, a miracle is a remarkable and welcome event that seems impossible to explain by means of the known laws of nature and is therefore attributed to a supernatural agency. Of course, the supernatural agency is God's crew of angels. Miracles come in many sizes and in various ways. There is a popular bumper sticker that reads: "Expect a Miracle." This is good advice for those of us who are becoming aware of angels, for angels are the engineers who organize and manage miracles.

Love is the force behind miracles. When love is converted into pure, unconditional energy, it heals whatever it touches. Miracles teach and perpetuate love. Miracles can transform those who doubt and hate into those who hope with love. Love, in and of itself, is a miracle. When angels choose insufferable human beings for miracles, they are always trying to teach them that they are loved. Think of Scrooge; he denied love every day until those spirits got a hold of him.

Each time we change our thinking from a negative to a positive program, we have brought about a remarkable and welcome event. Life is a miracle all around us, every day. When you make the choice each day to be happy and not worry, realize what a miracle it is to choose the positive. Over time, small miracles add up to large ones. Miracles do happen, and miracles teach love, unconditionally, through God's agency of miracle engineers.

Chapter 7

Angels Who
Embellish Human Life

Worry Extinguishers

*And which of you by worrying and being anxious can add one
measure to his stature or to the span of his life?*

Matthew 6:28

Angels love to destroy worry and anxiety. To worry is to torment
yourself with disturbing thoughts. Worrying means you are
harassing yourself with anxiety over what might happen, or
over the consequences of what has already happened. Worry
muddies the water of your creative nature, because it takes up
too much time and energy. Worry defeats its supposed purpose
by not giving you the chance to solve the problem that is worrying you. For if you are in a state of worry the problem will continue to exist, and it will own you.

If you are worrying all the time, you are taking life too seriously. Why stay up nights worrying about a problem when the

solution may be available only during dream time? It's easy to fall into the trap of worrying. When you find yourself worrying at a time when you would otherwise be happy and peaceful, call on the worry extinguishers. These angels will take care of what is causing you worry, reworking every issue for the highest good of all concerned. Also, if you are worrying about a situation you have yet to face, send the worry extinguishers before you to pave the way. Then notice patterns of how everything works out. If you are running late to an appointment, the other person will be even later—so why fret on the way? "Let go and let the angels," so that you can use your time for happiness and creativity. (Part Three includes specific methods for releasing worry.)

Happiness Trainers

A father and son who live on a well-traveled highway somewhere in Illinois are called "the wavers," because all they do all day is sit in the front yard of their junk shop and wave and smile at anyone traveling down the highway. Sam Chapman and his father Clarence spend up to twelve hours a day just waving at passersby. Frequent travelers on this road say that it is a welcome treat to have the wavers wave and smile at them; they say that it changes their mood to a much lighter state. What the waving does is wake them up—wake them up to happiness, wake them out of their present state of worry and tight time schedules. Just thinking about the wavers makes me happy; I can see their smiling faces in my mind.

When asked about their job, the wavers say that they had to *train* themselves to be happy and to sit in one place and wave at people all day long. We could all use some happiness training, and luckily for us there are flocks of angels whose sole purpose is to train humans in the art and practice of happiness. These angels want to wake us up to happiness, just as the wavers wake up passing motorists. (Could it be that the wavers are angels?) Happiness without reason, regardless of the circumstances in your life, gives you an ease of being in the world. This is the ultimate freedom — to experience a state of happiness you can carry with you wherever you are, whatever you are doing, whoever is with you — the freedom to be unconditionally happy. Claiming and accepting happiness is difficult for most of us. There may be several reasons why some people can't accept happiness into their being. Quite often, they feel they have to do everything for themselves without any heavenly help. They don't realize that they can "let go and let the angels." Accepting happiness may require reprogramming or changing the way you think about life, which may involve reevaluating your priorities and beliefs; this is why we need happiness trainers. Happiness trainers help us identify the things we do that keep us from true, unconditional happiness. They make us aware of the reactions we have to situations that take away happiness. To be happy means being in a state of fascination with life, where situations are simply interesting, not necessarily good or bad.

Happiness is now; it doesn't happen tomorrow or depend on circumstances. The happiness of the past is spent, so happiness training requires full awakeness in the now. Part Three offers some specific methods for happiness training. Get to know the happiness trainers, ask them to come and help you train in the blessing of happiness, and then read about Happiness Training in Chapter 17 to guide you in developing your own working model of happiness.

If you find yourself in a serious mood, look up at the sky and visually imagine all those happiness trainers waving and smiling at you!

Fun Executives

Have you ever really thought about fun? The *Oxford American Dictionary* defines fun as that which provides lighthearted amusement and enjoyment. When we do something we like, we say, "This is fun." Sometimes, work can become play; if we like it, then it is fun. Wouldn't it be great if everything we did provided lighthearted amusement? Well, that might be taking it a bit too far, but in this day and age we definitely need more fun. Angels' work is their play. The fun executives are always ready to provide light for your heart in any situation. They get their name from knowing how to manage fun and put it into effect.

When we set aside time for fun, sometimes we don't know what to do. We might go on vacation, expecting to have lots of fun, but instead we become bored. How ironic life can be! Adults often say, "I'm too busy to have fun." Games are supposed to provide fun, and most jobs are like games—there are rules, scores, players, and goals. So why isn't work fun? Work isn't fun because we take it seriously, and serious things usually aren't fun. Fun is like happiness; it depends not on circumstances but on our being in synch with ourselves and the universe. Fun is Zen; it requires full, effortless attention to the moment. Once again, children can serve as our teachers. Watching children play can make time stand still; children are right in the moment, letting their imaginations run wild, taking cues from their friends, and creating fun. Children at play scream with glee and laughter. Angels want us to have fun—fun we can take with us to work, to leisure time, to any activity. Angels provide us with lighthearted amusement. Life is funny, especially when it is fun, and we can laugh wherever we go.

Think of a time that was really fun. It probably came unexpectedly, with people you never imagined you'd enjoy. Maybe it started out as an adventure, exploring new ground. Maybe you were by yourself, cleaning your house, and it turned out to be fun. Fun is possible anywhere, anytime; it really is. When you are in a situation that isn't fun and you want it to be, take a time-out to get into synch by relaxing into the moment. If you're suffering from boredom, then do something about it. Get out, and ask the angels for a change. Don't grow up; regress if necessary. Find that child within you and learn to play again. Fun is contagious; let it start with you and then spread to those around you.

Call in the fun executives whenever you need good, old-fashioned, childlike fun. Ask and you will receive. Whether you're at a party, at work, or on vacation, just call on the fun executives and let your imagination speak to you. Take your cues from these angelic friends who represent the true essence of fun!

Mirth Makers

Mirth is like a flash of lightning, that breaks through a gloom of clouds, and glitters for a moment; cheerfulness keeps up a kind of daylight in the mind, and fills it with a steady and perpetual serenity.

Joseph Addison

Mirth is a little different from fun, although the two often go together. Picture a large round oak table lighted by lots of candles. Around the table are a party of friends who are practicing the "eat, drink, and be merry" religion. Joyful music is playing, and the laughter is on the verge of uncontrolled hilarity, exceeding the limits of propriety and reason. Everything is amusing and thus provides an excuse to laugh and giggle. Glee, the effervescence of high spirits and ecstatic gestures, is alive at this table. Good nature, good spirits, benevolent joviality, and a sense of love for all hold reign as the sights and sounds of merriment continue. Joy, merriment, glee, laughter, and fun equal mirth.

Mirth goes a step beyond fun. Mirth is like a magic spell cast over those participating in fun. It involves the merriment of the moment, not necessarily wit and fun making. You may find the example of mirth given in the above paragraph a bit too gustatory for a book on angels, but angels understand that we are humans and that we need to eat and drink together. Angels appreciate the sense of communion we experience when we share meals with others. Mirth is meant to be shared, and angels create it to share with us. If we could see the angels at the party described, they would be dancing, giggling, and singing with joy right in the midst of all the human activity.

Of course, we don't have to be eating to be graced with mirth. Being in love or taking a long walk with the one you love can be quite mirthful. Actually, anything you do when you are in love with life can be mirthful.

It would be difficult to have mirth without the angels; it is their invention. If you need mirth in your life for you and those you love, ask the mirth makers. Mirth makers are always ready to celebrate by adding extra joy and laughter to happiness. You may need to be the instigator, so follow your heart to the gleeful side of life, to mirth.

The Cupid Force

Cupid is the Roman god of love, the son of Venus. Cupid is an angel; he is portrayed as a young angel with wings. True romantic love is the greatest gift available to humans on earth. Where do we find this greatest gift? If you go looking for it, you won't find it; it has to find you.

If romantic love is the greatest gift from heaven, why does it cause us so much trouble? One reason is that it involves other humans. Other humans cause us trouble when we expect them to provide us with happiness. Only we can generate and accept our own happiness; others can embellish our happiness, but they can't give it to us. We have to have it first. Love comes to those who already possess love. Love comes when it can multiply and create an abundance, so there is enough to give away.

Sometimes, Cupid causes us so much trouble we want to re-name him "Stupid Cupid." You have heard the saying that, under the spell of romance, "love is blind." We don't notice the obvious, until later. We attract what deep down we feel we deserve, so look at the obvious. What have you attracted? Have you attracted some-one who is loving and generous in every way, or someone who is draining your peace of mind and wreaking havoc on your life?

Often, we hold on too long to someone who is not really compatible with our true self, and by holding on there is no room for anything better to come along. Keeping an atmosphere of freedom and release around you when you are in love opens the channels. When we love others, we must set them free so that they can come and go, and we must release them with forgiveness when they do something we don't like. Work on finding your true worth, and the Cupid force will find your true love. Don't limit Cupid by asking for someone specific. Let the angels chose your partner; you won't be disappointed, and most likely you'll be pleasantly surprised.

Prosperity Brokers

Prosperity is the art of being financially successful and fortunate. Prosperity doesn't mean having hoards of money; it means that the money you have is managed in a positive way. Regardless of what we have on paper, it's the way we live that makes us prosperous. Money is like energy: If it is used, it creates more; if it is stifled and stored, it withers (the interest rate earned on money in a bank often doesn't keep up with the rate of inflation). To use money as energy, we cannot be attached to it. We must be willing to release money with the positive thought that it will continue to work for us, that the energy cycle will not be broken. If you want freedom but you work all day with the belief that only money will give it to you, when will you ever have the time to be free?

Money is an apparition, a dream; if you chase after it as if it were real, you become part of a dream, different from what you are. This dream can become a nightmare and can cause a person extreme detriment and desperation. The belief that having money is good and not having money is bad is limiting and mistaken; having money is totally useless unless you have a use for it, and if the use you have in mind is a negative one then money can be destructive. By the same token, not having money is a problem only at those crucial moments when money is needed. Prosperity brokers can help move those crucial moments around to the times when you have money—hence, no problem.

Call in the prosperity brokers to teach you the true essence of wealth and abundance. Wealth and abundance come from an attitude of seeing our life as its own fortune, rich and plentiful with enough to go around. With a prosperous attitude comes a knowing that the universe will take care of us. The prosperity brokers make invisible deals for you, which may involve transferring your wealth—that is, converting time, energy, and ideas into more negotiable commodities. Or they may make deals to enable you to enjoy your wealth more with love. Or they may need to teach you about gratitude, to be grateful for what you do have rather than focus on scarcities. They may teach you to be grateful for each moment as a precious gift and thankful for each situation as a valuable lesson.

There are many excellent books written about spiritual prosperity and financial abundance; some will be mentioned in Part Five. If you decide to explore this subject further, take the prosperity brokers and your guardian angel as guides and helpers with the methods written in these books. So often, in employing "the power of positive thinking," humans forget to employ angels as well. Good luck and good fortune to you!

Chapter 8

Angel Psychologists

Brain Program Editors

I've said before that angels are like thoughts and that they inspire us by instilling ideas into our thought processes and patterns. Angels would never interfere with our thought processes without our asking, so ultimately we are in charge. If we make a conscious choice to let them in, angels can help us eliminate negative and worrisome thoughts in many ways. One way is by acting as brain program editors.

If you want to be a happier person, it is important to know exactly why negative thoughts need to be edited. These are some of the ways negative thoughts affect our well-being:

1. Negative thoughts depress vitality, including the immune system.
2. Negative thoughts and statements influence other people around you.
3. Negative thoughts and ideas bias your perceptions in favor of detecting and focusing on the negative aspects of existence.

Therefore, you expect and search (consciously or unconsciously) for negative results to confirm your negative expectations.
4. Negative thoughts distract you from the pursuit of positive goals. For example, you might waste time and energy preparing to cope with a possible negative situation, instead of pursuing a more valuable positive opportunity.

If you are aspiring to be your higher self, changing negative thoughts and editing the programs in your brain that don't work well are valuable pursuits. If you are using creative visualization techniques to connect with the abundance in the universe, it is important to know how and why visualization and positive thinking work. The benefits come mostly from eliminating negative belief programs that make you feel undeserving of your highest good.

Brain program editors, if you allow them, can have access to your brain and mind. They can go into your brain like technicians and improve your programming. If you put yourself in a receptive state, these angels will reprogram your brain by adding new information and discarding negative and stale programs.

You might think this sounds ridiculous—letting angels into your brain to change things! Many of you, however, allow more questionable things (such as mind altering chemicals, outmoded beliefs, and T.V.) to enter your brain, so why not angels? Visualize angels having the same effect as endorphins on your brain. These methods can introduce new brain-wave forms, improve molecular structure, and program inspiring beliefs that will give you a mission of greatness in life.

Archetypal Angels

For many years, I believed that the gods and goddesses of ancient Greece and Rome were actually angels. Then I came across support for this idea in several of the books I've read on angels. Dorothy Maclean, in her book *To Hear the Angels Sing,* writes: "I realized with joy, excitement and awe that the mythological gods of Greece were members of the Angelic world. This recognition was another instance of the truth of the oneness of all life — a leavening of the coded virtues of the Old Testament with the grace and beauty of the pagan world."

Jungian psychology studies the effect archetypes have on human personality. Archetypes are inherited from universal ancestors, such as the gods and goddesses of ancient Greece, India, and Rome. Archetypes are lodged in our unconscious as patterns of ideas, thoughts, and physical images. Archetypal energy, in the form of angels, stores the original models or prototypes from which human personalities are designed. In general, all mythological beings can be discussed as angels who represent our personality drives. By understanding these aspects of our personality, we come to a deeper understanding of ourselves and our drives. If we understand the archetypes, we can use this information to fill in the blanks of our personalities and strive for greatness.

When looked at as angels, archetypes come alive as a form of guidance. Each archetype you possess has a higher aspect that can manifest under the proper conditions. Also, if you study all the aspects of a particular archetype you've inherited, you may find the clue to certain behavior patterns you want to change. Astrological signs are also archetypes, and each planet is associated with one of the archetypal gods and goddesses of ancient Rome. One way to study the various archetypes is to read about them in mythology books or to consult books on Jungian psychology.

The archetypes are not meant to limit us; they are simply personality blueprints we inherit from the universe; we can trade them in for new ones if we choose, or we can rise above their influence completely. The inheritance of personality traits in various combinations makes us unique. We can supplement our basic personality traits by calling to us an angel for an archetype we may be lacking, and we can learn to love the archetypes with which we are born and in turn love ourselves more.

Chapter 9

Angels of Nature

The Devic Kingdom

The devic kingdom is the perpetuating life force of nature. It has a hierarchy of its own. Devas are the royalty of nature; they hold the archetypal patterns of every species on earth. Devas oversee entire landscapes. The smaller nature spirits, such as fairies, elves, gnomes, wood sprites, nymphs, and fauns, are given the blueprints of various plant forms, and they become the craftspeople who tend to the smallest details of each plant. In a sense, what angels are to human beings these little spirits are to plants and animals — sources of guidance and perfection.

The devic kingdom wants to share nature with us in a harmonic way, bringing us joy through the glorious creations of flowers, trees, fields of wheat, tropical forests, and so forth. The devic kingdom helps teach us respect for the earth and its energy currents.

Have you ever been inside a building that didn't feel right for some reason? Outside, the landscape held a barren, empty feeling in places and the plants didn't seem to grow very well despite ample watering and care. On the other hand, maybe you have noticed how some houses seem to fit right into the natural setting of the land; the plant life around them is lush, and the ambiance feels "right." Or maybe you have a favorite park with these characteristics. The Chinese have a word for this subtlety: *feng-shui* (which, translated literally, means "wind-water"). When the *feng-shui* is right, there is an alignment with the wavelike *ch'i* currents of the earth. In the West, this understanding is referred to as geomancy, which is based on the premise that humans do not act upon the earth, they interact with it. The devas can help you get the *feng-shui* right in your own environment by sending you messages concerning exactly where to build and plant and how to landscape. As always, the best way to receive messages from the devas or from any angel is to pay quiet attention to your intuition. If you are planting a garden, take your time to find the right spot for it by listening to nature. Open your heart and mind to the devic kingdom, and the devas will give you creative ideas for the *feng-shui* of your place in the universe.

For more information about the devic kingdom, read Dorothy Maclean's *To Hear the Angels Sing*. This inspiring book relates messages Dorothy received from the devas on how to grow the miracle garden at Findhorn.

Chapter 10

Designer Angels

There may be some areas in your life that the angels described so far don't seem to fit. Well, no problem! You can simply ask that an angel suited to this area take over. Basically, all you have to do is define the situation and name the angel who is supposed to take charge of it. A custom-designed angel will arrive and take on the job. In this way, you can draw to you your own personal flock of angels.

Designer angels can help for a variety of situations. For example, if you are a teacher, you may want to name an angel of education to watch over and guide you. You might name the angel something like Socrates or Horace. If you are a student, you can call upon a designer angel to help you study.

If you are a writer, call in a specific angel to help you write. Give the angel an appropriate name, maybe the name of a character in your next best-seller. Also, it is always helpful to get in touch with the angel of the typewriter or word processor you use when you are writing; this angel will help you in a variety of ways. According to best-selling angel novelist Andrew Greeley, Gabriel(la) is the patron angel of electronic gadgets.

You can also call upon designer angels for help with the communication arts or communication in general. Send angels with the letters you write and the phone calls you make.

If you're an artist, you can get very specific and name angels for your paints, for certain colors you are using; you can even assign angels to your favorite paintbrush and to each masterpiece you create.

If you are a businessperson, assign an angel of profit and an angel of customer increase or customer service to your business.

Think of your hobbies and the way you spend most of your time. There's room for angels in every activity and in every moment of the day. Some angels like to cook, even though they can't eat what they create!

Assign an angel to be the guardian of your hearth and home — to create a loving atmosphere where peace prevails. You can even assign an angel to each room. Set a place at the dinner table for your home guardian and designate a place where this angel can sit in your living room.

Angels are always ready to assist in the process of birth, especially in the birth of human beings. Angels like to be included in the miracle of creation from the very beginning. Invite them in. Of course, your guardians will be there anyway, but they enjoy company.

Angels can be assigned to groups or organizations that have an objective purpose of promoting well-being. Any group with an enlightened cause, whether it be promoting healthy fun for the individuals in the group or working toward world peace, has a group mind. If you belong to a group fitting these criteria, then acknowledge the group angel. The group angel represents the group mind. You can regard the group mind angel as the guardian of the group, and you can send this angel before you. Also, be sure to ask the group angel to guide you into the group mind to work out problems and create new awareness.

In contacting designer angels, pretend that there is a big adoption agency in heaven from which you can adopt an angel or that there's a catalogue of angels you can peruse. Have fun and think of this like a "star registry," where by naming a star it becomes yours. Look up to the sky and name an angel or a flock of angels to preside over the areas of your life that make you who you are.

Part Three

Attracting Angels
Into Your Life

About Part Three:

Keeping an Angel Journal

The main objective of Part Three is to help you clarify your goals, aspirations, and deepest desires and then discover ways the angels can help you create a sustainable positive energy (faith) toward attaining them. Angels have very creative ways to let you know they are providing what is necessary for accomplishing your ultimate mission. The key is recognizing the signs that show they are working (playing) with you through your higher self (or your own guardian angel). These signs include peace of mind, feelings of great hope, fortunate coincidences, and favorable meetings. Such signs confirm that you are on course and that your angel channels are open and fine-tuned to the universe of radiant bliss.

To employ the methods in Part Three in a personal way, it is helpful to keep an angel journal. Your angel journal will become a workbook for understanding your goals and for visualizing the future, as you learn to focus on what you want instead of worrying about what you don't yet have.

In your angel journal, you can free your imagination from the trap of seriousness. In it, you can challenge, accept, and reach into the galaxy of your imagination. Your imagination is your direct line to God. Cultivating and harvesting your imagination will save you from boredom, and will help you become attuned to your intuition.

Use your angel journal as a reminder to become less serious by listing ways to take life as lightly as the angels do. Keep track of everything you discover about happiness and lightness in your journal; record sayings and excerpts from books and articles that inspire you. Keep track of all angel experiences, synchronisms, and thoughts about angels. Use your journal to discover other dimensions to your sense of humor and lightness through angel awareness.

Part Three tells you how you can work (play) with the angels to rebirth yourself into angel consciousness, where we realize that happiness is in ourselves, not in our circumstances. You will learn about how angels can guide and assist you every day of your life.

For a moment, think of life as an experiment, one that is set up for the experience of enlightenment. There is nothing you can do to bring about enlightenment; enlightenment is serendipitous — a pleasant discovery made by accident. But accidents of this kind are more likely to happen when your life is set up for conducting a spiritual experiment rather than a worldly or physical one.

Perhaps we set up the experiment before we are born, finding proper parents, locations, and other opportunities for our growth and then climbing into our bodies and growing according to our experimental guidelines. Most likely, we set high standards for ourselves, higher than we can imagine now that we are actually doing the experiment. One fortunate aspect about this experiment is that it is personal to you, and you can change the rules, take away limits, set new records, or change the course completely because you have free will. Another fortunate aspect concerning your growth experiment is that you have invisible assistants from the heavenly providence who remember the highest goals you set for this experiment. They are always there to remind you in their inspiring fashion just how wonderful and important you are. These invisible assistants are the angels.

Your life is not a serious experiment; it is a light, optimistic, and humorous experiment. By attracting angels into your life and consciousness, you will experience the radiant bliss and humor of the universe.

Chapter 11

Becoming an "Optimystic"

Becoming an "optimystic" means taking a light and hopeful view of your spiritual path. When you are an optimist, you expect good results. When you are a mystic, you seek union with God (whoever and whatever that means to you, of course). When you combine optimism with mysticism, you become an optimystic. When you take a light and hopeful view of your spiritual quest for enlightenment, you create a positive environment where good things thrive—good things such as hope, good luck, good fortune, fun, wishes that come true, dreams that are realized, wonderful visions of a paradisiacal heaven, and unconditional, blissful happiness.

Do you remember wishing upon a star as a child? Walt Disney appropriately used a song about wishing on a star as his theme song. Do you remember throwing coins in a wishing well or pond? Pulling apart a wishbone? Making a wish as you blew out the candles on a birthday cake, or blew the seeds of a dandelion to the wind? A wish is a desire or mental aim. A wish is also a blessing. You have heard people ask others to wish them luck. When you wish people luck, you express hope about their welfare and hope that they will prosper. Wishing is a way of expressing a desire. Wishful thinking means you are expecting the best to happen. Start to be aware of your wishes. You may say, "I wish I could. . . . I wish I had. . . . I wish I was . . . " quite often and not even notice that you are wishing. Wishes might not always come true the way we'd like, but often enough they come true in ways beyond what we could even imagine. Wishing is one of the optimystic's main tools.

Hope is a feeling of expectation combined with desire. Wishing will not bring you anything without a burning desire. A strong desire will set your mind in action toward attaining your goals. You need hope for your wishes and desires to come true. Bernie Siegel, who has helped many people heal themselves from cancer, says, "There is no such thing as false hope." He also states, "Optimists live longer. Pessimists have a more accurate view of the world, but they don't live longer." Becoming an optimystic changes your mental chemistry, so your thoughts are changed and the situations in your life are rearranged to fulfill your hopes, desires, and wishes. Becoming an optimystic, means you have decided to live a "charmed" life.

Another tool of the optimystic is to interpret everything that happens in a positive light. This may seem impossible, but with practice you can do it. Give yourself "good luck." That is, find good luck and be ready for it. Interpret situations as lucky, even if they seem far from it. Don't say, "This is the worst thing that could happen; this is just my luck." Figure that in some way whatever happened might have been worse. If you think you are unlucky, then you tend to find more back luck. Good luck comes from taking advantage of opportunities offered and from passing through the low times with a light and cheerful heart. Walking under ladders has always brought me luck, and I've found that wonderful things always happen on Friday the thirteenth. Max O'Rell put it this way: "Whether or not it's bad luck to meet a black cat depends upon whether you are a man or a mouse."

Magnetize good luck to your life; it's up to you. Be aware that superstitions are in opposition to angel power. If you insist on being superstitious, the angels feel that you are not trusting them. Try eliminating all superstitious behavior from your life. If you believe that doing one thing will cause another thing to happen, change your thinking, do the one thing, and see that it does not cause the other thing.

Becoming an optimystic means eliminating suffering. Suffering is not a virtue. Suffering means you are subjecting yourself to pain, loss, damage, and disadvantage. Sometimes, sufferers even take on someone else's pain if they don't think they are suffering enough on their own. Suffering and sadness are habits that afflict many of us. Suffering can teach us lessons, if we can identify what is causing the suffering and release it from our lives. God does not make us suffer; we make ourselves suffer. An optimystic knows that suffering cramps one's style, and interferes with hope and happiness. Make the choice to suffer less and fulfill hopes more.

Integrating fun and play into your spiritual pursuit and developing a keen sense of humor are other tools of the optimystic. *Lila* (pronounced "leela") is a Sanskrit word meaning the divine play of creation, or the divine play of the universe; it is the reason God created the universe. Translated, it means pure fun. (That seems like a good reason to create a universe!) Part of the optimystic's job is to promote fun and play in the universe. The seriousness of life is forever removing fun and play from view. The optimystic can reclaim play, fun, and humor and make the world a happier place. The angels want to teach us how to play and have fun, two areas of their expertise.

Mystics are known to most of us as people who have spiritual visions or intense religious experiences. Mystics see beyond the popular explanations held by their social group. The *Oxford American Dictionary* defines a mystic as someone who is initiated into the mysteries and who can transcend ordinary human knowledge using intuition. A mystic enjoys moments of spiritual ecstasy and peak experiences of love and joy. By becoming optimystics, we can transcend the ordinary and accept the unusual in a light and happy manner. Angels will provide spiritual ecstasy and peak experiences for us if we want them. Don't be afraid to get carried away once in a while; getting carried away can be a lot of fun, and it is one of the best "highs" available. We can all become mystics in our own way by attracting angels into our lives.

A spiritual quest for enlightenment is easier when you expect the best and always look on the bright side. The bright side is where the angels are, and they are always there to help you become the optimystic you really are. Share your wishes and dreams with the angels, and they will relay your hopes to the highest good in the universe and help you cultivate a positive environment where "good things" thrive.

Because you are reading this book, I can assume you are seeking spiritual growth on some level. Becoming an optimystic will set the pace of your quest; it will help you understand the nature of angels and the ways to attract them and to connect with their realm. As you read about the ways to attract angels, think of your role as an optimystic and how you will bring optimism and mysticism to your experiences with angels.

SUMMARY

Method
Becoming an "optimystic," cultivating an environment where wishes, dreams, hopes, good luck, and good fortune thrive. Setting the stage for the right attitude to use when practicing any of the methods for attracting angels into your life.

Angels who can help
Guardian angels and spiritual guides, fun executives and happiness trainers, call them all in at one time or another; they are all able to provide optimism and mystical experiences.

Tools and ideas

1. Take a light and hopeful view of your spiritual path.
2. Refamiliarize yourself with the power of wishing and of hope.
3. Cultivate and harvest good luck; interpret everything that happens as a lucky situation.
4. Suffering interferes with the spiritual growth of the optimystic.
5. Incorporate fun, play, and humor into your spiritual practices.
6. Accept and "go with" mystical visions and peak experiences of joy and love; these are the ways an optimystic has direct contact with the angels.
7. Always look on the bright side of an issue; the bright side is the home of the angels.
8. Get rid of any superstitions you may have by becoming aware of them and changing your thinking about the outcome.

When optimystics are backed by faith and imagination, they become powerful forces in the universe, forces that can change the world around them with one positive thought, idea, or action.

Chapter 12

Cultivating Imagination and Faith

Imagination is more important than knowledge.

Albert Einstein

To cultivate your imagination and faith means spending time and care developing them for harvest (use) in your life. Faith and imagination must become intimately familiar to you, because they are the main ingredients in realizing and following your truest desires. Your desires must become clearly realized in your imagination so that the seed of hope has a place to germinate. When you know what it is you want, ask for it. Asking means you've planted the seed; then you can water the seed with hope and faith. Imagine and visualize your desire in its completed form, and know by faith that it is yours.

You may be thinking that you don't have faith and imagination, but you do. Every human being has faith and imagination. They may be lying dormant from nonuse, but they are there and can be cultivated for harvest. Faith, it is said in the Bible,

66

can move mountains. Faith is *knowing;* any doubt ruins it. Concentrate on knowing, not believing. Believing has limits; it raises doubts in and of itself and always becomes an issue. But if you *know* something, you have it; it is part of you, and this is where true faith begins. (Knowing leaves the doors open to alternatives.) Faith is the ability to sustain a state of inner awareness (consciousness) and positive energy toward realizing your goals and desires in life. Faith involves keeping the energy strong enough so that worries and doubts are blocked and the channels of visualization remain open and clear. Faith is the projection of your intentions into the future. It is the assumption that things are managed so that they work out in the long run. Faith is the trust that God is unconditional.

Imagination is the art and practice of producing ideal creations and forming clear mental images. Your imagination is your future. It is the only place the future exists. When you want something, you must be able to visualize it and produce an ideal image of it in your mind. When you use your imagination with faith, you will know without effort what you want and how to attain it because you already have it in your mind. Imagination is your direct connection to the angels.

With faith, imagination, the angels, and God, you can do anything. If you are having trouble experiencing angels, use your imagination and faith to get to know their ways. Imagine everything you can about angels — what you already know and what you want to know. Imagine meeting an angel; imagine what the angel would look like, what you would talk about, and what the angel would sound like, smell like, and feel like. Visualize floating into the etheric realm and flying with the angels through all the heavenly colors. If you aren't having much luck with this, keep trying. Write about your feelings in your angel journal; describe your faith, your imagination, and your impressions about angels.

Develop your own system for knowing angels. To know is to notice, to recognize, and to feel positive. You don't have to convince yourself. There is no need for effort; just relax and pay

attention. Building and developing your faith and imagination
may take time, but think of it as something fun to do. Know
that you will be taken care of, know that you are loved unconditionally by God, and know that you are worth it. If you have
beliefs that contradict your sense of worth, work on eliminating
them. (Review the section in Chapter 8 on brain program editors
to help in eliminating negative programs and beliefs.)

To attract angels and get them to play for you, remember to
cultivate and harvest your imagination. Then think positively
and become an optimystic. Plant the seed of hope, and the angels
will water it. Create your future; you already have the resources.
You can create heaven; all it takes is a little harvesting.

SUMMARY

Method
Cultivating and harvesting your faith and imagination. Attracting angels by developing your imagination and faith.

Angels who can help
Call on guardian angels and spiritual guides to keep you on
course; worry extinguishers to cast out doubts, fears, and worries; brain program editors to edit out negative beliefs about
yourself; creativity ministers and fun executives to remove effort
and force; and any angels who have entered your imagination.

Tools and ideas
1. Examine faith and imagination, think about what these
   powerful concepts mean to you, and write about your thoughts
   in your angel journal. Become one with faith and imagination; develop effortless knowing.
2. Clarify what your desires are and what you want out of life.
   Imagine you have what you want now (you do). Then complete the following statement: "Angels, I am asking that
   _____, and that the stream of faith and positive energy I
   have focused on this desire remain clear and constant."

3. Create the energy in your imagination for what you want and let yourself visualize it. Start a fund of energy, like an energy bank account. Deposit positive thoughts and visualizations of actual steps that can be taken for realizing your goals. (Ask the angels for a high interest rate and return on your energy.)
4. *Know* that you will be taken care of; trust the angels to connect you with the abundant loving force in the universe.
5. Use your imagination to meet an angel. Imagine everything you can about the angel, including what you would say, do, and see. Then fly with the angel up through the clouds to the heaven plane.

Things of heaven cannot be attained by perseverance; they are the grace of God. To open to this and trust in it is how belief is crystallized into faith. We cannot pay for it in any form, in any way, by our goodness, by our piety, by our great qualities, merits, or virtues; nothing. It is a gift, and all we can do is receive it.

Hazrat Inayat Khan

Chapter 13

Angel Mail

Keep on asking and it will be given to you;
keep on seeking and you will find . . .

Matthew 7:7

Angels are special request agents. Special requests cover a wide range of issues, from immediate tasks such as finding your lost keys to help with achieving a long-term goal. When we involve angels in our special requests, we are acknowledging the desires of our higher self. It is fine to ask angels for help with your goals and aspirations. You may think that angels should already know what you want and that you shouldn't ask, but asking is the positive step that sets the action in motion. There is no harm in asking the angels for something, because they only do things for the highest good of all concerned. Catherine Ponder has said, "Your ships come in only after you have sent them out." Asking the angels for a special request is like sending your ships and asking God to bless them. You are protected from greed with the angels, because they see into excesses and are attuned with your higher consciousness.

With angel mail, you write your special request on a piece of paper and mail it to the angels. The written word is said to have a special power of its own. Declaring your wishes on paper and addressing your letter to the angels is a good way of clarifying your goals and truest desires. To make a special request to the angels, simply take a piece of paper and address it to your own highest angel and the highest angels of the others whom your request involves. In your request, be specific and define what it is you want as clearly as you can. Always add the phrase "for the highest good of all concerned" to your note. Then express your gratitude. Thank the angels as if the request had already been granted. Also, thank God, and anyone else who has something to do with the request.

A story about one of the Catholic popes describes how he prayed to his guardian angel every day for guidance. When he was scheduled to confer with someone he thought might be troublesome, he would ask his guardian angel to speak with the other person's guardian angel regarding the upcoming meeting. The two guardian angels would work out the disagreements beforehand, and the meeting would proceed without needless arguments.

Apply this idea to angel mail. If there is someone in your life—your boss, your spouse, your child, your coworker, or your friend—with whom you have trouble communicating without disagreements and arguments over trivial issues, try writing to that person's guardian angel and ask that the situation be understood on the highest level. Then pay attention to what happens the next time you see the person. Look for any subtle or obvious change of heart that person suddenly has concerning the areas of disagreement.

You can use this technique whenever you feel resistance from other people. Write to their angels, and state clearly what you want from them, what it is you want them to understand, how you want them to react, and what you want them to do. By writing to a person's guardian angel, you can get past any emotional blocks either or both of you may have in the situation. Use this technique for helping those you care about to do something positive for themselves. If people you know need healing, release, love, or knowledge, write to their highest angels and ask that they be blessed with what they most need. This technique is especially useful if people you know have created situations for themselves that you can't talk about face to face. Maybe the situation involves something that you can see clearly from the outside but that they are in denial about.

When writing to angels with regard to other people, keep in mind that they have free will. We experience pain when those we love disappoint us by doing something we don't appreciate. If you have expectations about people, eventually you are going to be disappointed, one way or another. On the other hand, if you don't expect anything and give and release freely, loving others unconditionally, you will not allow their negative actions to affect you. If you are trying to influence someone romantically by writing to his or her angel, the best thing to do is bless and release him or her with unconditional love. If you are meant to be with this person, he or she will come to you freely with no conditions. The angels want you to be happy, but they also know that no other person can make you happy; you must claim your own happiness first.

You can write to any of the angels described in Part Two with special requests. You can write to the prosperity brokers for abundance, the healing angels for healing, the humor transformers for humor, and the miracle engineers for large or small miracles. Of course, you don't always have to write your requests; you can also voice them, pray them, or think them.

When you are ready to "mail" a written request, the first thing to do is to fold and seal it somehow; then find a special place for it. Some people keep their requests in books like the Bible; others use a jewelry box, their wallet, their journal, or their altar. After your request is mailed, be prepared for action. You have asked the angels, so listen intuitively for messages regarding your request, or just mail your request and forget about it until it pops into your mind again.

SUMMARY

Method

Angel mail and special requests. Attracting angels by writing to them and making special requests.

Angels who can help

Write to whichever angel is specific to your request.

Tools and ideas

1. Define your request.
2. Write your request on a piece of paper. Specify the angel to whom you are writing: for example, "to the guardian angel of _____" or "to the prosperity brokers" or "to the highest angel of _____." Somewhere in your request, include the phrase "for the highest good of all concerned." Close your request with an expression of gratitude.
3. If there are any people who might interfere with the fulfillment of your requests, write to their guardian angels and ask that anything that might block your progress with this person be removed.
4. Fold and seal your letter, find a special place for it, and consider it mailed.
5. Wait for a response, which may come in the form of intuition, opportunities for action, or feelings such as peace of mind and knowing that all is well.

Chapter 14

ANGEL® Cards

A deck of ANGEL® cards (copyright © 1981 by Drake and Tyler) consists of fifty-two very small cards. Each card has a key word representing a special essence or quality from the spiritual path. The cards are colorfully illustrated with angels in actions pertaining to the spirit of the individual cards. ANGEL® cards were developed as a part of a board game called "The Game of Transformation," which was created by the originators while living at the Findhorn Foundation. The game is a tool for exploring your inner life and consciousness. ANGEL® cards and "The Game of Transformation" are available at most New Age bookstores and are easy to order by contacting:

Music Design, Inc.
4650 North Port Washington Rd.
Milwaukee, WI 53212–1063

ANGEL® cards can provide an effective means for bringing angelic essence into your life. Some of the key qualities listed in the deck are joy, humor, peace, light, surrender, and trust. There are also two blank cards, which can be used to request a specific quality or essence not included on the other cards, or you can use them to ask the angels to send you a gift from the universe.

Right away, you can probably think of several ways to use the cards. There are no rules, but it is best not to ask about the same situation over and over again. (Again, the master speaks but once.) The cards reflect what is presently happening in your internal and external reality, and the list of key words contains nothing negative or dark. Keeping this in mind, here are some suggestions for using ANGEL® cards as tools for spiritual growth.

The first thing to do is find a quiet place to sit where you can spread the cards out in front of you. You may want to place them systematically into rows or just swirl them all around. Make sure they are face down so that your unconscious mind has a chance to come through. Or hold them fanned out in your hand, letting your energy run through the whole deck. Then pick the cards when you are ready.

To begin with, you may want to do a reading on your present state of affairs. Think about eight areas or situations in your life for which you would like guidance from the angels. I write down the following eight domains and life issues as follows:

The past
The present
The future
A gift from the universe
Love/romance
Money/prosperity
Work/career
Play/Recreation

Then I focus my thoughts on each area and pick a card when I feel ready. You may want to add or subtract areas to make the reading more personal. After you have picked the cards and written them down, study the reading for clues to any actions or breakthroughs the key words represent. You may want to leave the reading for a day or two and then return to it.

Think of a situation or question in your life for which you want guidance. It can be anything from money to love. Or ask for a reading of what is in the forefront of your consciousness, with no specific question in mind. Or ask for a set of gifts to develop in your present state of consciousness. Concentrate on your situation and pick one card to be the "trump card"; set it aside and don't look at it. Now, pick three more cards and turn them over. Think about what they mean to you and then turn over the trump card. The trump card represents an overall guiding light for the situation. Write the essences down in your angel journal and reread it in the future when you want more insight.

Do a "virtue request" with your ANGEL® cards. Look through the cards and pick out the ones representing virtues you want or need in your life. Then study the cards and the pictures drawn on them; meditate and ask for insight on these virtues. Write them down and declare this request to the angels, and be ready to explore your virtues.

Pick an angel of the day, year, month, cycle, birthday, or season; pick an angel for any special occasion you want to lighten up.

Pick an angel to help with an obstacle to be overcome; to help with a new venture, a new relationship, or a new house; or to bring inspiration and creativity to your work, schooling, and play.

Remember to have fun and keep the experience light so that the angels can truly respond. If you get stuck on what a card means to you, sometimes it is helpful to look the word up in a dictionary for insight into the word itself. The two blank cards can be very significant, because with them you can ask for something specific or for a gift from the angels or for a clean slate for the future. Invite the angels to join with you in celebrating your spiritual growth, and use the cards to communicate with them.

I showed the ANGEL® cards to a very creative and brilliant friend of mine, and he came up with a game based on the card game "War." The name isn't very appealing, but you can ignore it. The game is played with two people. First, shuffle the cards and deal them out face down. Each player turns over one card each time. With the two cards facing up, you must decide between the two of you which virtue or essence is "more important." The player with the "more important" card gets to take both cards. After the cards have been used up, the player with the most cards win. Of course, this game could stir up a few healthy arguments, so it is important to keep it a fun learning experience.

My first experience with ANGEL® cards was very memorable. I had seen the cards several times in my favorite bookstore, but I had never bought them because I was skeptical of what they might represent. I waited until my best friend and witness came to visit me for a vacation, and the first thing we did was to buy a deck of the cards. We opened them in the car and the first one we picked was a blank card, so we asked that our vacation week be filled with synchronisms (it was!). We weren't really sure what to do with the cards at first, and then we came up with the idea of giving them out wherever we went that week.

We had a great deal of fun leaving cards with tips in restaurants and handing them out to friendly people up and down the coast of Virginia and North Carolina. We also gave them to people we knew, and we had friends pick out a card without looking. Giving ANGEL® cards to people led to many discussions about angels. So we had an angel-filled week of fun, lightness, and synchronistic events.

The cards we gave to friends turned out to be very meaningful in their lives, as they later told me. To give is to receive, so giving the cards gave us much in return.

For more information on "The Game of Transformation" and to find out about the Facilitators' Training Workshops offered by InnerLinks (which include extensive work with the ANGEL® cards and with angels in group settings), please contact:

> Kathy Tyler or Joy Drake
> InnerLinks
> P.O. Box 16225
> Seattle, WA 98116

Chapter 15

Holding an
Angel Conference

A conference is a meeting for discussion. When people know where they are going and why, they can become powerful forces in the universe. And when people are on a straight course, angels can cooperate with them in a more complete way. To help us know where we are going and to help us explore the reasons for going there, we can call an angel conference to chart out our goals and discover how the angels can help us achieve them.

An angel conference can be thought of as a chance to develop a business plan for your life. If you think about it, each human life is like a business (some small and some large), and like every business a human life needs a plan stating goals for the future. Calling a conference with the angels is a way to plan for your future, to define what you want to accomplish, and to recognize key people in your life. Angels act as your consultants and your staff of employees. The conference is a way to assign tasks that your staff can handle for you. It is also a way of defining what may be limiting your creativity or free time.

First, define your board of directors. A sample board of directors may include your version of God; Mary, Jesus, or particular saints you like; important archetypes, gods, or goddesses; ancestors or personalities from the past who intrigue you; spirit guides, gurus, biblical characters, superheroes, and sages; and so forth. Your board of directors will be inspirational, and it will be personal to you. Think of your board as an association of spiritual advisers and consultants who can help you carry out the main purpose (essence) of your business (life).

Napoleon Hill, the author of *Think and Grow Rich*, held an imaginary council meeting with his group of "Invisible Counselors" at night before going to sleep. His council was comprised of nine men whose lifework most impressed him. The object of these meetings was to reshape his character by trying to imitate these nine great men in some way. Hill wanted to become a composite of these men (see the section on soul angels in Chapter 5.) In his imaginary council meeting, Hill was able to sit among great men and dominate the group by serving as chairman. This idea can be incorporated into the angel conference.

To hold an angel conference, it helps to have a chart to follow. I take a piece of paper and draw a circle with a compass so that I end up having a mandala with sections. In the sections, I write down goals for specific areas of my life. Then I assign angels to help in the realization of these goals and desires. I also assign angels to keep certain people from interfering, so that a barrier of protection is formed. If there are people who can help you, this is a good time to address their highest angels.

The Angel Conference Diagram is an example of one form I designed for use when holding an angel conference. I also make up other forms, and sometimes I don't use a form at all. You can design one that works for your own needs. You might want to keep your forms with your angel journal and date each one so you can monitor your progress.

Angel Conference Diagram

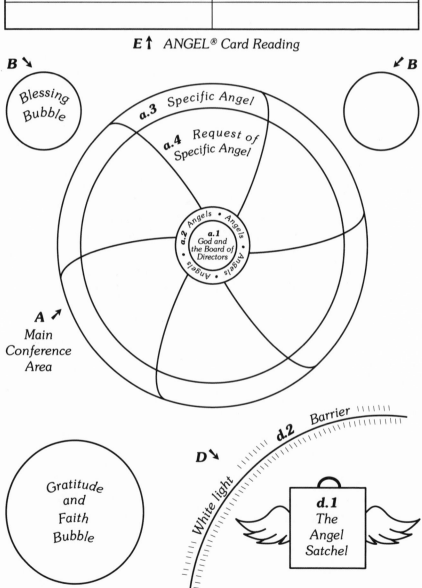

E ↑ ANGEL® Card Reading

B ↘ Blessing Bubble

↙ B

a.3 Specific Angel

a.4 Request of Specific Angel

a.2 Angels • Angels

a.1 God and the Board of Directors

Angels • Angels

A ↗ Main Conference Area

D ↘ White light

d.2 Barrier

d.1 The Angel Satchel

Gratitude and Faith Bubble

C ↗

KEY TO ANGEL CONFERENCE DIAGRAM:

A = The main area for your conference. I write God in the center circle (**a.1**), and I also write in the names of the members of the board of directors. In circle **a.2**, outlining **a.1**, I write in the word "Angels" a few times. In the space (**a.3**) on the edge of the large sections, I define the angels for whom I have specific requests. In the large section (**a.4**), I write in my specific requests, goals, or objectives.

B = The blessing bubbles. In these bubbles, I ask the angels to bless special situations and humans.

C = The gratitude and faith bubble. In this bubble, I ask for faith and thank the angels and God and myself and anyone else for the realization of the goals of the conference.

D = The angel satchel section. This section is used to keep other humans (or other aspects of yourself) from interfering or blocking your progress. You can also use this technique to avoid people you fear and loathe. When you use this satchel (**d.1**), repeat the affirmation, "There is no such personality in the universe." Then put the name of the person who owns that personality in the satchel. *This does not mean that you want anything bad to happen to him or her!* On the contrary, it means that the angels are in charge now and that they will make the energy positive. Basically, the barrier means that you are not going to acknowledge the part of the other person's personality that conflicts with yours. Also use this area to write in any blocks you might encounter from yourself, such as fear, doubt, procrastination, and resignation. On the border of this section (**d.2**), you can write the words "White Light" or you can write the affirmation to the archangel Michael: "Divine light of the highest order under the protection of the archangel Michael." This gives you protection and sends the light of transformation to the person in question.

E = The ANGEL® card reading. You can number the sections to correspond with the sections of the main conference. Pick a card to represent an essence you can bring to enlighten the situation or request of each section.

You can convene an angel conference any way you choose. Sometimes, just starting out with a blank piece of paper and being spontaneous is a fun way to hold a conference. Also, if you have an active imagination, you can do the whole process in your head using visualization techniques.

There are no mandatory conditions for holding angel conferences. You can hold them anywhere, anytime, anyhow, but keep in mind that angels are not to be worshipped. They appreciate ceremonies, but they do not want to be worshipped; they only want to assist and help without interfering in human free will. With this in mind, here are some ideas to use for getting in the spirit of the angel conference:

1. An angel conference is not a serious and confining ritual; it is a chance to be light and to connect with the beauty surrounding angels.
2. Angels love candlelight, so light some candles for the conference (white or pink candles are especially nice for an angel conference).
3. Surround yourself with beauty, setting up a table with flowers, pictures, incense, rocks, and angel figurines to provide a nice setting for the angel conference.
4. A recording of harp or flute music is nice to play during a conference.
5. After the angel conference is complete, do a reading with ANGEL® cards. If you have several categories, pick a card for each one. Do an overall reading of the conference for additional insight.
6. Incorporate anything that will promote happiness, beauty, peace, lightness, and love into your conference.
7. Angel conferences are meant to be light and humorous, so laugh as much as you like. Invite the mirth makers and humor transformers to attend.
8. Hold the angel conference with a friend, so that you have a witness and someone who will giggle with you.

9. Pay the angels who attend with wages by doing something nice for yourself and those around you. Plant a flower garden, paint a beautiful picture, or give love and lightness away, and the angels will consider themselves well paid for their services as consultants on your staff.

10. For updates on the main conference, hold special meetings with specific angels whose help you are requesting. For example, if you need extra help in the area of career and finance, have a "power lunch" or breakfast meeting with the angel you have assigned to this domain. Take notes during the meeting if you like, and make it as real as possible. If you go out in public for the power lunch, ask for a quiet and private booth.

Chapter 16

Adventures in Antiseriousness

*Not a shread of evidence exists in favor of the idea
that life is serious.*

Brendon Gill

People can waste a lot of time taking life seriously and worrying about perceived problems. My friend Charlie reached a period in his life when he felt burdened by problems and worries. He spent most of his time seriously worrying over what he was going to do. While driving on some treacherous mountain curves one day, pondering over the serious issues he faced, he took one curve too fast and found himself looking down several hundred feet of mountain with his van up on two wheels. In that instant, Charlie realized that he was probably going to die and that all the situations he was worried about would never be resolved. Then a sudden force (his guardian angel, no doubt) pulled Charlie's van back into control, and he was saved from imminent death. After the shock subsided, he found himself laughing hysterically at how absurd his worrying was. Nothing seemed so serious anymore; suddenly, he was struck by how funny everything was, and he laughed and laughed. Charlie realized that the moments he had spent worrying were wasted time, which could just as easily have been spent in enjoyment.

Those of us who become consumed with the illusion of seriousness in our lives usually reach a turning point. Sometimes this turning point happens dramatically, as in a near-death experience; other times, it happens less dramatically, as in a sudden realization that you have spent weeks and months without having any fun. If you are not planning to have a near-death experience any time soon but you are plagued by seriousness, pay attention to the time and energy you spend on seriousness. Start by writing down all the serious issues you are dealing with in your life at the moment. Now look at how funny these issues look on paper, and let yourself laugh out loud. If the issues don't strike you as funny and you can't bring yourself to laugh, just look for some aspect of humor and lightness, however small. Sometimes when we start laughing at our lives, we end up hysterical, and we may cry, scream, or shout out the window. The point is we need a release now and then and laughter is a good one.

Give up, give in, and let go. Pretend that you are filled with helium and that the only thing keeping you on the ground are the serious issues in your life; let yourself rise above them for a different perspective. If you saw the movie *Mary Poppins*, think back to the scene with the song "I Love to Laugh"; the more people laughed, the higher they rose until they reached the ceiling. When they wanted to come down, they had to think of something sad and heavy. Take a break from the seriousness of life; the angels will encourage it. Remember G. K. Chesterton's words: "Angels can fly because they take themselves lightly."

Laughter has many benefits. It exercises the lungs, releases superfluous energy, bathes your being in endorphins (natural pain relievers), and promotes healing. (See *Anatomy of an Illness* by Norman Cousins.) If you need help bringing laughter into your life, start by surrounding yourself in humor. Do your own study on humor. Make a list of the movies, comedians, television shows, books, friends, and situations that make you laugh, and always search for more.

In your angel journal, keep track of the humor and seriousness in your life. If you catch yourself becoming plagued by seriousness, examine your behavior and that of others. Find out what keeps happening in your life that isn't funny. Whenever you like, ask the angels to release you from seriousness and connect you with humor. The plague of seriousness is everywhere: in our churches and schools, on the news, and at work. It is hard to escape from it. But there is always a way to introduce humor into any situation, and you may need to be the instigator.

Keep a page in your journal labeled "trash bag" and draw a trash bag on the page. Whenever you have a nagging worry or negative thought you want to release, write it into the trash bag. If other people are causing you grief, put them in the trash as well. Bad habits, seriousness, complaints, and anything that disturbs your peace of mind belongs in the trash. When the bag is full, or on a weekly basis, call the angel trash collectors for a pickup. These trash-collecting angels will take your trash bag to the universal transmutation dump. If you are truly willing to part with the contents of the bag, the energy will come back to you clean and charged with a positive force to use for something creative. The angel rubbish collectors can turn one person's trash into another person's treasure. Form a clear visual image of your trash bag being carried away into the universe for the highest good of all concerned and say, "Good riddance!" Another way to take out the trash is to burn the trash bag page, and as the smoke rises visualize yourself free of all the trash you've accumulated.

Angels are antiserious; there is no weight in their realm, and they simply can't take anything seriously. This means that they can't take us or our problems seriously either. This doesn't mean they will ignore our problems; they will do what they can to help us remove the serious worries so that we can solve problems creatively and take ourselves lightly. The *Oxford American Dictionary* defines serious as solemn and thoughtful, not smiling, not casual or lighthearted, causing great concern, and of grave and somber disposition. How could anyone want to be serious after reading that?

SUMMARY

Method

Adventures in antiseriousness. Attracting angels by lightening up your load of life issues.

Angels who can help

Humor transformers, fun executives, and worry extinguishers are all antiserious; call on any of them.

Tools and ideas

1. List all the serious issues you face at the moment, and laugh at them.
2. Take a laughter inventory, and find new ways to laugh. Also, learn how to have a good hearty laugh as often as possible.
3. Keep a trash bag page in your angel journal for serious trash such as worries, negative thoughts, and negative personalities that you want removed from your life. Then take out the trash.
4. Cultivate lightness in your life.

Chapter 17

Happiness Training

Happiness is not in our circumstances but in ourselves. It is not something we see, like a rainbow, or feel, like the heat of a fire. Happiness is something we are.

John Sheerin

How many times have you heard yourself or someone else say, "When this happens, I'll be happy"? Well, it doesn't work that way; you must first be happy now — without reason. Happiness without reason is the ultimate freedom. This freedom from conditions and contingencies means that you aren't waiting for the right ingredients to make you happy; you just *are* happy. No matter what the circumstances, you feel blessed and happy. If you are truly happy without reason, you are freed from the domination of outward conditions. You are free to live happily in the present tense, in the now.

Happiness without reason requires training. The state of happiness requires that you know yourself and that you identify precise moments when you switch from being happy and at ease on this planet to being uncomfortable and out of synch.

The problem with true happiness is that there is no key to its door, there are no rules to follow, no steps to take, and no conditions for it to exist. There is no manual or cookbook with recipes to read. True happiness is a state of grace. It's a bit like having a naturally occurring chemical in your bloodstream that feeds your brain and bathes your soul in positive energy. There is nothing to swallow, breathe, look at, smell, or do to become happy. Happiness comes and goes. We cannot plan it; it is a naturally occurring product of living in the present tense, free from external conditions. We can, however, train ourselves to be *available* and *open* to happiness.

Happiness training is accepting everything the angels have to teach: humor, love, beauty, lightness of being, and joy. It requires living in the now and being *awake*. You must get off autopilot. Autopilot is a personality program some of us adopt to avoid pain and to avoid living and experiencing the now. By subscribing to set routines and predictable patterns, some people are sleepwalking through the day. You won't find these people rocking the boat or moving and shaking the world; that isn't safe in their minds. Going on autopilot does not get rid of the pain and suffering in your life; it only delays and diffuses it. Sooner or later, the voids will come back to haunt the person on automatic pilot. When we see children on autopilot, we call it mental illness. Young children normally don't resist life. When they feel like crying, laughing, screaming, or singing, they just do it. Angels and children go together; they are happy and creative. Angels see this happy state as the way we are meant to be (all of us). Step number one of happiness training is: Get off autopilot. Wake up and experience your senses. Stop and smell the roses; wake up and smell the coffee.

Happiness (or unhappiness) is largely a result and function of how we *relate* and *react* to events in our lives; it does not reside in the circumstances or the events themselves. Overreacting to an adverse event makes it worse. Overinterpreting circumstances with an attitude of what should be according to a given set of conditions is a sure way to deter happiness. We must not react with fear, anger, or disappointment to the events of the day. Choose to see whatever arises in the moment with fascination and interest, and know that it is neither good nor bad. Events and things are only bad or wrong when they are compared to a standard in your imagination of what should be. Step number two of happiness training is: Don't overreact, overinterpret, or compare. Adopt a sense of lightness and humor in every situation you encounter, and the angels will be there to help.

The happy mind is free of judgments, expectations, and worries concerning other people. Other people's actions can only hurt us when we have a preconceived notion of their intent toward us. When we are happy with ourselves, then we can see others as innocent. If someone sends you a carton of horse manure, just assume they forgot the horse! Worrying about people doesn't help them or you. Expecting people to act certain ways will only disappoint you. Judging yourself and others is a waste of time. Step number three of happiness training is: Don't let other people affect your happiness. Just as events are neither good nor bad, the same is true of people; see people and their actions as interesting and fascinating, originating from a source of innocence.

You must be willing to give up suffering and worrying. Suffering is the opposite of happiness. Many people have resigned themselves to live with low-grade, chronic suffering. This suffering may stem from physical pain, mental anguish, regrets, bad habits, or emotional blocks. Whatever the cause, the result is constant suffering. Angels are frustrated with suffering because until humans are willing to give it up angels can't work their magic. When you discover a cause of suffering and worry, and you are willing to give it up, get in the habit of stopping and releasing. Stop and release; you can repeat this process in your mind and visualize the angels taking your suffering away. Once the decision to stop suffering is made, angels jump in for the transformation; whether the transition is from sickness to health or from bondage to freedom, the angels are waiting to help. The change can happen in an instant. Make peace with yourself so that if anything is making you suffer it will be gone, and you will be available to experience happiness without reason. Your suffering teaches only a temporary lesson; don't keep it around longer than needed. Step number four of happiness training is: Recognize what is causing you to suffer and work on giving it up so that the angels can help you become one with happiness. Stop worrying about yourself and others. "Let go and let the angels."

Go and love some more. Giving love on any level is a sure way to happiness. This love must be unconditional love, of course, and as always with giving you receive. Anne Frank once said, "Whoever is happy will make others happy too. He who has courage and faith will never perish in misery!" Have the courage and faith to spread your happiness and love around, and you will create an abundance that will continue to give throughout the universe. Love and happiness are synergistic; their combined effects exceed the sum of their individual effects. Step number five of happiness training is: Be generous with your love and happiness; spread it throughout the universe.

Training yourself to be available and open to happiness without reason requires that you remove obstacles such as those discussed above. Unconditional happiness is the ultimate freedom. It doesn't require that you live anywhere special, that you dress a certain way, that you ingest a mind-altering substance, or that you do anything other than make yourself available to receive it, anytime and anyplace. Happiness has been described as a butterfly; when you pursue it it is always just beyond reach, but if you sit quietly it may alight upon you. Angels are natural happiness trainers, so sit down quietly and ask them to help you develop a habit of happiness.

SUMMARY

Method

Developing a habit of happiness, so that the angels will be able to play effectively in your life. Use the steps of happiness training to recognize the precise moment you become uncomfortable and unhappy, and then change the way you think of the situation so that the angels can jump in and make you one with happiness. Write out a declaration of happiness in your angel journal.

Angels who can help

Call on your guardian angel, the happiness trainers, worry extinguishers, mirth makers, humor transformers, and cheerleaders.

Tools and ideas

1. Wake up and stop any automatic behavior that keeps you from experiencing life. Autopilot behavior is a way of resisting life and avoiding pain; it avoids the present.
2. Do not overreact to or overinterpret situations that come your way. Compare them only with themselves; in this light, they are neither good nor bad, and you can find them interesting and fascinating—and therefore positive in some sense.
3. Don't let other people's behavior interfere with your happiness. Perceive others as innocent, and adopt an attitude of optimism regarding their intentions. They are neither good nor bad, just interesting and fascinating. In most situations, people and circumstances can only hurt you if you let them.
4. Discover the causes of your suffering and worry, and be willing to give them up; the angels will step in and help you. When you feel uneasy and out of synch, stop and release whatever is blocking you.
5. Love and do as you will. Give from your abundance of happiness. As David Grayson says, "Make one person happy each day and in forty years you have made 14,600 human beings happy for a little time at least."

The quotation that follows is from Barry Stevens's book *Burst Out Laughing*. Stevens once received a rejection letter for one of her books that stated, "You write like an angel, but you just won't say the right things."

I choose to give up suffering.

This dosen't say the same thing as I choose to be happy.

One is a negative.

The other is a positive. Always be positive! But then I start with a picture in my head of what happiness is and I limit myself before I start.

Whereas when I choose to give up suffering – a strongly positive act, I see now that I have written it – I notice when I am suffering, look into the cause of it in myself, and give up whatever makes me do it, leaving the space wide open to whatever comes in. It isn't easy, but surely is a ladder to heaven.

Of course, I'm also giving up luxury – the luxury of feeling sorry for myself. I am then one step beyond where feeling sorry for myself is possible, seeing the whole thing clearly.

I burst out laughing.

                                                              Barry Stevens

Chapter 18

Light-Heart Training

A light heart lives long.

William Shakespeare

Light-heart training teaches you to attract angels by becoming angelic. Think of light-heart training as a process of growing feathers! Being angelic is a sure way to attract angels (birds of a feather flock together). As we know, angels take themselves lightly, but what can this do for us? Simply put, developing a light heart brings out our natural ability to be entertaining, charming, and clever, and allows us to rediscover our innate sweetness. Most children have all these qualities working for them, unless something awful is happening in their lives. So this means that most of us were charming, clever, entertaining, and sweet at one time in our lives. Some of us still are!

Essential angelic qualities come to the surface only when we are authentic and genuine. Radiating sweetness and light brings you more of the same. Being authentically charming and sweet will energize those around you. Have you ever noticed those special individuals who can enter a room full of people and put everyone at ease? A true social genius makes others feel comfortable and important, regardless of their social status. Why? Because he or she is genuinely interested in people. Have you ever met someone you thought was truly charming and interesting, only to realize later that *you* did all the talking? True charm involves listening to someone and noticing the dimensions of that person's personality. Human beings *are* fascinating. Anyone living on this planet for more than a couple of years has a fascinating story or two to tell. All people on this earth have something very special and interesting to teach us. If we get bored around people, it is not because they are intrinsically uninteresting; it is because we have lost our ability to find fascination in every moment.

The key elements of lightness training are charm, sweetness, a sense of humor with an infectious laugh ready to erupt anytime, and wit — the ability to see the humor in a situation. These key elements are all interdependent.

Charm can be defined as the power to arouse love and admiration. Charm makes you attractive and fascinating, influencing others as if by magic. The *Oxford American Dictionary* defines magic as a mysterious quality that seems to enchant. To enchant means to delight completely, to enrapture with joy — literally, to encircle in song. A truly charming personality is magical and mysterious, and has an alchemical effect on the surroundings. Above all, charm attracts people to you because you are genuinely interesting and engaging. Charm also attracts angels.

Innate sweetness is another element of lightness. A sweet personality will attract angels, and a bitter one will repel them. Think about sweetness. It is agreeable, fresh, unsalted, and kind without effort. When it is artificial, we say it is saccharine, too sweet, a substitute for something real, with a bitter aftertaste. But when sweetness is integrated and real, it is purely delightful. We all have it in us. Just smile and think of something sweet like the fragrance of a flower, and you will instantly become sweeter.

Having a sense of humor and wit is the essence of a light heart.

There is, however, a very fine line between making fun and true wit. Both find the absurd and the ridiculous in life, but wit does this in a comfortable way so that no one is offended. Being witty and having a sense of humor do not mean you are making fun of anyone. Ridicule is not charming, even when you are ridiculing yourself. Ridicule makes people very nervous and uncomfortable. The source of true wit comes from a basic love of life; it is not meant as an attack on anything or anyone. Being witty means having the ability to combine words and ideas in a clever way that appeals to the intellect. On the other hand, a sense of humor does not necessarily mean that *you* have to be the one who creates humor. It means you have the ability to perceive and enjoy amusing situations, and the ability to have a good laugh. Having true wit or a true sense of humor is charming, because both bring out the best in others and lighten any heart.

The following qualities never make for a charming personality at any time, ever:

1. Criticizing means to find fault, looks for flaws, and form negative judgments. There is no such thing as "constructive criticism" unless someone is sincerely asking you for a critique, in private, and even then it is hazardous. If you engage in criticism of *anyone* in other people's presence, people will wonder what awful things you are saying about them when they aren't present.

2. Pointless complaining (or bitching) means talking in a futile, negative vein. No one but your best friend or therapist should have to listen to pointless complaining. In a group situation, complaining is totally uncalled for, and the angels will definitely make themselves scarce if you indulge in this unpleasant behavior.

3. Boredom is never welcome or necessary. If you are bored with people or a situation, the best thing you can do is to leave.

4. Tattletale behavior or ganging up on someone is terribly un-

charming. On the other hand, defending someone who is being attacked in a diplomatic way (dissolving the attack) is quite charming and clever (if you can do it right).
5. Be wary of talking politics and religion in your social circle. If such a discussion gets out of hand, be the one to change the subject.

Think of a truly charming person you know, one who is a social genius. I'll bet he or she rarely falls into any of the traps mentioned above. You may think I'm sounding a little like Miss Manners, but there are a lot of people who could use some coaching in manners. A charming manner will bring you good favor, which in turn will bring you good fortune. Charm seems to be dying out on this planet, so help keep it alive; give to the charm fund by becoming a person you yourself would like to be around.

Above all, remain true to yourself. When you are truly authentic, your charming side comes to the surface. Having a light heart leads to freedom, for it means that you are on the lighter side of life. When a heart is light, you can almost see the angels surrounding it. Ask the angels to follow you into any situation, and keep your heart light.

So shall you find favor, good understanding, and high esteem in the sight of God and Man

Proverbs 3:3–4

SUMMARY

Method
Light-heart training. Enhancing one's charm, sweetness, and wit—in essence, becoming like an angel to attract more angels.

Angels who can help
Your guardian angel, the mirth makers, the happiness trainers, the cheerleaders, the fun executives, and the muses can all help.

Tools and ideas

1. Know the key elements of lightness: authentic charm, sweetness, wit, and humor. These key elements put people at ease and create comfort in any situation. Know that they must stem from a ground of love.

2. Be aware of the difference between true wit and humor, and the barbs of making fun of someone or something. When you make a conscious choice to find more humor in your life, the angels will help you systematically. If you are stuck in a situation that seems to lack humor—for example, in a long line that doesn't seem to be moving—turn to the person next to you and say something light and funny. It takes practice and a conscious effort to find the humor in life.

3. Eliminate the following from your behavior: criticism (it is never constructive), pointless complaining, boredom, and attacking or tattletale behavior. Avoid contentious topics of discussion in groups. When you train yourself to be aware of the critic within, you can train the critic to remain silent.

4. Maintain your integrity, and be authentic at all times. (If you detect any of the nasty behaviors mentioned above in yourself, don't cover them up; *eliminate them*. That way, you can be genuinely charming and pleasant.)

5. When you "make an entrance," do it with an entourage of angels.

Chapter 19

Declarations to the Angels

You shall also decide and decree a thing and it shall be established for you, and the light [of God's favor] shall shine upon your ways.

Job 22:28

When people make declarations, they are stating clearly and formally what it is they want known. Making a declaration to the angels means that you are openly announcing what you want known to heaven. Declaring your goals and statements of things to come will establish a plan of action with the angels. A declaration can be an outline or map that you can follow. The angels will bless the declaration and add higher inspiration and aspirations to it. There are many ways to create a declaration to the angels. In this chapter, I will expand on three declaration ideas that I have used with success.

The first is a declaration to abolish stale patterns, limiting beliefs, and negative brain programs. (First of all, read about brain program editors in Chapter 8 to familiarize yourself with the ways angels can help change programs and eliminate negative behavior.)

If there is something we want to change about our personality or a habit we want to get rid of, then we can openly announce our willingness to change in a written declaration. Just the act of being willing opens a new awareness channel in your brain to detect those elements that contribute to the behavior you want to change. With this awareness, you can choose something different.

List any behavior patterns, negative brain programs, or bad habits you want to change. If you have a clear idea of any actions you can take to end them, list these as well. Now formulate a statement of your intention to end the behaviors and replace them with positive behaviors or patterns. Use this formula: "I, _____, formally and willingly choose and am open to change. I would like to eliminate the following behaviors and patterns from my life: [fill in your list]. I also agree to take action in the form of [put your list of actions here] to help facilitate my progress. I ask that a new awareness channel be established in my brain to detect the patterns when they start so that I can choose a different way of being and so that I can see how or if I have been limiting myself and sabotaging my progress. I hereby ask the angels to bless this declaration and to instill positive inspiration in place of the stale patterns that were detracting from my happiness. I ask that these angels in particular be on hand to guide me in the right direction: [list specific angels whose help you desire]." End by formally thanking the angels and the higher power in the universe, and know that you are blessed.

A second possible declaration is to state goals, desires, and hopes for the future—creating a map or outline to follow. For this declaration, you can write a formal letter to the angels, stating the path you are going to take and the quality of life you expect. Your letter can go something like this:

Dear Angels [and other interested higher parties, including yourself],

I will live a long, healthy, and prosperous life. I will create peace and harmony, and I will be blessed with the grace of happiness.

I will follow through with my lifework [describe] and see it come
to pass with success and abundance. [Now add the details: the
goals, accomplishments, and rewards you desire.] I will release
any fear, worry, and attachment that is holding me back. I will
be open to the gifts of the universe. My work will be for the
highest good in the universe. All limiting thoughts are now
replaced with loving thoughts of abundance.

Yours truly,
[your name]

Get as flowery as you want and have fun with it. Create an agenda
or itinerary to follow, including specific dates. And, as always,
remember to thank the angels. Finally, make sure you really want
the things you put in your letter!

A third kind of declaration you can make involves composing a "let go and let the angels list."

*Casting the whole of your cares – all your anxieties, all your
worries, all your concerns, once and for all – on Him; for He
cares for you affectionately, and cares about you watchfully.*

Peter 5:7

A "let go and let the angels list" is a declaration to release cares
and worries that you want out of your life. It's a very simple
procedure. Just make a list and after each item write or say,
"Yours." Your list can be as simple or as specific and detailed
as you would like; either way, the angels will hear you. For
example:

Dear Angels,

I am asking you to take over the following situations and work
them out for my highest good:

Money anxieties: Yours
Moving question: Yours

"Bad back" problem: Yours
Health in general: Yours
Career: Yours
Fun: Yours
Disagreement with _____: Yours
Car troubles: Yours

Thank you, angels, for taking over these situations. Thank you for finding the highest solutions and guiding me in pursuit of higher ground without petty worries.

Sincerely,
[your name]

Check the declarations you have written every once in a while. Monitor yourself and congratulate yourself or any progress. You may need to update or change things, so go ahead. Yes, you can change the declarations. They are not set in stone—only on wings. One time, my friend and I had to make a formal apology to the angels for asking so adamantly for something we ended up not really wanting. Of course, the angels didn't mind because they understand human nature, but we wanted them to know that we recognized how funny and silly we had been.

Chapter 20

Bedtime Angel Review

Once asleep man has no real freedom of choice. His entire slumber is dominated by his last waking concept of self. It follows, therefore, that he should always assume the feeling of accomplishment and satisfaction before he retires in sleep.

Neville

My three-year-old niece once told me not to worry about how late she was staying up because when she finally went to bed she would go to sleep with two angels. I asked her about the two angels, and she explained that they fly all around her bed, keeping the monsters and ghosts away from her so that she can get a good night's sleep.

Sometimes our days are filled with monsters in the form of worries, stress, hostile people, and work deadlines. When we go to sleep still carrying these monsters, dream time can be a battleground. Humans need sleep because of gravity. We have a constant force field keeping us from floating off the planet, and just by standing up we are working against this force. We need sleep to recover from the day's gravity and seriousness. Thus, it is of the utmost importance that we allow our sleep time to be as calming as possible. If we review our day with the angels before we sleep, the process of resolving our worries works more efficiently. Dream time becomes more creative, brilliant ideas come to us, and dreams are more pleasant. (Some people actually do their best thinking in their sleep!)

Reserve some time before you go to sleep for a review of your day. Go over what worked and what didn't. If you are still holding onto worries and disappointments from the day, ask the angels to release them for you. Ask the angels for the chance to work things out in your dreams creatively. After you've gone through the gravity checklist—that is, your seriousness review of the day—switch your focus to the positive and give thanks for the blessings in your life. Think of things that happened during the day that were humorous and meaningful. Ask the angels to keep you in a sweet and light state when you fall asleep. Ask them to keep your dreams sweet and peaceful—taking you with them to the plane of heaven.

If you are worried about the upcoming day, try this technique: Take a piece of paper and write about the upcoming day as if it had already happened. For example: "This morning I woke up fresh and alert at 7:00 A.M., which gave me plenty of time to enjoy my morning coffee and think peacefully about my life. At 9:00 A.M., I left the house; the traffic was smooth, with every car in synch. I found the perfect parking place, and I even got to work early. At 10:00 A.M., my meeting with _____ went perfectly, and she agreed to _____. During lunch, I had more than enough time to take care of some errands, to eat, and to socialize. The rest of the day was very productive and creative. My drive home was wonderful, and dinner with _____ was incredibly romantic and sweet. . . . "

I hope you get the idea. When your script is done, ask the angels to bless it. Then, at the end of the "perfect" day, go over your list and see how well you did. This is a good technique to use when you have an important day coming up and you want some unseen help with it.

A similar technique involves visualizing the next day in your mind. As you do this, ask the angels for insight into the people you'll be seeing. What are they really like? Is there a common ground between you? What are their deepest desires? Ask the angels what phone calls you need to make, and how you can manage and remember the big and little details that so often elude us and end up causing us more work in the long run.

When you try this technique, think of yourself having a meeting with your invisible secretary (your copilot angel) and discuss ways your copilot can help you with the day ahead. This technique works! It works because you have loaded your unconscious mind with a program to follow. Our unconscious mind can follow time schedules quite well. Think of a home office that exists in your mind, taking care of the little details while you are out promoting yourself in the world.

Many people watch the news or a violent and stressful show on television right before going to sleep. News is rarely edifying and usually leaves us with a feeling of fear and discomfort, as does a show with violent images and messages. This is not a good way to fall asleep. Reading something inspiring or listening to relaxing music are good alternatives to the violence and degradation of late-night television. If you must watch T.V. before you go to bed, at least pick something humorous and light — if you can find it.

At bedtime, clear your mind and gather the angels around you, so that you can go to sleep in a higher state of consciousness. When you are no longer worried about the day you had and you've planned the upcoming day, cultivate a time of peaceful silence and fall asleep. Imagine the angels putting you to sleep, covering you with a warm, cozy blanket of golden love light, and flying around you all night, keeping away the monsters and ghosts and sprinkling gold dust on your hopes and dreams.

SUMMARY

Method

Bedtime angel review. Ask the angels to purify the atmosphere while you sleep, to bring you sweet dreams, and to help you bless the coming day.

Angels who can help

Call on your guardian angel and any other angels who will aid you in sleeping in peaceful bliss. The worry extinguishers, co-pilots, and brain program editors can help you sort out the day and plan the day ahead.

Tools and ideas

1. Review the day. What worked and what didn't? Go through a gravity checklist in your mind, releasing the heavy burdens you've accumulated. Call in the angels for insight and peace. Be thankful for the humorous and meaningful experiences you had during the day.
2. If you have a big day scheduled tomorrow and you are a bit worried about getting through it, try the technique of writing about exactly how you want everything in the next day to go as if it had already happened, as if you were entering it into your diary the following night. Then ask the angels to bless it, and to bring you insight in your dreams.
3. Manifest and visualize the next day in your mind. Meet the people, make the calls, and send the letters in your imagination, and then ask the angels to give you heavenly insight into what you will accomplish.
4. Find something edifying and inspiring to do or read before you fall asleep. Or just listen to relaxing music or watch something humorous and light on T.V.
5. Read about brain program editors in Chapter 8 for more assistance in eliminating the negatives.
6. Sweet dreams!

Chapter 21

Listening to Your Inner Guidance

Most of us never stop to give ourselves a quiet moment; we rush through our days and never process the information we absorb. We ignore ourselves with the hope that we won't have to "face the music" anytime soon. Facing the music is a lot easier when the angels play it for us. By meditating, centering ourselves, and praying, we can plug ourselves into the heaven circuit and process our information for the highest good.

There are a variety of approaches to meditation, such as focusing on a mantra, on imagery, or on physical objects, or simply paying attention to one's breathing. You may already be familiar with meditation and practice it regularly. Being centered comes from meditating and from taking the time to breathe and process information as it comes up, in a nonattached manner. Praying is a way of expressing our longing for insight and peace from the realm of heaven.

Angel Meditation

Start by finding a quiet and comfortable place to sit. Close your eyes and just be. Try not to think; if thoughts come to you, allow them in and then release them and go back to not thinking. *Pay attention to attention.* Never let attention become an effort, or try to force thoughts away. Don't let thoughts disturb you; just let them come and go. Now let your attention focus on angels. At this point, you may want to use the word *angel* as a form of mantra. Allow the word to take you wherever it will. Let a smile come over you, and notice the feeling of peace that comes with it. As you smile, feel yourself lifted and surrounded by white light. Ask the angels to lift you into heaven so that you can meet them. Ask to be an angel for a moment, and experience the lightness and happiness of the angels' realm. Get to know your guardian angel as you would a friend. Do this in whatever manner comes to you; there are no set rules. Ask the angels to guide you with their inspiring wisdom, and listen quietly for any messages they have for you. The messages may not come to you in words; often angels speak to you with feelings and images. Sometimes, the benefits of meditation come to the surface hours later. It may be that an idea was planted into your subconscious for use at a later time. During meditation, the angels sometimes spread out the pieces of your life, like the pieces of a puzzle, so that you can see what you have to work with. As you go through each day, another piece will fit into place, bringing you closer to the whole. (Then you can start another puzzle!)

When you are just getting to know angels, meditation may be a time for clearing out negative belief systems and emotional blocks that keep you from connecting with the heavenly realm. (See Chapter 19 on declarations to the angels.) Be patient, and do the work. Purify your consciousness of whatever is limiting you. Eventually, your inner wisdom will come through loud and clear, and the light and happiness of the angels will stay with you throughout the day.

Angel Centering

Being centered means your spirit is in alignment with your body. It means there is a balance: your head is not totally in the clouds in an avoidance of life, but neither are you completely grounded to the earth and overreacting to life situations. Centering is a way of synchronizing our energy. If our energy is scattered, we are going in different directions within ourselves; we are going in circles, so to speak. If we synchronize our energy, we can head in one direction and accomplish our goals. Centering synchronizes our energy with our higher self and with the angels who guide us.

Centering harmonizes our body/mind. When we are centered, we cannot be knocked off balance or fall over easily. We are able to accept the reality of our situations and to use our inner resources and creativity to deal with that reality. Sometimes, just a change of scenery will center you—for example, going outside for a breath of fresh air, or admiring a beautiful garden. Exercise and movement can center you—for example, taking a long walk on the beach, or dancing to your favorite song. Playing a musical instrument, painting, cooking, and writing (especially in a journal) are ways to find your center by paying attention to the activity, and thinking of nothing else.

Centering yourself is a good habit and talent to develop. Meditating is one way of centering yourself. During the course of the day, however, you may not have time to do a full meditation. Taking a time-out is like doing a quick meditation. If you feel yourself getting off balance, take a time-out. Find a place where you can close your eyes and calm your breathing. Clear your mind and ask for immediate angel guidance and insight into what knocked you off balance. Now, bring a smile to your being and relax. When you are centering yourself, ask the angels for creativity and peace and then accept it and go back to what you are doing with a refreshed attitude.

Get in the habit of not overreacting to situations; get away from the "everything is either good or bad" syndrome. Adopt the perspective of: "This is interesting; let me stop and center myself for a moment so I don't freak out." Step back and observe the situation from an objective position. Realign your spirit with your body/mind. Pull yourself together by taking a time-out with the angels.

Praying

Prayer is our chance to talk to the higher power in our lives, whether we think of it as God, the angels, Buddha, a saint, a bodhisattva, or simply the Universe. Prayer is something we can do alone or with others. You can pray by singing or writing a poem. You may experience prayer as a peak experience when you are giving thanks and blessings. Sometimes, we pray and don't even realize it — for example, when we're feeling down and we cry out for release.

F. Forrester Church talks about three kinds of prayer in his book *Entertaining Angels: A Guide to Heaven*. The first kind of prayer is confession, through which we make peace with the enemy within us. The second kind of prayer links self to others; this happens when we ask for blessings for others and for situations we want. The third kind of prayer involves saying "yes" to life and giving ourselves over to God; this is how we express gratitude and trust in the universe.

Prayer is personal: We all have our own ways or praying, but basically prayer involves expressing ourselves verbally to God. We can be specific in our prayers, relaying exactly what we want, or we can ask for blessings from God's abundance and trust that everything will work out. Prayer can center us and guide us back on track. Prayer is the way we talk to angels, and by meditating we listen to their response. Prayer is asking for divine intercession, both for ourselves and others.

When you pray to the angels, pray as if "it is already done"; in other words, thank the angels in advance for taking care of your burdens. Pray that it will be done on earth as it is in heaven, for the highest good of all concerned. When you pray to the angels, remember that they work for a higher power (meaning God or whatever term you use to describe the highest spiritual force in your life). So always thank God and the angels in your prayers, and ask that you be blessed with peace.

Creating an Altar

An altar is a space of spiritual focus. Altars in churches are tables on which offerings are made to God, such as the bread and wine of communion. You may already have an altar or shrine in your home; a lot of people do these days. If you don't, you may want to create one so that you can have a place of spiritual focus. Gather small objects that are sacred to you, such as pictures, statues, a vase for flowers, prayer beads, crystals, rocks, shells, plaques, icons, an incense burner — whatever feels right to you. Now, find an empty space to create your altar. A small table, an area in a bookcase, the top of a dresser, or a windowsill can all work well. If you are uncomfortable about having people see your altar, find a subtle place in your room. You can make your altar so simple that no one will even notice it. It helps to have a beautiful cloth to add inspiring colors. Always make room for a candle. Angels love candlelight. Candlelight illuminates and purifies the atmosphere and attracts angels.

After you have created your altar or shrine, light the candle and sit quietly in front of it. Draw in the beauty and ask the angels to join you. Put on some inspiring and peaceful music — harps and flutes attract angels. Burn some incense if you like. Let yourself find joy, love, and divine humor in your spiritual contemplation, and inhale the golden light you've created.

SUMMARY

Method

Meditating, centering, and creating a space for spiritual focus as a way of attracting and getting to know angels.

Angels who can help

Call on the angels to join you in your meditations.

Tools and ideas

1. Do an angel meditation as a way of connecting with the heaven plane.
2. Learn to take time-outs during the day to center yourself and connect with the angels for inspiration. Center yourself whenever you feel the urge to overreact to or to label any situation as good or bad.
3. Pray. Verbally express your longing for peace and communion with the angels.
4. Create a shrine or altar as a place for spiritual focus and centering.
5. Connect yourself to the spiritual beauty in life with flowers, music, and candlelight — the elements that attract angels.

Chapter 22

Noticing Angels in Everyday Life

It's fun to notice the way angels are sung about, portrayed in art, and talked about in our everyday life. By everyday life I mean the routines in our lives involving external reality — for example, listening to the radio, watching T.V., going places each day in our cars, noticing people on the street. When we become aware of angels, it is fun to notice how often we hear the word *angel* each day, and how often we see angels in art and even in people.

Most of us leave the house at least once a day. And most of us listen to a recording or to music on the radio in our home or car. Most stores and restaurants have music playing. Start noticing how often you hear the word *angel* in the songs you hear. Go through some of your old records and notice how many times you come across titles with the word *angel* in them.

When you go to the grocery store or pharmacy, start noticing all the products that use the word *angel* in their name. They range from toilet paper and perfume to pasta and liqueur. One time, my friend and I decided to have an angel food dinner, with angel hair pasta as the main dish and angel food cake for dessert; we added other appropriate items to go with the theme. Many products have heaven or paradise as their theme, or use the names of specific angels on the labels. Celestial themes are also popular.

When you see paintings and statues, look for angels. You might walk by them all the time and not even notice. You will see angels in magazines and on book covers. It is fun to see how contemporary artists portray angels. The New Age visionary artists have created especially beautiful paintings of angels. There are greeting cards with angels pictured on them for all seasons and occasions. Museums flourish with angel statues and paintings.

You can also find angels on television. There is even a prime-time show about an angel who comes to earth as a human to help people. Movies about angels, both new and old, often make their way to our T.V. sets. Occasionally, you can hear about an angel of the moment on the evening news or on a T.V. magazine show. An angel of the moment is a human who is a rescuer. Whether these angels rescue people from danger or from the darkness, either way they are inspiring to hear about and deserve more time on the air. Also, if you are watching a news story about a disaster in which miraculously only a few people were hurt be assured that there was unseen help from heaven.

Visualizing angels in the clouds is fun. Sometimes, angels show up in reflections on glass or water. I have taken pictures of strange blobs of light that appeared for no reason and that looked to me like angels. One time I took a picture of two friends of mine sitting at a table, in what I thought was the same light, but one of them came out so overexposed in the photograph that I could hardly see her image. This didn't really surprise me, though, because this friend is full of light and very much like an angel. Stains on old buildings, paint splatters, rock formations, and strange lights in the sky—all can hold the visual image of angels.

Increasing your awareness of angels in everyday life will help you formulate your own concepts about who they are and how they can help you. If you become highly interested in angels, you will want to read more about them. Several books about angels are listed in Part Five, along with other sources of information that will increase your knowledge and understanding of angels.

Chapter 23

Recognizing Signs of Angels' Play

An angel's work is actually play. When you want to attract angels into your life, you must recognize the signs of play that mean they are with you. Recognizing and acknowledging angels is important for keeping your relationship with them alive and prominent in your life.

One meaning of play is "free movement." Play does not restrict or control anyone. Play is also a means for interspecies communication—for example, humans and dolphins play together, and dogs, cats, and humans play together. Another example of interspecies communication through play is between angels and humans.

Synchronicity is one way the angels play with us. For a detailed description of synchronicity, read about synchronism agents in Chapter 6. Basically, a synchronism is a coincidental event that seems to take on a meaning beyond the obvious. When angels are playing with us, they communicate by arranging coincidences and favorable meetings.

Another way angels play with us is by providing humor at our most serious moments. They may arrange for something hysterically funny to occur just when you can't take it anymore.

Unexplainable feelings of peace and well-being mean that angels are at play around you. Visualize them playing all around you, scaring off the negative thoughts and worrisome situations that interfere with your peace of mind. Visualize them catching the negatives and turning them into positives before they get to you.

Good luck and good fortune are fun games the angels play with us. Luck seems to be a gift from the universe, but actually we create our own good luck by believing we deserve it. When we believe and know we deserve good luck and fortune, the angels help it along. The reason luck is a game is that it involves a certain kind of work on our part to play it. As with playing any game, there are opportunities we must grab and actions we must take to win. The angels help us understand just what luck is all about.

Hope is present when angels are around. There is always hope. Hope is a seed the angels plant in our consciousness; then they water and fertilize it to grow and flourish in our lives. Hope and faith can heal physical and mental maladies. They give us the will to find the way.

Playing with the angels can give us the feeling that we are so light we might just float away. The lightness is so prominent that we may even forget we have bodies. Experiencing this light is pure joy. It is a peak experience of love. It is a gift the angels give us to let us know they are near and that we deserve to feel good.

Understanding and recognizing the signs that mean angels are at play in our lives will help us prolong the positive feelings and bring us a deeper and closer connection with them. Each time you ask the angels to help you with something, look for clues of their play. Then thank them, and tell them to keep up the good play.

Chapter 24

Wearing Clothes Angels Like

One way to attract angels is to wear the kinds of clothes they like. By now, you probably have a sense of the qualities of the angels that surround you. Wearing something that the angels will like is a personal choice based on your own perception and idea of angels. Here are some ideas I've found in the books I've read on angels and from talking with people about angels.

COLORS TO WEAR TO ATTRACT SPECIFIC ANGELS

> Guardians: rose or pink (an aura of divine affection), and
>   soft green
> Healing angels: deep sapphire blue
> Angels of birth: sky blue
> Ceremonial and music angels: white
> Nature angels: apple green
> Angels of art and wisdom: yellow

The seraphim (the "burning ones" are the first choir of
  angels, and are the closest to God's throne): crimson red
The cherubim (the next choir): blue
Archangel Michael: deep green, vivid blue, gold, and rose
Archangel Raphael: pale blue and soft greens
Archangel Gabriel: tans, browns, and dark greens

COLORS TO WEAR TO ATTRACT MOST ANGELS

Study the colors of an abalone shell (mother-of-pearl) and select
clothing in various combinations of these colors. These beautiful
light pastel colors will make you feel light and heavenly. When
you feel this way, you will surely attract angels.

TYPES OF CLOTHING TO WEAR

Clothes that flow and drape your body
Breezy clothes that catch the wind and make you feel a part
  of nature
Clown suits that make others laugh
Angel costumes with wings and halos
Clothes that make you feel and look good
All-white clothing that helps you reflect light around you

FLOWER FRAGRANCES THAT ATTRACT ANGELS

Jasmine and rose are said to be noticeable when angels (especially
guardian angels) are near. Pine is said to attract healing angels,
and its scent is noticeable when they are near. Sandalwood is
the fragrance that the creativity ministers or muses are supposed
to like.

Assign fragrances to the angels you want near you, and bring
flowers into your home, burn incense, or wear perfume with
these fragrances. For example:

Honeysuckle: the messengers
Gardenia: worry extinguishers and prosperity brokers

Hyacinth: soul angels
Lilac: happiness trainers

OTHER IDEAS

When you are in a difficult situation, imagine yourself wearing a halo and surround yourself with white light. Imagine your car wearing a field of white light to protect you on the road. Imagine your house wearing an aura of white light to protect you from negative forces.

Wearing something angels like is all in fun. It works because angels like to participate in fun. It is your own game and your own rules. So use your intuition. If you feel strongly about a certain color or fragrance for attracting specific angels, bring the color or fragrance into your life and the angels will be near.

Part Four

Living an
Angelic Life

About Part Four:
An Angelic Life-Style

Part Four is about living an angelic life-style. This doesn't mean that all of a sudden you are a perfect little angel in all you do; it has nothing to do with perfection. Perfection is boring, and the angels know this. Living an angelic life only means that you have chosen to incorporate lightness into whatever you do. To bring lightness into your life, you may need to make more room for it. By bringing in lightness, you bring in angels, so it is impossible to have one without the other. Part Four discusses ways to make room in your life for lightness and angels.

Chapter 25 is about forgiving yourself and others as a means of releasing the past. Forgiveness equals release. By practicing forgiveness, you open up many channels to lightness.

Chapter 26 explores the difference between empathy and sympathy. Chances are good that you are a very sensitive being who can fall into periods of heaviness if those around you are in pain. We can't ignore our friends when they are in pain, and we would not want to be ignored ourselves. It helps to know some techniques for dealing with other people's pains and problems without going down yourself. In fact, by remaining light you will be able to help them more.

But helping others requires remaining light in a responsible way. Chapter 27, on the consequences of light behavior, tells you about the balance to strive for when you've adopted the philosophy of lightness.

Chapter 28 looks at enlightenment in connection with angels, as another way to incorporate lightness into your spiritual path.

Random angel testing is a game the angels play with humans and is described in Chapter 29. This game has the objective of lightening up and waking up the participants.

The angel health and beauty program in Chapter 30 lists ways you can lighten up physically, leaving room for even more lightness in your life.

Chapters 31 and 32 address issues that get in the way of lightness, which are not very fun at all. The topics discussed need to be looked at for insight into how and why we humans experience the "downs" in the "ups and downs" of life. Ideally, the more we learn about the down side, the easier it will be to stay away from it and incorporate more levels of light—more "ups"—into our life-style.

The information in Part Four is compatible with the methods in Part Three and will help you expand and personalize these methods. Also, as you read Part Four, consider which of the angels described in Part Two can help you lead a more angelic life.

Welcome to the life-styles of the light and angelic!

Chapter 25

Practicing Forgiveness and Release

Look at the humans on this planet as either extending love or as fearful and sending out a call for love.

Gerald Jampolsky

Forgiveness means ceasing to feel anger and resentment toward others about offenses you feel they have committed. The act of forgiving releases you from resentment and anger so that these negative emotions don't consume you. True forgiveness is a difficult lesson if we are convinced that others have harmed us purposely. We want them to ask us for forgiveness, but they may not agree with our perception of the situation. Whether or not a negative action was purposely directed at us doesn't matter. Facts surrounding the situation don't really matter either (unless you are in court); it is how we perceive the situation and how it makes us feel that causes trouble. The pain, anger, and resentment that is stored in our consciousness when we won't forgive and release can cause big trouble in our lives.

Current research is finding a link between unexpressed anger and resentment and a tendency to get cancer and other illnesses. Anger and resentment chip away at our happiness and cloud the present. It is difficult to be happy when our minds are stuck on past situations that have caused us pain. Practicing forgiveness releases us from the limitations of the past, clears up the negatives, and gives us a clean slate for the present.

Sometimes, the people we love the most are the hardest to forgive. If there are some people who you find especially unforgivable, write a note of forgiveness to their highest angels. The problem may be that you don't know *how* to forgive them. Cultivate a willingness to release the situation. Write or speak to their highest angels and let it be known that you are willing to forgive and forget and go on with your happiness. Imagine your highest angel talking to the other person's highest angel and working out the differences between you, ending in peace and laughter. Willingness is the key ingredient on your part; let the angels take care of the rest.

According to Emmet Fox, "When you hold resentment against anyone, you are bound to that person by a cosmic link, a real though mental chain. You are tied by a cosmic tie to the thing you hate. The one person perhaps in the whole world whom you most dislike is the very one to whom you are attaching yourself by a hook that is stronger than steel." Resentment and anger can have a snowball effect in your mind. Just as a snowball picks up more snow as it rolls down a hill, anger picks up more fuel as it grows in your mind, picking up misperceptions. In other words, if a small offense is not taken care of and released immediately, it can grow into a huge offense in your mind, one which will be difficult to forgive later.

Abraham Lincoln was once criticized for the manner in which he dealt with his "enemies." He answered the criticism by saying, "Do I not destroy my enemies when I make them my friends?" At some point in your life, you may have been told, that you must love your enemies. This is a lot easier said than done, especially if *we* are our own worst enemy. When the enemy is ourselves, we are usually the last to know because we can't step outside ourselves with total objectivity to see the attacks we wage on ourselves.

One day I was driving my car and I kept noticing things that were wrong with all the other cars on the road. One had a taillight out, one was spewing dark smoke out of its tailpipe, and another had a bad tire. Then I realized that if any of these things were wrong with my car, I wouldn't know it because I was busy driving. I, too, could have a taillight out or a bad exhaust system, and not even know about it. Unless I were to stop the car, get out, and watch the car in action, I would not really know what is going on with it. Well, how can we get out of our lives and really notice all the things we need to fix? We can't exactly get out and walk around, but we can become more aware of the ways in which we sabotage ourselves and act as our own worst enemy.

The key is to adopt a pattern of awareness so that we can detect and change negative thoughts directed toward ourselves. Learning to forgive *ourselves* is extremely important. When it comes to forgiveness, we are hardest on ourselves. If guilt is keeping you from forgiving yourself, then work on releasing guilt first. Guilt consists of unexpressed resentment and fear or anticipation of punishment or a harsh reaction from others. If a situation with someone is making you feel guilty, this could mean that you actually feel that that person is trying to control or sway you into doing something you don't want to do. This breeds resentment. We resent it when our time is wasted, but most of us do things for others because we believe we "should." Situations involving "shoulds" or trying to live down to another's expectations breed resentment, resentment breeds guilt, guilt looks for a way to punish, and punishment means pain.

Guilt can also surface when we feel "too good." You may have a brain program that tells you you don't deserve to feel good: "How dare you feel good when others feel bad?" You may feel guilty for having so much when others have so little. You imagine them disapproving of and envying your happiness. Forgiveness is an act of unconditional love. This means we must love ourselves unconditionally and treat ourselves well. Ultimately, guilt has the same effect as unexpressed anger and resentment; you can literally make yourself sick with guilt.

The bottom line is that you won't be as happy as you deserve to be if guilt and hatred are taking up space in your consciousness. Whatever the hate results from, get rid of it; don't punish yourself needlessly. Ask the angels for release and be willing to let the hatred go. Call on your cheerleaders. They like you no matter what. Their main cheer is: "Don't give up; we like who you are. We are proud of who you are!" Cheer with them and learn how to love yourself unconditionally regardless of any stupid mistakes you have made in the past. We all have the right to make asses out of ourselves as long as we can have a good laugh about how funny we are. So lighten up and don't be so hard on yourself!

Make a list of the things you have done for which you want forgiveness. Think of the things you have done that may be keeping you from unconditional happiness. Declare formally that you are forgiving yourself for the situations listed. Ask your guardian angel to help you release the situations and take care of the how, while you concentrate on being willing to release your list. Here is a sample list.

I formally and willingly forgive myself for the following situations:

1. Complaining
2. Forgetting to count my blessings
3. Listening to and internalizing criticism
4. Forgetting that at any time I can change my perception and see other humans and myself as innocent
5. Blaming
6. Feeling guilty
7. Getting angry

8. Being conditional
9. Worrying
10. Feeling envy, jealousy, and greed
11. Overeating and jeopardizing my health
12. Being in denial
13. Losing faith and not following through
14. Harboring negative brain programs
15. Forgetting to call in the angels when needed

After you have made your list, try to see how funny and endearing you are. Love your humanness. If there are people you find difficult to forgive, make a list of their offenses and then release them, and remember to check out the humor in their lists. Always ask the angels to help you release your lists and transmute the energy.

Practicing forgiveness brings you closer to happiness without reason. It frees you from the past. It allows freedom in the present. It takes away limits, and so frees the future. Forgiveness allows us to be happy in the now without guilt, anger, and resentment causing us pain. Forgiving yourself and others without condition is the key to releasing the past and healing the present. Forgiveness is an act of love. As Louis Gittner says, "Love can build highways out of dead ends."

PRACTICE IDEAS

1. If there are people or loved ones you are finding difficult to forgive, then write a letter of forgiveness to their highest angels.
2. If there are people you need to forgive, visualize meeting with these people or their highest angels to clear the air.
3. If you are being hard on yourself for one reason or another, write down a forgiveness list as described above, and hand it over to the angels.
4. Adopt a pattern to detect and intercept negative thoughts directed toward yourselves and others; then transmute the thoughts or throw them out.

5. If you are your own worst enemy, make friends with yourself. If there are too many "shoulds" and feelings of guilt in your daily life, this is a sign that you need to forgive yourself for not being "perfect" and to incorporate the angels into your life. This is also a sign that you need to play and have fun. Attain a feeling of lightness toward yourself by calling on the angels or by writing a formal statement to them regarding your forgiveness of yourself. Read and internalize any information you find about loving yourself and raising your level of self-esteem.

The following Loving Kindness Meditation, from the tradition of Theravada Buddhism, is quoted from Rick Fields's *Chop Wood, Carry Water.*

If anyone has hurt me or harmed me knowingly or unknowingly in thought, word, or deed, I freely forgive them.

And I too ask forgiveness if I have hurt anyone or harmed anyone knowingly or unknowingly in thought, word, or deed.

May I be happy
May I be peaceful
May I be free

May my friends be happy
May my friends be peaceful
May my friends be free

May my enemies be happy
May my enemies be peaceful
May my enemies be free

May all beings be happy
May all beings be peaceful
May all beings be free

Chapter 26

Empathy Versus Sympathy

There is a fine line between empathy and sympathy. Empathy is understanding another person's feelings without getting caught up in the feelings. When we have sympathy for others, we connect with their pain and we suffer if they are suffering. If we have empathy for others, we can remain happy even if they are sad, and we can still help them by understanding and recognizing their pain without feeling it ourselves. Remaining happy and light as long as we are not pushy and forceful will help others lighten up in due time.

Sympathy includes an element of pity or feeling sorry for someone. Pitying others is not helpful; it is condescending. Sympathizing with others can have the effect of continuing a downward process. It is like a man coming by on a sled that is heading downhill for diaster and stopping to pick you up. If you get on, you go down with him. If you turn him around or stop him by helping him recognize the end result, you help him.

Empathy conveys a message of equality and strengthens self-esteem. You are not putting yourself above others and saying, "Let me help you." Nor are you lowering yourself and feeling bad, too. Empathizing means you are allowing a person to be and to explore. You will be there as a caring and unconditional listener. Unconditional listening is a rare and delicate art. Listening with an open heart and mind without expectations, projections, emotional investment, or judgments is difficult to master. The angels can help.

Are you someone people come to with problems and sorrows? Are you someone others seek out to talk to about themselves in general? If you are, consider it a high compliment. It means you are trusted. Learning how to listen without it damaging or interfering with your own psyche is important. It is also good to know the way angels can help you help someone else.

First of all, ask the angels to protect you from reacting emotionally to someone else's problems. This means you must stay centered within yourself when you are listening to others talk about their lives and their perceptions. Practice listening to people without thinking things like "that's good . . . that's bad . . . you should . . . he should . . . she should not . . . do . . . don't"—in essence, try to free your mind from judgments of any kind. See the situation as it exists by itself; free it from your projections as much as possible. Try not to "react and relate" to information that involves people, regardless of how much you care about them. Don't take sides if someone is talking about a relationship. If you take sides even in concept, you will soon find yourself sinking into identification with one person or the other and becoming emotionally involved in the discord, thus amplifying the problem of the person you are trying to assist, and reinforcing the bad feeling between the two people.

Here is one technique that will make it easier to hear people fully while avoiding the trap of becoming emotionally involved in their conflict: When you listen to somebody talking, listen for what they are really saying. Repeat key phrases back to them. For example, if a friend says, "_____ really made me angry today because he went somewhere without me and he knows I wanted to go with him," repeat back to her, "You are really angry

because you wanted to go to _____ and _____ didn't take you."
Then she will know you are listening to her, and she'll go a step
further: "He always does this to me, and I'm afraid he doesn't
want to be with me anymore." Repeat back, "You are afraid
_____ is going his own way without you." You have gotten even
more information, and you now know that your friend is dealing
with the fear of potential rejection. By repeating information
back to other people, you allow them to direct the conversation
to the areas where the real issues lie.

When it seems to be the right time, you can confront people
about the real issues that are upsetting them. Remember that the
feelings are real, that they are experiencing pain, and that it
doesn't matter whether you or anyone else agrees with them.
The facts do not matter; the only thing that matters is *how* and
why the situation is causing them pain. Of course, no one is
expecting you to be a professional counselor, but it never hurts
to learn and practice ways of listening to others that let them
know they are heard and cared for—and to do this without
involving yourself in the pain. In this way, you are practicing
empathy for others and leaving sympathy out.

If people are talking on and on about the behavior of others
in their lives, notice how often they are actually describing themselves. If you feel compelled to point this out to them, do it in
a loving way.

The angels can help you in a variety of ways. When you are
with people you care about who are having a rough time, ask the
angels to surround the room in the white-pink-gold light of healing and love. Ask your guardian angel to confer with the other
people's guardians to give you insight into their pain and suffering
and to guide you in the best ways of helping them. Ask that the angels and your guardian keep you centered and free from identifying with pain that is not yours. Ask the other people's guardians
to let them know that you can be trusted, that you will be unconditional, and that you will not judge or react—that you will just
listen. Ask your own guardian to help you be this way.

Your overall objective will be to bring in humor at some point — to "leave them laughing," so to speak. Do this with the utmost delicacy and ask the angels to help you; it is one of their specialties. Ask the guardians of both you and the other people for the release of laughter every once in a while. Laughter will help you clarify the issues. Laughter will free both you and those you are helping for creative problem solving. Laughter is a good way to introduce "angel help" to others if they aren't already aware of its existence.

When the people see the light and lighten up, they will be receptive to angels. Think of any of the methods in Part Three that could help these people. Think of any angel stories you could tell them. Then let them know that they have a guardian angel and that this guardian angel is around to protect them and lead them to a happier way of being. Encourage them to try a few methods together with you, such as writing to the guardians of people who have hurt them and writing some declarations to the angels stating positive changes they want to make in their lives. Ask that the angels bless all of you with healing and light.

When all is said and done, think of how much you learn from listening to others. Examine any tension you feel is clinging to you from time you've spent with others and their problems. Write about it in your angel journal or just meditate on it. Somehow, let yourself process the information you absorb. Know that you can protect your center and remain happy when others are sad. Know the difference between empathy and sympathy. Know that you can help others by simply listening unconditionally to them. Know that the angels can help you achieve all of the above.

Chapter 27

The Consequences of Light Behavior

Enlighten up!

Steve Bucher

Taking yourself lightly and behaving in a lighthearted way has a favorable effect on all aspects of your life. Lightheated people would never want to offend or hurt others with their behavior, so it is important to examine just what is meant by taking yourself lightly and almost nothing seriously.

First of all, why is it that angels want us to become more like them by taking ourselves lightly? This is mainly a matter of trust. As humans, we have basic survival issues to face on a daily basis. We have to make sure we have water to drink, food to eat, and shelter and safety to protect us. For some people, these needs are taken care of without a worry; most of us work for money to pay for these basics. With working comes a certain amount of stress and worry — worry about having enough to get by and still having time for some fun and creativity. The way angels see it, if we can trust and have faith in them and the laws of an abundant universe, we will be taken care of without all the worry. In turn, we won't have to take these survival issues so seriously, we can have more fun in life, and our work can be play.

Angels provide protection in the form of a personal guardian who is always by your side. They provide food and shelter by sending messages through your higher self, guiding you in the direction of the right career and opportunities. Of course, they will only do this for you if you want them to—so somehow you or your higher self has to ask them. The only thing angels can't do is live your life for you. Angels want to help us with the serious issues we face each day so that we can be lighter and more creative—and in turn more fun to be around.

Angels want to remove from our lives the solemnity and pessimism that result from reacting to too many things in a serious manner and creating a heavier gravity field around ourselves. This doesn't mean that if your children come to you hurt you can't take them seriously or that if someone is truly asking for your help or empathy that you can't respond to their request. (See Chapter 26 on empathy versus sympathy and basic listening techniques.) It means take your loved ones to heart (a light heart) but not with gravity.

When those we love come to us hurt or in serious trouble, we can keep a light heart and still help them know that we love and care for them. If we need to discuss a "serious" issue with someone, we can still be happy and optimistic. The angels will help you balance lightness in your life so that no one is hurt by your behavior (unless someone wants to be hurt by you). The angels want to see loving lightness in humans—not carelessness. Be carefree, not careless.

When people are in serious and solemn moods, they may be offended if you treat their problems and perceptions too lightly. Developing the right balance of lightness in relation to other humans is important. Have you ever been in a bad mood and had to be around a cheerful person? In a state of depression, being around a cheerful and light person can make people angry. One time I was sincerely angry at someone because of her behavior in a certain situation. All I wanted was someone to listen to me while I aired my anger. The person I chose kept saying, "Oh, what a silly girl. She is so silly. That is so silly." Well, of course it was silly—everything is silly—but I did not want to hear that at the time and it made me even angrier. I learned several valuable things about myself from this experience. Later I realized that I have probably done the same thing over and over to this same person and to most of my friends. While trying to make people see the humor (the light), I wasn't listening in the most caring and unconditional way that I could.

It is wise to adjust our lightness and cheerfulness to the right level around people who are having a hard time if we want to be true friends. Listen unconditionally and wait for the right moment; wait for a cue from them before you begin trying to cheer them up. This way, they can ease out of their pain and join in your happiness on their own. In other words, we wouldn't want to force-feed lightness to anyone.

Laughter is important for lightening up any situation. Just be sure you are not "laughing in someone's face." Find a way to get others laughing with you in serious situations; it is a great release. Call on the humor transformers if you are in need of laughter. In any crisis I've experienced, I have noticed that at some point the people involved needed a good laugh, and it happened naturally. Even at funerals, people find a release by laughing. This doesn't mean disrespect for those who are deceased; it's actually a good indication that they are greatly loved and appreciated.

When I hear myself say (or think), "This is a very serious matter," I instantly get the urge to laugh. When I am forced to go out and take care of "serious matters" and I run into people who are way too serious, once again I get an urge to laugh. This seems so funny to me, and they usually look funny too. A fun thing to do is to try to get a smile or laugh out of people when they are caught in the trap of seriousness. This takes some skill, but it can be done by anyone willing to try. Of course, always do this with a sense of love, never out of anger or as a punishment. First, try smiling yourself. As you smile, imagine light radiating from your being to reach out and zap the people. If this doesn't work, you can try telling a joke. If they get more serious after the joke, you may be in too deep and need to stop. If people have chosen to work with the public, I think they have a certain responsibility to be pleasant. This is just my opinion, but when we are out among others of our species an air of kindness and hospitality creates a pattern of magic in the universe — a pattern that attracts the angels.

When you go out in the world with a light heart, you want the consequences of your light behavior to be positive. It is not wise to lecture or preach! If people are feeling heavy, depressed, or even paranoid, there's nothing worse than laying your own belief system on them, as if agreeing with your doctrine or view of the world would help them. This can be especially bad if you come on with the self-righteous attitude of many people who attribute their own success or happiness to some belief they hold or some code of conduct they practice. People can become "belief dependent," and they are usually off base as far as their own explanation of their success goes. They become superstitious. It's easy to make other people feel bad, even worse than they were already feeling, by convincing them that the problem is their failure or inability to believe as you do. Well, now I'm lecturing and preaching! How does it make you feel? It's so difficult to be perfect, isn't it? So we might as well have a good laugh at ourselves and not take the process of belief so seriously.

KEYS TO RESPONSIBLE LIGHT BEHAVIOR

1. Angels want us to be less solemn and to worry less over the everyday survival issues we face, so that we are happier and

more creative. They remind us to give our burdens over to a higher power and to trust in the protection they provide.

2. We must do a lightness check to make sure that we are not taking things that require our loving attention too lightly. Carefree behavior is fine as long as it is not careless.

3. The consequences of behaving lightly must be positive, or it is not true lightness. In other words, take life lightly in the spirit of love.

4. Laughter is a great release for serious occasions, as long as it is not totally inappropriate. Cues from others let us know when to introduce laughter.

5. Be wary of force-feeding lightness to others when they are not ready for it, or not in the mood.

6. Beware of the "belief system" mentality in yourself and others. Practice not preaching about what you practice!

7. Allow the dynamics of change to operate in your life. Change the rules when you feel stuck in a systematic practice.

Chapter 28

Angels and Enlightenment

Since everything is but an apparition,
perfect in being what it is,
having nothing to do with good or bad,
acceptance or rejection,
one may well burst out in laughter.

Long-Chen-Pa

Enlightenment is a state of being in light. To enlighten is to impart spiritual (intellectual) knowledge — to shed light on something essential. To be enlightened means to be free from prejudice and ignorance and to possess the spiritual knowledge that sheds light. From the above, we can surmise that enlightenment is the state of being completely in light, totally and spiritually informed, and free from having to judge and compare. The opposite of enlightenment is a state of mental darkness; the curtains are pulled so that the light won't get in.

According to most spiritual seekers, attaining enlightenment is the goal of life on earth. When we reach the state of enlightenment, we will know the answers to the questions of ontology (the metaphysical category that asks the question "What's it all about?") and teleology (the metaphysical category that asks the question "Why are we here?"). This boils down to: Who is directing this big picture, and do I really have a starring role or am I just an extra?

Angels are constantly in a state of light. They shed lightness and spiritually awaken us every chance they get. Angels send messages that tell us to cease comparing, judging, and emotionally reacting to the serious issues we face each day. In essence, angels are the epitome of enlightenment. And they live in the same neighborhood (heaven) as the creator of the universe.

Angels are the perfect teachers for us if we are seeking enlightenment. The catch is that according to the angels the experience of human life is ridiculous and absurd—and way too serious. By the angels' standards, once we really understand this, we will be enlightened. So what is the point of striving to attain a state if everything is seen as ridiculous? Well, one reason is that you will burst out laughing, because you will be one with the divine humor that permeates the universe.

We usually run into blocks on the path to enlightenment, because we forget to take along our sense of humor. Humor is definitely needed at all stages on the path of enlightenment. Angels can be of assistance by giving us a spiritual lightening up. Angels teach us that enlightenment releases us from the seriousness of life, and frees us from the traps of survival and emotional perceptions. All these traps occur first in our minds. Angels want to release us from these traps so that we can rest in the bliss of their realm.

When one connects completely with the angels (which only happens for brief previews if you haven't yet reached the state of chronic enlightenment), the peak experience of joy and bliss is indescribable. It is a moment of total freedom. The angels' message is: Give up and rest in God's love, and be one with the divine humor of the universe. The closer we come to a state of divine humor, the happier we will be. Any step we take freely toward enlightened humor will multiply our understanding of the ultimate question.

Enlightenment is the state in which you have merged completely with your higher self. Your higher self is able to have constant contact with angels in the realm of heaven. Just think of that—a chance to joke around with the angels whenever you want!

Enlightenment is hilarious, and life *is* absurd. We humans love a challenge and a game. Each time we get closer to being released from the human qualities that block enlightenment, something else comes up. For example, you finally get to a point where you aren't attached to the pain and suffering of others. You can be carefree, and you feel that you can go anywhere in the universe and survive with total freedom. Then you add a child to your life and everything changes. Now you have a whole new set of emotions and instincts to follow and integrate—as well as a new capacity for love.

Apparently, you will never run out of lessons to learn on this earth. But that is what makes human life fun and meaningful. If you attain enlightenment, you still have to go on living. The closer you get to enlightenment, the closer heaven gets to your reality of living on earth, so enlightenment is worth pursuing. Angels teach us to enlighten up! Loving humor makes everything seem a little easier to take and understand. Most of the lessons we have to learn on this earth are lessons that will increase our capacity for love. Love isn't heavy. Love is light; it is the highest angelic ideal.

Practice finding loving humor in all the things you do in the name of enlightenment. In each person you talk to, each book you read, each holy teacher you seek out, look for lightness and humor. If you miss it or find that it isn't there, go on to something else quick! Solemn spiritual rituals and the solemn people who practice them take enlightenment far too seriously.

Have you ever been involved in a serious religious ceremony and in the middle of it you got an urge to laugh hysterically?

Some churches and religious organizations seem to think that acting in a serious manner means respect for religion. Some religions take all the joy out of worship by demanding that people listen to a serious, solemn service talking about how bad humans are. This is supposed to lead us to "perfection"—but who wants it? Not I, and not the angels!

Angels are the ones who want to make us laugh during serious religious ceremonies. They are all over the place wanting to spread joy and humor. Their message is that we are loved unconditionally by God and the universe (and this love has nothing to do with being perfect). This message deserves lighthearted celebration and mirthful expression whenever it is heard. I would guess that there are more angels around people who are having fun and laughing, regardless of the circumstances, than in churches where people are being indoctrinated in seriousness.

Humor bypasses the need for strict and rigid spiritual practices. A day spent laughing will bring us closer to God than a day of heavy soul-searching. This is because laughter brings us closer to the real us—the lovable us, the happy us, the free us, the us others want to be around. Laughing frees our creativity so the soul-searching process unfolds in a natural, rather than a forced, manner. No need to push the river. Just build a raft, hop on it, and burst out laughing at the bends and rapids along the way.

Chapter 29

Random Angel Testing

*Do not forget or neglect to extend hospitality to strangers –
being friendly, cordial and gracious – for by this some have
entertained angels without knowing it.*

Hebrews 13:2

It may seem dangerous these days to acknowledge strangers in
any way, especially to be hospitable to them, but most of us have
developed a way of knowing intuitively when we are in danger.
If you know and believe that you are protected, being friendly
and helpful to strangers can be fun and quite enlightening. I'm
not suggesting that you do anything unintelligent, such as thaw-
ing out a frozen snake in an act of kindness and then getting
bitten. Within the bounds of safety, however, being kind will
bring you great rewards.

One day, I was sitting in my car at a stoplight when I saw
a strange-looking creature on a bike in my rearview mirror. My
first reaction was to ignore him. He looked like he was in his
fifties, and he was dressed just like a little child playing cowboy.
He rode right up to the stoplight, which seemed to be taking

143

a very long time to change to green, and he was now parallel with my open window on the passenger side of the car. I turned and smiled at him, and in return he smiled a beatific smile and said, "Greetings from the Master." I was so astonished at what I heard that of course I had to ask, "What?" So he repeated it: "Greetings from the Master." I said thank you and continued smiling. The light changed, and I swear he just disappeared. The feeling I had after this greeting can only be explained as a peak experience. I felt so tremendously happy and joyful I almost had to stop the car. Later I realized that if I hadn't acknowledged this stranger I would have missed a marvelous experience.

Sometimes, being aware of the ways of angels seems like belonging to a secret society where you never know when, where, and how another member of the organization will show up. If you feel like being rude or unkind to a stranger, be careful; he or she just might be an angel. Angels like to appear randomly at various locations to test our reactions. They usually do this in places you wouldn't normally identify with angels, such as gas stations, bars, airports, movie theaters, and street corners. The test itself is not serious. If we miss it or fail it, we have nothing to worry about. The only reason angels do random testing is to teach us love and respect for all human beings. They also want to wake us up to happiness and the joy of being alive.

Angels may give you hints or signs of an impending test. Things to watch for include an intense feeling of lightness in their presence; some form of radiance shining out from behind their eyes and face like one big smile; a knowing look — as if they knew you and you knew them from somewhere; a feeling of timelessness, as if you were suddenly in a movie or a different reality; a very distinctive, mirthful laugh, almost like tinkling bells and extremely contagious; a feeling that all the worldly events around you are ridiculous; and a stirring, sweet aroma resembling jasmine left behind after they disappear.

I bet that many of you have met angels without realizing it. Think back on any experiences you've had that seemed inexplicable, illogical, mysterious, or inconsequential at the time, and see if they fit the angel-testing paradigm. If they do, try to enjoy them *now* and get ready for more. Practice for the future. Many are called but few are chosen for random angel testing. So be prepared!

Chapter 30

The Angel Beauty and Health Program

Every night and every morning thank your own Guardian Angel for peace and for the regeneration of all the cells in your body, and for joy.

Dorie D'Angelo

Mental gravity is the foremost destroyer of health and beauty. Mental gravity equals stress. Stress in the form of negative thoughts, negative circumstances, worries, and tension weighs down your spirit. Beauty and mental gravity are negatively correlated. This means that when the mental gravity load goes up, beauty goes down. Stressed-out people seem to age faster than normal. The process can be reversed if stress and mental gravity are taken away and replaced with spiritual relaxation, lightness, and harmony.

Some people show stress in their faces, some in their bodies, and some in their voices. I call some of the people I know shape shifters. Their shape (body) changes with the outward conditions in their lives. Some days they look like vibrant, youthful spirits,

146

and the next day they look about twenty years older — wrinkled, sunken, and tense.

Angels can help alleviate the problem of mental gravity in our lives. Angels do this by bringing us awareness of our unnecessary worries and, by providing creative solutions to problems that consume time and energy. (All of the methods described in Part Three help lighten mental gravity in one way or another.)

When people remove the seriousness of survival issues from their lives and replace this with living happily in the now, they will naturally become beautiful and radiant. Nuns are known to look much younger than they are and to have very few wrinkles, if any, on their faces. This is because they have given up the ways of the world (such as material possessions and worrying about meals and bills and emotional relationships) for a spiritual life of prayer and service; this shows on their faces. (Of course, this description represents an ideal and not all nuns have the true luxury of a spiritual life.)

It is not feasible for most of us to lead a life of prayer and constant spiritual practice, but there *are* ways to integrate beauty and spirituality into our everyday lives and in turn to radiate more beauty. Meditation is a practice that can keep you young and help you reduce the ill effects of stress. Meditating for as little as twenty minutes a day can reduce the stress that shows up in your face and body. Listening to a relaxation tape can be helpful. When you use these practices, visualize beautiful angels transmitting beauty into your soul. Also, when you look in the mirror, see your face as young and beautiful. Shift the shape in your mind if you want a change; imagine the face of your most beautiful angel superimposed on your own reflection in the mirror.

Physical release like exercise is also a way to reduce mental gravity. You may find this hard to believe, but angels can help you exercise. They can also help you carry things, by lightening the load. One day, I was carrying a heavy table top down some stairs, and I decided to do an experiment. I asked the angels to help me carry it — to make it lighter. It worked! The table top became lighter and easier to carry. Then one day I was hiking up a hill; it became very strenuous at one point, so again I asked the angels to help me. I suddenly felt like an energy force was gently pushing me from behind and releasing my focus on how difficult the climb was. You can try this with every form of physical movement. If you are a dancer, imagine that the angels are lifting you up and making you one with the music. (Maybe this was Fred Astaire's secret!)

Angels can also help you if you are on a diet. You might think this is going a bit too far — angels helping you cut back on food? I know someone who lost weight and kept if off and who gives the angels credit for this feat. I admit that one subject does not make a scientific study, but I know others who are trying this now and experiencing success. I think this works for two reasons. First, when you ask the angels to help you accomplish something, they know you are ready for success and will stick to the program. They assist you by distracting you from eating too much and by helping you change your eating habits. Second, angels help you go after what the food has been replacing in your life. If it is love and romance, they will lead you on the right path to fulfillment, which means they help make you aware of the blocks and problems that are keeping you from what you really want.

Angels don't eat food, but they can put on the appearance of a feast for you. Imagine angels having a great party, drinking nectar and eating angel food cake with delight and merriment. They're having a wonderful time gobbling up enormous chunks of angel food, which is really just foam, or thin air, or imagination. This will make you feel so silly that you won't want to eat for some time.

Angels will lighten the field of gravity around you. This will help you in all the areas of your life. It will enable you to display your true natural beauty, and it will keep you healthier.

Chapter 31

Cosmic Jokers: Archetypes of Evil

Legend has it that the father of evil was once God's second in command, chief among all his angels, the beautiful and beloved archangel Lucifer. Lucifer means "light bearer," and Lucifer was to be a teacher to humanity. God needed a volunteer to come to earth to strengthen and enlighten mankind through the use of tests and temptations. Lucifer volunteered. He began to delight in the tests he was giving. Eventually, he was testing humanity not for God but to feed his own pride. And, in feeding his own pride, he created a separation between himself and God. So God kicked him out of heaven. He had to go somewhere, so he created hell.

Eventually, Lucifer became identified as the deceiver (an independent force to destroy humanity). Legend also has it that Lucifer took other angels out of heaven along with him—hence the fallen angels (or cosmic jokers). Lucifer is also known to some as Satan. *The Dictionary of Angels,* by Gustav Davidson, lists Satan as a fallen angel having nothing to do with the archangel

Lucifer. Other books make no distinction between the two. *Satan* is the Hebrew word for *adversary*, and Satan is an adversary to God's love. For Satan, love is something foreign to fight against.

The debate of good and evil strikes a different note in all of us. I have read many books that dismiss evil as something we make up in our minds that manifests in our lives only because we let it and that has no real life force of its own. I used to think that there weren't any real victims on this planet. Now I think that we need to expand our language and come up with several different words to represent the various types of victims that *do* exist. The reason that victims are victims is because of a force that is evil. Regardless of whether we ourselves create this force, it is as real as its victims.

It is difficult to ignore the concept of good versus evil. It is the theme of many movies and books, and it is the theme of many human lives. This battle of the dark versus the light goes on around us all the time. But when it goes on inside us and divides our own being, we are weakened, off balance, and unintegrated.

The fear that if we are not "good" we will be punished can start to haunt people who are doing their best to be good. But who is going to carry out this punishment? God does not punish. God gave us free will and cannot punish us even if we won't accept God's help. And God cannot stop us from punishing ourselves and others. Free will means that God won't interfere, not even when the force of evil is after us. The only thing God will do is offer us unconditional love, and this love can be our refuge at any time we need it. The catch is that *we* have to *ask* for God's love and be open to it.

The Cosmic Joker Syndrome

Cosmic jokers are the fallen angels, or you could call them demons if you like. Cosmic jokers help us punish ourselves when we think we have done something bad or wrong. They don't do this by addressing the obvious; they get to us through our humanness and our pride. Cosmic jokers are not very angelic; they exist to test and punish. They work out the consequences of our negative beliefs and toy with our egomaniacal fantasies. The trick is to spot the humor in their little games and get away from them. They only understand practical jokes, ones that are not on them but on us. Furthermore, they have no understanding of love. So if we fall prey to a cosmic joke, the best thing we can do is increase self-love and acceptance.

Cosmic jokers are brats who teach us to laugh at ourselves through their practical jokes. We may have to eat some large slices of humble pie before we realize how funny we are. If we are too serious, fearful, obsessive, hateful, or prejudiced, the cosmic jokers have a field day teaching us lessons. If we dabble too long in darkness, or in an altered state of mind resulting from ingesting chemical substances or deprivation of sleep, the cosmic jokers will get us with their bratty lessons. We give them the power by weakening ourselves with fear and loathing. Their lessons can have a positive outcome by guiding us back on track, the track of awareness and awakeness. But it is up to us to find the positive side of these lessons. Cosmic jokers can be ruthless, just like Lucifer's original group of fallen angels.

Keep in mind that we all have our little battles, and when we get sidetracked by them we open ourselves up to negative consequences; it helps to be aware of these traps, so that our awareness can give us a choice. We attract the cosmic jokers when we fall into some of the following traps.

If we have a "worst fear" trap, one that haunts us and makes us superstitious, the jokers may choose to cultivate this fear for us. Fears come in many shapes, sizes, magnitudes, and conditions. Fear is a powerful negative force, one that can consume your spiritual energy. When we spend our energy on fear, we make it worse. Fear varies profoundly in each of us, and it is difficult to understand how deeply our fears can dig into our souls. If you have a fear haunting you, start to examine and confront it. Tell it in no uncertain terms to get the hell out! If we attach power to our fears by being superstitious, then the cosmic jokers have no choice except to use that power to make a joke. Get to the point where you can laugh at your fears, and then they won't have the power to destroy otherwise peaceful moments.

If we fall into the trap of taking ourselves too seriously, we will be the brunt of several cosmic jokes. Being serious means that we have great concern over everything. Comedy makes fun of serious behavior; that is what makes good comedy. Think about Jackie Gleason's character Ralph on the "Honeymooners." The humor in the show came from situations Ralph took too seriously, and at the end of each episode Alice helped Ralph laugh at himself with love. Seriousness is also the trap of thinking we are always right, and many times the joke is on us.

Cosmic jokers also love to play with the trap of prejudices and expecations in any form. The prejudice or expectation may be about race, religion, occupation, or gender, or it may even be one you don't realize you have. Whatever we prejudge will be fair game for the cosmic jokers. If you are prejudiced against a certain race of people, the jokers may see to it that you or your child marries someone of that race. Or you may have a dramatic experience of someone from a religion you don't respect rescuing you or your child from danger. The lesson is simple: Don't judge! Each situation with each human being exists as it exists, so expect the unexpected or cease expectations and gain everything.

If you are obsessed over something or someone, you are just asking for trouble. Obsession is the seduction of your mind by some desired or feared object. The value you have placed on this desired or feared object is skewed in an unrealistic fashion. You may have obsessive thoughts that haunt you throughout the day. The bottom line is that obsession disturbs your peace. And the cosmic jokers will only make it worse by giving you confusing signs and indications about the object of your obsession. Obsessions can get so bad that we may need professional help, and when it has gotten that bad it is difficult for us to realize

help is needed. Common, everyday obsessions are something
we can get rid of ourselves; this process depends on a sense of
humor toward the obsessive behavior. When obsessions become
a trap in your life, return to simplicity. Release the obsession:
Who cares whether you locked your door or not—just send some
angels over to house-sit if you are worried. If you are in a state
of obsession over another human being, release him or her; if
he or she comes back to you, then take your cue.

Cosmic jokers are quite creative in playing with humans "under
the influence." We may be under the influence of chemical substances (for example, LSD, alcohol, tranquilizers, and pain killers)
or we may be under the influence of sensory deprivation or of
not having had enough sleep or the right foods. When we move
ourselves into an altered state of consciousness, we sometimes step into cosmic joker territory. The cosmic jokers turn
into a movie crew, to make a movie—not necessarily for your
enjoyment—with you in the leading role. You might find yourself
in a science-fiction movie complete with aliens, or in a horror
film complete with demons and monsters. Or you might be cast
as the king of time and space or as a spiritual mystic who has
cosmic consciousness and becomes one with all creation. These
movies seem real, but look at who the directors and producers
are. They are the cosmic jokers, and they will oblige you in acting
out your fantasies and fears until they seem real. Sooner or later,
however, you may get sick of being an actor in these epic thrillers
and want to get back to a consensus reality. You've realized you
have had enough of the lessons the extraterrestrials and dark
characters have to teach. Welcome back; it was all a joke: You
are simply you, not the king of time and space, not the victim
of aliens and monsters—just good old you. All is well; now you
are back in your own movie as director (with your higher self
as producer), and you have stories of different worlds to tell and
pictures to paint.

I have talked to people who have had cosmic jokers appear
to them. This is unusual, but it can happen. It only happens

from a source of deep fear. Seeing the image of a demon or ghost can be quite frightening and elicits more fear. Fear gives these beings power, so the best thing to do if you see one is to get centered, take a deep breath, and then tell them and the fear to leave. Release the fear by taking refuge in something sacred to you. For example, Christians can use the name of Jesus or the image of a cross. The affirmation to the archangel Michael (found in Part Five) recited three times is also very effective.

The only reason I am adding this chapter on cosmic jokers to the book is that more people have experienced their antics than I originally thought. I think it is important to address the power of what negative thought patterns can do in a worst-case scenario. Whether people really see or hear cosmic jokers or whether this is just their imagination does not matter. What does matter is the stress and fear in their lives that brought them to that point. Unconditional love is the one and only true cure for every negative thing imaginable. If you can't find this love from another human or yourself, find it from God and the angels. The angels will never let you down if you open your heart to them. They will teach you to love yourself unconditionally, and this in turn will draw in love from the world around you.

Chapter 32

Reminders About Life on Earth

Truth is a pathless land. (There is no need to seek it through any occult hierarchy, any guru, any doctrine. . . .) The important thing is to free your mind of envy, hate, and violence; and for that you don't need an organization.

J. Krishnamurti

The main themes I've been stressing in this book are that life is not to be taken seriously, that we need to play more, and that we can learn to be happy-go-lucky with a little training. This is much easier said than done. Changing our thought patterns requires training and effort on our parts. To get anywhere near a state of enlightened grace, we must be willing to grow and to do our spiritual work. Angels are guides and teachers, but they will not do or interfere in work we must do for ourselves. Sometimes our work is not very fun and can create discomfort, but this only means we are changing and awakening to our highest personality and happiness.

155

Change can create a certain amount of pain and upset in our lives. The pain and upset that results from change is growing pain. When growth brings pain, we can either "*go* through the pain, or *grow* through the pain." Changing our way of thinking so that we can be happier and more awake in life may entail going back in the past and healing or letting go of pain we stored as a child or young adult; instead of just going through it again, we can grow through it. To become less critical of ourselves, we must remove pride and take a good look at our lives through loving eyes.

The ideas in this book about how angels help us create heaven in our lives are for people who are not afraid to experience growing pain and who are not afraid to give their burdens over to a higher power. People can laugh even while they're in pain; it isn't easy, but if you practice on a regular basis you can master the technique. Pain is a teacher. Pain teaches us to let go and not be so attached to emotional burdens. Avoiding pain is a human instinct; we tend to put pain aside for later and ignore it at precisely the time when it is easiest to confront. Don't worry about it! There is always a way out, and seeking loving divine humor is the best shortcut I know.

If you visualize yourself on a path to enlightenment in this lifetime, go easy on yourself and take along the angels. Burst out laughing at every new growth point on your path. In this New Age, we have many choices and opportunities presented to us in the name of spiritual growth. Explore where the information is coming from and whether it really fits into your path. If you choose to have psychic readings (aura readings, tarot card readings, past-life readings, or astrological counseling), beware of the limitations of this sort of information. Too often, information from a psychic reading turns into a self-fulfilling prophecy, because we are all suggestible to some degree. If the information doesn't seem right to you or is something that you don't want in your life, rise above it.

Rise above it by knowing that you have free will and can create miracles in your life. Go for the highest potential in your life.

If a psychic tells you something you don't like, use this information as a gauge for the middle point. That is, say to yourself, "If I only want to go halfway with my life, this is probably what I'll end up doing, but if I go all the way to the top there are no limits to what I can achieve." Sometimes, psychic information relates to doubts and fears we have in the present. When the information is confirmed by a psychic reading of our present state of affairs, our doubts and fears are reinforced.

Keep in mind that, in time, you always get what you really want. Realize how ridiculous it is to believe, on the one hand, that anything is possible and that miracles of love can happen, and then to turn around and limit those thoughts by listening to the advice given in a psychic reading of your future.

With the angels' help, you can visualize and create the future as you want it. Angels won't give you past-life information or tell you about your future. They will give you this-life inspiration to live your life fully and happily in the present tense. When you get your information from the realm of heaven, the highest of spiritual planes, only you, God, and the angels are involved. The information you receive will never take away or interfere with your free will. The information will set you free, free from the projections and expectations other humans have on you. Information from heaven will inspire you to become strong, creative, and centered within yourself, so that your choices and decisions will benefit you and those around you.

Finally, the insight and advice in this book is directed toward people who are basically mentally healthy and who function well in their world. If you are going through pain that is not easily removed or you are blocked by compulsive behavior, it never hurts to talk to a trained professional, such as a good analyst or counselor. Be sure to ask the angels to lead you to the right type of outside help. Look for someone loving and experienced. The reason I recommend finding someone other than yourself to help you is because one requirement for keeping ourselves healthy (besides getting the right vitamins) is loving contact and relationship with other members of our species.

Part Five

Angel Forum
and Annex

Chapter 33

Angel Personality Profiles

The Angel that presided o'er my birth,
said "Little creature formed of Joy & Mirth,
go and love without the help of anything on earth."

William Blake

Human Angels and Aspiring Angels

Angels are formed of God's joy and mirth. Sometimes they love humans so much, they decide to become one. They might do this with a specific intention, such as helping the humans they love achieve happiness. Or they may want to assist in a global mission. The choice to become human is a risk, because then they have to abide in the human body and experience the emotional turmoil humans go through at times. Because they are highly evolved and extremely sensitive, angels may have adverse reactions to the everyday life of humans. Psychic repair and help comes from realizing their connection to the heavenly circuit. They must go and love spiritually without the help of anything on earth. They made the choice to be humans, and now they must stay linked to God's unconditional love so that they don't self-destruct.

Human angels are optimistic about human ideals. They chose to be a human to experience the joys of being human, so they will do their best to live a full life. The funny thing is that they haven't yet got it down, so to speak, and they sometimes get themselves into humorous situations. They always seem to be in the process of learning the language of human behavior. Children experience them as kindred spirits in this learning process. Children and babies are drawn to human angels.

Human angels are naturally charming, sweet, gracious, loving, and witty, and they love a good laugh. Life for them is about the joy of the moment. They feel an affinity for angelic ideals and want to arrange a happy ending for everyone. Human angels expect and seek to see the forms of heaven all around them, wherever they go on planet earth.

Human angels know that they are protected and guarded on earth. The number thirteen is always lucky for them. They have a practice of turning all superstitious beliefs to work in their favor. Their lives are full of synchronistic events and favorable coincidences. In essence, they lead charmed lives, because they know how to attract love and happiness to themselves.

Their homes may be decorated in the heavenly colors of an abalone shell. They display rocks, pebbles, stones, gems, shells, or fossils somewhere in their house. This habit deepens their connection to the earth realm, the realm in which devas, elves, and fairies play, and helps keep them grounded. Otherwise, they would have a tendency to want to float away into the ethers.

Light is a constant in the life of a human angel. If the lighting isn't right in a room, they will not be comfortable until they can design and sculpture it the right way. Human angels reflect light off their bodies in a powerful or unusual way, noticeable in sunlight, moonlight, and candlelight, and in photographs. They often talk about light — the light of the sun, neon lights, lighting, prisms, crystals, pink light, items that glow in the dark, and moonlight on water or snow.

You will often find human angels looking up at the sky and noticing magnificent birds in places you don't expect, clouds that look like angels, rainbows when there hasn't been rain, an abundance of shooting stars at night, and strange beautiful sights you can't explain. Human angels have a reverence for beautiful things, like moonbeams, sunsets, and nature at its finest.

If you feel like a human angel or a human aspiring to be an angel, keep in mind that your help comes from heaven. This means that if you get exasperated with being human, you must remember you chose this to help enlighten up the humans here on earth. You loved them so much you decided to become one. Or, you have decided to create your humanness into angelhood. Either way, remember that your goal is to bring heaven and lightness to earth, and remember that you are now human and must abide by the lessons your humanness will provide.

CLUES TO HUMAN ANGELS AND ASPIRING ANGELS

1. You feel light and airy at times, and you are convinced you could fly or float up through the clouds.
2. You have experiences of heavenly joy and lightness that leave you laughing hysterically.
3. You see other humans and yourself as innocent, and it is easy for you to forgive and forget.
4. You have trouble taking the concept of money seriously; you are inclined to play all the time rather than to be motivated by money.
5. At times you find yourself lovingly observing life as if you were invisible. Occasionally, adults seem to see right past you as if you were transparent. Children and babies always notice you and are drawn to you in a special way.

If you resonated with one or more of these clues, then you have definite angel tendencies. You can develop them further with the help of this book and the help of your spiritual brothers and sisters in heaven, the angels.

Sensitives

Everyone is sensitive to some degree, but a *sensitive* is someone who is ultrasensitive. Being a sensitive is not very easy at times. Sensitives receive impressions easily and quickly. They receive impressions that others miss. They start to feel responsible for having received a strong inner knowledge about something or someone. Their intuition is extremely keen, to the point where they purposely doubt it at times, so as not to be burdened. Sensitives are usually highly intelligent and creative, but, being so sensitive, it can be difficult for them to bring forth their gifts and face possible rejection and other adverse conditions.

Some sensitives can take on another human being's physical pain and sensations, or feel another's emotional hurt sometimes more deeply than the person truly experiencing it. This may force the sensitives to go on autopilot, creating an automatic routine to protect themselves from feeling too much. This isn't necessary. Sensitives can learn to understand themselves, and they can learn ways of removing themselves from another's pain without going on autopilot.

Sensitives are attracted to the ideals and thought patterns of the New Age movement, or to other forms of religious and philosophical idealism and mysticism. Sensitives who want to understand themselves are inclined to seek past-life information and psychic readings about their future. This need for a feeling of certainty and guidance can become a problem in itself. Card readings and other information given through psychics can become a crutch or an addiction; worse yet, such practices can keep you from living fully in the present as captain of your own ship. Eventually, sensitives may find that the New Age is just not enough for some reason; something is missing.

One reason for this sense that something is missing may be

that they have lost sight of their initial reasons for exploring the New Age. If they were looking for spiritual truth in different directions because organized religion left them cold, they may find that they are still left cold. Sensitives want the truth, but at times they get sidetracked because they are so sensitive, susceptible, and psychic. Sensitives need to love and accept their sensitivity as a special gift and learn to fine-tune their gift so that it serves them and those around them.

The sensitives' higher self resembles that of a saint. They came to learn similar lessons, and their inner nature is similar. Their houses may even have the feeling of a mission, monastery, or chapel. The problems of the sick, the homeless, and the impoverished can either drive them to work in one of the helping professions or overwhelm them to the point that they don't even want to go out their front door. On the high side, sensitives may be able to lapse into states where they have beatific visions and mystic raptures that leave them with feelings of awe, reverence, and perfection.

Sensitives are very gifted in the fine arts. The problem is that their sensitivity and saintly natures keep them from sharing their gifts — often for fear of rejection or fear of success for which they feel unworthy. Sensitives can use angels to help them understand themselves better and to develop tools for their own growth and for living successfully in the often insensitive world around them. Angels can help sensitives develop their gifts so they can share them and enrich the world around them. Also, sensitives sometimes need armor, and the angels can provide the armor for protecting them in everyday life on earth. Angels can help sensitives become the ultrahumans they are meant to be.

CLUES TO THE SENSITIVE PERSONALITY

1. You find yourself merging with others to the point where you can feel their physical and emotional pain. You feel sorry for everyone, not just for yourself.
2. You seem to be psychic, and you pick up impressions easily.

Very often you think something and the person you're with will say it, or vice versa.

3. People frequently remark on your extreme sensitivity.
4. Experiencing life can be completely overwhelming at times, to the point where you have to space out or "give up."
5. You are attracted to astrology, psychic readings, tarot cards, metaphysical phenomena, and you like dark bedrooms for isolation and restoration.
6. You have a strong, ineffable sense of the truth. You know, but you do not say.

If you resonated with any of the statements above, then you are a sensitive. This book was written to help you the sensitive enjoy life more and develop your gifts and creativity to their highest good. Part Five lists some other books that might be of interest to you. Please use the angels for your psychic repair and learn to trust yourself. All the answers lie within you; all you have to do is trust. You have everything it takes to be an ultrahuman, so bring in the angels and you will be on your way.

Chapter 34

Practicing Love and Kindness

To love for the sake of being loved is human,
but to love for the sake of loving is Angelic.
Alphonse de Lamartine

I asked my four-year-old niece to tell me what she knew about angels. She told me, "They probably glow in the dark. . . . And, of course, we know they have feet." But most important she told me she knew that angels love little kids. I agreed, and I asked her, since she was a little kid, if the angels had any messages for all of us here on earth. She quickly replied, "Yes. Be kind for another, and love one another!"

Soon after she gave me this message, I had the chance to hear the Dalai Lama speak. The Dalai Lama is the spiritual leader of the Tibetan Buddhists, and he is living in exile from his homeland. The overall feeling emanating from the entire audience lifted my soul from the minute I walked into the building—I felt like I was floating in an ocean of love. I had the privilege of sitting near the front of the auditorium, where the Tibetan families were sitting. The look on their faces when the Dalai Lama came out to speak was incredibly moving, and I felt like I had merged into their world. I felt a sense of true compassion even before I knew this would be the subject of the Dalai Lama's talk.

Basically, the Dalai Lama had the same message for us humans that my niece relayed from the angels. The title of his talk was "A Human Approach to World Peace." He talked about practicing compassion for others as a way to develop inner stability and a sense of responsibility for the human family. Compassion provides security and inner stamina and allows us to reduce fear and develop self-confidence with awareness. What the Dalai Lama means by compassion is actually altruism. When you show kindness and act upon a feeling of empathy toward a very poor person, your compassion is based on altruistic considerations. On the other hand, love toward your partner, lover, spouse, friend, or children is usually based on attachment. When the attachment changes, your kindness also changes (and may even disappear). Real love is not based on attachment, but on altruism.

The Dalai Lama said that the main source of supreme happiness and joy is mental stability and mental peace. Several things can interfere with mental peace. One such thing is anger. The Dalai Lama said that anger diminishes mind—that it is of no use at all and appears as protection from something that *might* happen. Anger deceives us. A person can destroy your property, your body, your friends, and all the supposed sources of your happiness, but real mental stability and peace of mind cannot be destroyed, unless your brain is physically injured. We are minds; we are consciousness. The real enemy to our peace of mind is not external but internal, such as anger.

The foundation for solving human problems lies in transforming human attitudes. If we are happy, truly happy without external reasons, with our minds at peace, then we can give kindness and love to other people effortlessly because we are drawing upon an unlimited source.

I felt compelled to share this information with you because it sums up the angels' message for us. First and foremost, the angels want us to know that we must find our own center within ourselves—the place where we no longer need to judge everything as good or bad and where anger does not interfere with our inner peace. With mental stability comes true peace and happiness. With true peace and happiness comes the drive to be kind to ourselves and love ourselves, so in turn we can love and be kind to others. This is truly the first step toward world peace. This is a crucial and timely message. We must not continue selfishly destroying and overpopulating the earth for a short lifetime of supposed happiness, only to leave the earth in a worse state for our grandchildren and our grandchildren's children.

I don't want to detract from the simplicity of the original message, so I will leave it to you to arrive at your own mental peace and stability. I hope this book will prove helpful in some way. The message is timeless and transcends all cultural and physical barriers. So, please, let it start with you: "Be kind for another, and love one another"—now, before it is too late. Let this be your call to become an angelic force on earth.

I would like to thank Frankie Lee Slater for loaning me her notes from the Dalai Lama's lecture.

Chapter 35

The Angel Forum

The angel forum in this chapter presents an open discussion on angels. In it, a variety of people express their points of view on angels. Their stories illustrate the various ways angels interact with human beings. The topics and opinions expressed do not necessarily match my own. And the people expressing their views do not necessarily agree with everything I've written in this book. The first contribution is a poem written by my eight-year-old niece.

Angel Poem
  by Elizabeth Ann Godfrey

Angels are very holy and they are ten feet tall.
They wear beautiful white dresses and a halo.
They guide you every minute of the day.
Even though you can't see them, they are still here.
And I know you can't put your hand out and touch them.
They make you happy when you are sad.
Angels help and love you very much.

Sometimes in pictures Angels have wings, but I'm not sure if
they have wings in real life.
They live on the earth with you, except they're still in heaven, too.
I know it's confusing to you — it's confusing to me, too!

Attracting Love and Romance
by Mary Beth Crain

Whenever I think of calling in the angels to do my romantic
bidding, I remember an episode of "Gilligan's Island" in which
the professor builds a large robot that supposedly does everything you ask. Of course, everybody on the island agrees that
the robot should build a boat that can take them all home. They
all pack up, say their farewells, and meet on shore at dawn.
Sure enough, the robot has followed instructions and designed
a luxury liner. The only problem is that it's about twelve inches
long. "Whoops," says the professor. "I guess I forgot to give him
the dimensions."

Never forget to give the angels the dimensions. Because, as
we all know by now, our metaphysical friends are incorrigible
funsters and only need the smallest excuse to turn the drama
of our lives into one big cosmic joke. They try to put a lid on
it, and sometimes God or Mother Mary or a particular saint
known for something sobering, like gruesome martyrdom, is
called in to give them a talking to when their little pranks get
out of hand.

At least I hope that's what happened when I prayed for a man
who really loved me to come along, and I got somebody who
wore cologne that smelled like bug spray and who had a big,
fat wife nobody, not even the angels, would want to tangle with,
in alleys either dark or light.

Needless to say, this was distressing. Not only was I completely repulsed by the answer to my prayers, but his obsession
knew no bounds. There were gifts, cards, phone calls, entreaties.

I wanted to run off to Gilligan's Island myself, just to escape him.

At my wit's end, I called Terry Taylor, who told me that it was definitely time for an angel conference. I told her that I thought it was definitely time for angel reform school. But I called in my angel of love and romance, and our conversation went something like this.

Me: Thanks a bunch!
ALR: Well, you asked for a man who really loved you.
Me: But he wears bug spray!
ALR: Sorry. You didn't specify.
Me: Specify? Just how specific do we have to get here?
ALR: As specific as you need to be to attract the right person.
Me: Listen, you guys are supposed to know everything I'm thinking anyway.
ALR: We want *you* to know what you're thinking. To be very clear about it. Otherwise the things you attract will be slightly off base.
Me: I guess I'm lucky you didn't send me a chimpanzee or something.
ALR: Go back and meditate on the man you really want. See him, feel him, call on him. We'll get the message.
Me: Just make sure *he* gets the message. Okay?
ALR: Scout's honor.
Me: Your fingers are crossed.
ALR: Whoops. Didn't think you'd notice.

Believe me, you have to watch these guys. Anyway, I went back and thought about where I'd gone wrong. I'd asked for an older man who shared all my interests, who was spiritually in-clined and passionate, and who had a career of his own. But I hadn't specified marital status, and I hadn't specified that I should be equally attracted to him. You'd think the angels would assume such obvious details, but no. You absolutely have to spell it out.

So, I did another meditation. I got relaxed, felt golden white light coming through me from my toes to my nose, went to my favorite mental imaging place, which happens to be a grassy field by a beautiful stream, and imagined my perfect mate. I saw his face and his eyes; I felt his gentle, unconditional love. I made a list of all his qualities, and I made sure that he smelled nice and didn't have a wife the size of Mount Rushmore. Then I mentally summoned my angel of love and romance.

"That's him," I said. "Bring him to me. And no fooling around!"

Well, it took about six months. But I can cheerfully report that at the present time I am the proud companion of an adorable and adoring seventy-year-old man, who shares my interests, has a career of his own, is deeply religious, unmarried, and wears a cologne that knocks my socks off. In fact, I met him on Christmas day, at mass, which only goes to show you that when the angels decide to do things right they put on the whole show.

Of course, there's a bit more to attracting love and romance than just programming your angels. You have to feel good about yourself. You have to feel that you deserve the best. And you have to pay attention. One of my favorite cartoons shows a woman sitting on a rock, contemplating her Prince Charming. "Some day my prince will come," she daydreams away. "He'll be handsome and perfect, and he'll sweep me off my feet. . . ." And presently a man rides up on a white horse. "Excuse me," he says. But the woman doesn't hear him. She's too busy fantasizing about her prince. "Excuse me," the man says again. "I'm Prince Charming." But the woman is totally oblivious to him. "And he'll have blond hair, and he'll love to dance, and . . ." she's still going on. And with a sigh, Prince Charming turns his horse around and trots off.

So you have to notice when the angels send you someone. And then you have to work at the relationship, because nothing comes free, especially when the angels are involved in it. They like to see you earn your keep. In my case, the man I loved was very shy, and I had to work like the dickens to make him comfortable with me. In fact, there were more than a few moments when I was ready to declare defeat. But in every meditation I did, the angels confirmed that yes, this was the one. I just wasn't to lose faith. And sure enough, one day a miracle happened and he asked me, very shyly, if I might like to play golf with him, and life has been one big birdie ever since.

Oh, yes, here's another thing you might try if you're having relationship questions and you want "yes" or "no" confirmation from the angels. Just ask them to send you a sign that the person is or isn't the one the universe has picked out for you. In my case, I asked for the angels to send me a rose to confirm that this fellow was "the one." And about five days later, a nun friend of mine and I met for lunch and the first thing she did was to hand me a novena card of St. Therese. I opened it up and there, inside, was the sweetest little pink rose.

Big chill time! "Jan," I said, "Why are you giving me this?"

"It was the funniest thing," she replied. "But yesterday I was driving and I got lost and I ended up at a hospital run by an order of sisters devoted to St. Therese. There was a chapel in the hospital, with a shrine to St. Therese and roses all around it. And suddenly I felt I had to pray for you, that God gives you a relationship that's beautiful, fulfilling, and challenging. And I picked this rose from the shrine."

So the angels are listening. Just keep an eye on them because, as I've said, their humor can sometimes be more than you bargained for. Actually, I think they may have written the entire "Gilligan's Island" series, and that they rerun it down in hell, for eternity. So I'm going to be very good from this day forth. Aren't you?

On Angels
by Francis Jeffrey

(1) JEFFREY'S SCIENTIFIC THOUGHTS ABOUT ANGELS

Angels and ideas

Angels are creatures of imagination. This does not mean that they are any less real than you are. Some esoteric teachers have said to their students, "You are nothing but an idea!" To which certain students have repleid, "Yes, but I'm a real good idea."

As Shakespeare said, "We are such stuff as dreams are made of." And angels are evidently made of the same stuff as the non-material aspect of ourselves. Angels can thus coexist with us in our individual worlds of ideas, thoughts, and images — where we exist, somehow mysteriously connected with our bodies and usually focused inside our bodies or, more precisely, "in our heads."

Angels in the brain

When philosophers and scientists have thought seriously about the connection between mind and body, they generally have pointed to the brain, and concluded that the brain is where the mind operates (or enters) the body. The brain is composed of a trillion little cells (called neurons), all packed together and tickling each other (chemically) with their tiny tendrils. As a flurry of activity (or conversation) runs through this group, it can produce results that resemble a computer running its program. A program is just a sequence of events, planned in advance, or a sequence of decisions, anticipated in advance. (In this respect, a computer program is not very different from a television program, except that in a television program all the decisions are made in advance, not just anticipated.)

Such "programs" result in what you do, or what you experience.

Now, imagine tiny angels stationed at each of these cells, steering the conversation this way or that. This idea is similar to the model of a guardian angel for a person, only these little angels are guiding individual cells. By giving a little nudge one way or the other, they might introduce a subtle change in your perceptions, or a small, but decisive, change in your behavior.

These tiny angels might do a little ornamental gardening with the tiny tendrils, and thus effect permanent changes in your brain programs. They are then acting as the brain program editors described elsewhere in this book. They will only do this when they are invited in by the person in question. When active, you will probably notice their presence as a warm, fuzzy feeling in the head, as a pink glow around everything you look at, as a melodious echoing of sounds, or as the fragrance of a warm summer's eve when the air is pregnant with the promise of unknown possibilities.

Angels and endorphins

Endorphins are a kind of natural chemical found in the brain; they are associated with pleasure and relief of pain. Actually, it seems that the presence of endorphins increases the brain's ability to "screen its messages"—to tune out unpleasant signals from pain nerves, and to focus your attention wherever you want it to go. Evidently, this freedom to attend as we please to whatever pleases us is the state we call "pleasure." Pain, on the other hand, is some hurt or sick situation *demanding* our attention, and jangling our brain in the process.

Angels can serve the same purpose as endorphins, positioning themselves at key crossroads in the brain, forbidding unwanted signals from passing. Of course, if you decide to use angels in this way, be careful not to get into the syndrome of "angel abuse," where you screen out so much all the time that you get "out of touch."

2) JEFFREY'S UNSCIENTIFIC OBSERVATIONS OF ANGELS

Healing angels

Imagine a globe of radiant light, way off in the heavens. Draw off a pinch of this golden glow, and form it into a tiny angel. Say,

"Hello, angel," and give it a name. Repeat this procedure until you have a whole line of tiny angels streaming toward you through space. Direct them into the part of your body that is unwell or painful. (Or direct them into someone else you wish to heal.) See the angels arrive on the scene and envelope the diseased or injured area, permeating the tissues and cells with their intense, warm golden light—driving out the pain and inflammation.

If the situation is really serious, take the emanantions of golden light from these angels and form it into vaster numbers of smaller angels, who can go to work at the cellular level, treating each cell individually.

If you're fond of the medical model of healing, try an angel I.V. (intravenous injection). Imagine a translucent tube coming down from the angel source, down through space, and into one of your veins (or right into the part of the body that is ill). Tiny angels—drip, drip, drip—float down through this tube and into your body, where they perform their healing activities, as above.

We are certainly not recommending that you substitute this practice for physical treatment in the case of serious, medically diagnosed conditions! Use it to supplement traditional medical care.

SANTA

Flying over Greenland in 1987 on the day of the harmonic convergence, I had a startling revelatory experience. As I gazed out the window of a 747 at 30,000 feet, I spied hoof marks and the tracks of sleigh runners upon the vastly white snow fields. Interesting, I reflected, they're still using sleigh and reindeer down there in Greenland.

Then, as the shadow of our plane fleeted across the path of the tracks, the full impact hit me: Those tracks were enormous! To appear that big viewed from that altitude, the sleigh must have been the size of an aircraft carrier! And the deer must also have been of titantic stature. And who was driving that sleigh?

And then I received the full revelation: Santa Claus! Yes,

of course, that's how he does it! He's huge! Santa has plenty of toys for everyone.

Later I reflected on the true meaning of SANTA, and I realized that it stands for Super Angelic Nocturnal Transport Agent. SANTA is a gigantic angelic being who moves stuff around at night. SANTA is a special-purpose angel assigned to planet earth.

The luminous cloud

Several months after my SANTA revelation, I was in Malibu, California, and a friend at the beach asked me to take my car to pick someone up who wanted to visit but didn't have transportation. This woman—I'll call her "K"—was staying at a house in the mountains.

I drove through the dark winter's night, and, as I looked in the general direction I was heading, I saw something I'd never seen before—something that mystified me. It was a luminous cloud towering above the hills, like a pillar of scintillating, multi-hued pastel light. At first, I thought of the aurora borealis, but that is never visible from the temperate latitudes of Los Angeles and, besides, this tower of light was clearly a local phenomenon.

The road wound through the mountains, and I could see it was bringing me closer and closer to the luminous cloud. I wondered if I would finally arrive at its base—like the end of the rainbow?

At last, the road turned beside a steep hillside, which blocked my immediate view of the tower of light. There, on the hillside, I found the appointed address. The house was totally dark.

I beeped the car horn, and soon there emerged a tall figure in a white robe, carrying a flashlight, and beckoning me up the path. The robe the woman was wearing turned out to be a bathrobe. She thanked me for coming and apologized that she was not quite ready to go, because the lights had gone out some time ago and she was unable to locate the fuse box.

I helped her find the fuse box and restore the electricity. When the lights came back on, I saw a tall blond woman who bore a certain resemblance to Brigette Nielsen.

On our way down to the beach in my car, "K" started telling me about angels. She spoke of them most matter-of-factly. She had been in close contact with them for years. In her meditations, she drew them around her, and as a cloud they clung to her wherever she would go. In my little car, I could feel this was true. (Later, over a dinner with our mutual friend, "K" seemed more like a normal, sophisticated woman. I learned that she was on vacation from her home in the snowy wilds of Canada.)

Several days later, drawn by a notable chain of coincidences to travel hundreds of miles, I was to meet a very angelic-looking young woman named "T," who had vague plans to write a book about angels!

Healing With Angels
by Linda Zwingeberg Fickes

All healers, be they microsurgeons, dentists, acupuncturists, or evangelical faith healers, work with the healing angels of the body. They must work with nature. Nature is life with intelligence.

An angel is simply an intelligence of Nature that guides a spark of life toward its perfect fulfillment. An angel may oversee the life spark of a cell in the body, an organ, the physical, mental, or emotional body, or the soul, the Inner Christ, or the I Am body.

An angel may be tiny or vast. But each angel has the quality of perfect synchronism with the good of that life and the good of all. No healing proceeds without the angels' care. Man, the "healer," simply removes the obstacles and opens the doors, so the angels can do their work.

The angel or intelligence that oversees the physical body directs and coordinates the angels that make up that body — the angels of the skin, blood, nervous system, and so forth. This angelic being also interacts with the angels of all our subtle bodies. The subtler the body, the closer to God and the more powerful and simpler the angelic life within that body.

All the subtle bodies are guided by their own natural tendency or intelligence. The mental body is composed of thoughts and ideas, each one of which has an angel to fulfill it.

The emotional body is a subtle body composed of emotional energy flows. Each flow of emotion has a guiding angel. When these angels are restricted, life gets bottled up. The energy becomes frustrated and consequently affects the grosser mental and physical bodies. Many therapists are discovering how to allow the emotional angels to assist in the process of emotional energy release, which always concludes with love.

The etheric body or soul is the perfect and original blueprint for an individual's existence. Therefore, it carries the original design matrix created for it by God. Look for the angels of the etheric or soul's body, and you will see a fine geometric matrix of stars. The stars set a tone of perfection and harmony for every part of our being.

On the Inner Christ level, beyond the soul, the body is still less complex and made up of the qualities of universal love and compassion. When we connect consciously with our own universal intentions, the Christ angels will help us fulfill them.

The I Am subtle body is even closer to God and therefore simpler and more powerful. On the I Am level, we find the pure qualities of our own God being. A feeding of energy from this level might be: "I Am Power," "I Am Love," or "I Am That I Am." To connect with the Christ and I Am angels and feel their consciousness and power is exalting and transformative.

The goal of all of the angels of each of our bodies is to fulfill the divine purpose of our God Self. For the Being we call Earth, as well as for the Being that is each of us, this simply means the complete and perfect functioning of Nature, of all of Nature. All of the angels of your own life stream of identity and those of your patient may be accessed for healing.

HOW TO USE THE ANGELS FOR HEALING:

1. Open your heart with love and trust to the angels of your own or your patient's I Am, Christ, or soul's body. Trust is important, for the angels will not adapt to your techniques. Your techniques must follow them! Your success will reflect how well you can follow Nature.
2. Close your eyes. Picture the body and locate its problem on the screen of your heart. Share with the angels the problem you are concerned with, for instance, a dairy allergy that gives sinus congestion, or ankle pain. The more specific the problem, the more specific the angels you will call forth. Start with an open mind, so that the angels can give you an overview of the case. They may show you something that at first doesn't make sense, but you will soon be surprised at its wisdom.
3. Ask for a vision of how the angels of the body would like to heal this problem. You may be very adept at this immediately, or it may take some practice. Remember your level of consciousness determines where you get answers. You will get a vision that powerfully magnetizes the necessary angels to work. This understanding will also magnetize your hands, your mind, and your energy bodies to speak the right words, to place your hands exactly where necessary, and to bring the perfect energy into the body to help remove the blockages or integrate the light that has already entered.
4. Ask where to start. Follow the angels' lead. The angels heal in waves that touch all the subtle bodies. We must respect the order in which the patient's angels want the care to be given. Keep asking questions. You will be shown how the healing will best unfold. You may be shown by feeling in your own body the next area to work on. This does *not* mean you are drawing the problem into yourself to transmute. Let the angels take care of it all. Your body just resonates with the healing and you get some healing, too.
5. Once you have opened the doors, ask the angels what kind

of support would help: nutritional therapies, specific exercises, rest, laughter, music, visualization, breathing, tones of color. We no longer need to do everything ourselves; angels are here to help. We cannot afford to believe that we know best. We have a partnership with the angels that can make earth a paradise once again. Let go of all the pictures you have stored of how you should be healed. Let Nature nurture you with joy.

The above contribution was excerpted with kind permission of the author from *Connecting Links*, vol. 1, no. 3. Dr. Linda Zwingeberg Fickes resides in Hawaii with her daughter and husband, Bob. Linda and Bob offer courses and seminars around the country. You may call them at (808) 262-7239 or contact them by writing:

> Council of Light, Inc.
> 1496 Humu'ula St.
> Kailua, HI 96734

El Shaddai — The God Who Is More Than Enough
by Daniel Kaufman

The Sufis have a wonderful word for God — El Shaddai, which means "the God Who Is More Than Enough."

El Shaddai is my favorite term for expressing unlimited blessings bestowed upon those willing to receive, the love that is heaped upon us if we are loving and willing to receive love, the bounteous beauty of the angelic world, and the exquisite beauty of our own earthly paradise if we are willing to experience it.

I have always felt that gratitude is the key to releasing any painful and stuck moments of self-pity. At such times, I ask my angels and guardians of gratitude to remind me of the numerous blessings in my life. It is impossible to indulge in self-pity when I remember that I have eyes that see, hands that can touch and paint and write, a mouth to kiss my beloved wife and baby, a brain to enjoy life (and to create problems to resolve), a heart that pumps millions of times automatically, and the ability to feel love. These blessings reflect the generosity of El Shaddai— that I should have such blessings, and also angels to help me, and friends and air and water, that for no other reason than my seemingly random birth on May 4th, 1949, in New York City, amidst millions of other randomly born others, I should have so many ways to find pleasure and love and fulfillment in a land of freedom and opportunity.

This is *more than enough*; this is the infinite love and benevolence of the Creator, of the Universal Principle—that I was born with the capacity to know myself, to find within myself the same beauty that I perceive in the outer world.

Two things inspire me to awe: the starry heavens above and the moral universe within.

Albert Einstein

This, again, is the generosity of El Shaddai, the God Who Is More Than Enough. And gratitude for this generosity of abundance and guidance (just remember to *ask* for it!) will heal untold frustrations and misery.

My favorite Jewish song is another exquisite reminder of El Shaddai—the God Who Is More Than Enough. On Passover (a most holy holiday celebrating the Jews' escape from slavery), we sing "Dayenu," which translates, depending on which Hagadah you look at, as "It would have been enough" or (in another translation) "We should have been more grateful." The song tells the story of all the miracles one after the next that made possible the Jews' escape from Egypt and their subsequent miraculous survival in the desert for forty years. After each miracle (the parting of the Red Sea, the appearance of food to feed them in the desert, being led into Israel, the land of freedom), the refrain "Dayenu" is repeated: "It would have been enough."

So, when my angels don't give me all the guidance I expect or demand, I back down and say to them, "Okay, you've been really generous already. If you'd just given me my life and not my wife or my wife and not my baby or my baby and not my health or my health and not my talent: Dayenu." It would have been enough; for any one of these gifts, I should be grateful.

And usually if the gratitude is sufficient and sincere, my angelic guardians (or whoever is showing me the way) will give me a new gift (if I am paying attention) as a bonus for saluting the God Who Is More Than Enough.

Dolphins and Angels With Kutira and Moonjay

The very day I was wondering about the connection between dolphins and angels, Kutira Decosterd showed up to shed light on the subject.

Kutira's life path is very much that of a human angel. One of the goals of her lifework is to help individuals cross personal boundaries that limit creativity and to help generate a more playful, rewarding way of life. A Tantric Yoga teacher for many years, she has found a way to combine this ancient practice of energy-raising with her interest in dolphins and whales, by creating Oceanic Tantra.

In one of the guided images she uses, Kutira takes people into the sea to meet a dolphin. You find yourself hanging onto the dolphin, and as you get used to the rhythms of the sea through breathing and relaxation you find you are now in a spiral motion with your dolphin. As the motion increases, you have been catapulted into space, flying with your dolphin into the realms of heaven, where time and space vanish and there is only freedom. Now the dolphin has become your guardian angel. When you are ready to come back to the earth plane, you ask your guardian dolphin for a gift to keep from the journey. Many beautiful gifts are bestowed on people in this way. One individual received a glowing crystal from her dolphin, which the dolphin then planted in her heart forever.

Kutira once took a video tape of dolphins dancing and swimming in their water ballet style and superimposed it on a video tape of a beautiful sky filled with magnificent clouds. It was at this moment that she felt the connection between dolphins and angels. Watching the dolphins flying and dancing in the clouds transported her into a realm where all life connects.

Kutira and her partner Moonjay gave me these insights into the ways dolphins are like angels — the angels of the sea:

> Dolphins inspire play and laughter.
> Dolphins can be used as a connection with a higher consciousness — a special state of being which they seem to carry around with them, and which they seem to open up for humans in their presence.
> Hawaiian mythology traces dolphins' origins from the stars in the heavens.
> Dolphins are known to be helpful to humans in distress at sea.
> Dolphins don't take things seriously; their field of gravity is lighter.
> Dolphins awaken the child within us; they open us to our playful self.
> Dolphins and children connect easily and naturally.
> When people see dolphins, their mood is lightened and a sense of joy, excitement, and love prevails.

The connection between dolphins and angels is definitely worth exploring. I'm convinced that the dolphins have a message for our species and that it is similar to the message angels have for us: Lighten up and play more!

If you would like to find out more about the wonderful things Kutira and Moonjay are doing, contact them at:

Kahula Hawaiian Institute for Inner Transformation
P.O. Box 1747
Mahawao, Maui, HI 96768

An Afternoon With Suzanna Solomon

Looking through a section of the local Malibu newspaper, I found the following ad listed under "Announcements": "You are not alone—your guardian angels are all around you. They want to love you, source you, inspire you, counsel you in all you are and do. If you are ready to go beyond your known reality, then come with me on a wondrous journey and meet with your angels. Suzanna."

I cut out the ad, and set it aside in a place where I would see it from time to time. A few weeks passed and spontaneously I called Suzanna. She was warmly receptive and agreed to let me come and talk to her about angels, with the possibility of writing about it for my book.

When I walked into her apartment, I immediately felt a strong presence of angels. Suzanna took me on a tour of her apartment, which looked and felt like it could be heaven. The colors I always associate with heaven were in every room, displayed in true artist's fashion. I noticed that Suzanna collected rocks, pebbles, and gemstones, and that they were displayed in each room. This was particularly exciting to me because I, too, have rocks, gemstones, and pebbles displayed throughout my living space. I asked what all these rocks could mean and she told me, "They represent the earth realm in which we live, the realm in which we can be in touch with the devic kingdom. The rocks also provide grounding for the incredible lightness of being that comes from being in close contact with the angels."

Suzanna has seven angels who come to her, and she has drawn beautiful portraits of these angels. Each angel has brought a profound experience her way, which she is going to put together with the portraits in a book she is creating.

Suzanna has helped hundreds of people connect with their guardian angels. She does this by taking people into an "altered state." To make sure that the beings who come are angels, Suzanna tests each entity. Some of the tests she uses (she says there are many) are basic questions such as "Are you from the angelic realm?" After that, she told me, "If the beings/entities are not from the angelic realm, they usually disappear, or the feeling of their presence leaves." Other questions include: "Are you here to give the experience of the God-self?" "Do you come for my highest spiritual good?" "Are you from the Christ vibration?" "Are you of the Love vibration?"

If angels are around, the person will get an incredible feeling of lovingness and lightness. Suzanna agreed with me that angels are full of humor and light. They are very funny beings. If an entity comes who is heavy and serious, she knows that that entity is not of the angelic realm.

Suzanna told me that some of the people she has helped connect with their angels have had the most amazing experiences, like cosmic consciousness expansions; then, six months later, they were right back with all the craziness in their life just the way it was before. The reason this happens, she explained, is that "they don't listen, they won't ask, and they don't do the meditations. To stay with the higher vibration, you must ask for the connection. The angels will not push you over: If you don't shift your vibration and raise it to their level, life will not change at all. Guardian angels are always around us, but only when we truly *acknowledge* and *ask* and *have faith* will they come to source the vibrations of our higher self." She added an analogy to electricity: "If you don't stick the cord into the plug, nothing happens. The electricity is there, but you have to connect with it; you have to turn on the switch for it to be any use to you. Guardian angels come to us in many ways to teach us. When we can allow that and stay awake our life will change."

Suzanna asked her guardian angels if maybe it wasn't the right time for these people to meet their own guardians. Her angels told her that the time was right to introduce them but that the people were not ready to change their lives just yet.

Connecting children and teens with their guardian angels is an especially rewarding experience. Some of the children Suzanna has worked with have readily seen and talked to angels and fairies since they can first remember. The father of such a child who had contact with the fairy world thought it would be interesting to see if this same connection could happen with the child's angels. So he brought the child to Suzanna. The connection was powerful because the child already accepted the world of angels and was ready to meet them.

Meeting their angels through Suzanna's guidance brings many positive changes to many people's lives, and lets them know they are not alone.

Animal Angels
by Nancy Grimley Carleton

My pet rabbit Willow is an angel. I'm convinced of it. At 2.7 pounds, he is a furry bundle of unconditional love. Willow has been my rabbit, and I have been his person, for three years now. And from the first time I saw him, he has filled my heart with lightness and love. Even in my most serious moods, when I see Willow come hopping into the room something inside of me opens up and I am overcome with gratitude and joy. No matter how I'm feeling, no matter what I'm going through, he is there as a steady source of acceptance and love. In the evenings, I get into bed and lie with him directly over my heart. His body sinks trustingly into mine, we breathe together, and both of us experience a piece of heaven.

I believe that many treasured pets are angels in disguise. Angels know that sometimes we humans need the comfort and warmth of flesh and blood. An angel came to me when I was five years old and desperately in need of a positive connection to life. She took the form of Tippy, a small black dog with white paws, white chest and nose, and a white tip on her tail. We owned her mother, Lucky, another probable angel, who gave birth to her puppies on our couch (a big mess, as I wrote in a kindergarten account of the event). I watched Tippy being born, and I knew from the moment I saw her that she had come to be my dog. She was the first of the three puppies to wag her tail, and for several weeks she wagged it only for me. She made me feel special and loved. My mother let us keep her (we could only keep one of the puppies) and for the next sixteen years, until I was twenty-one, she was my faithful and loving companion. We spent hours playing together; she had more patience than any other dog I've known, even allowing me to dress her in clothes (I seldom played with dolls). At night and in the mornings, she cuddled warmly with me whether I was sad or angry, happy or depressed. Tippy gave me many gifts, but foremost among them was unconditional love and acceptance. I will never forget her.

Today I opened the mail to a letter from Mary Kay Wright-Malear, a bodyworker in the Bay Area who has held two raffles in the past couple of years to raise funds for treatments for her much-loved dog, Brujo. The letter informed those of us who had contributed to the raffle that Brujo had died in July: "He was my best friend," read the card Mary Kay had printed in his memory. She also included a quotation from Meher Baba, which captures very clearly the quality of love animal angels can give: "Love is essentially self-communicative. Those who do not have it catch it from those who have it. True Love is unconquerable and irresistible and it goes on gathering power and spreading itself until it transforms everyone whom it touches." The love and acceptance pets give the people around them doesn't end there; it fills us with the kind of love that spreads out to touch others.

To close, I'd like to share a synchronistic experience I had regarding animals as angels. Last Christmas, two of my psychotherapy clients who know each other gave me a gift. Both of them knew I liked rabbits (my favorite pair of earrings are dangling golden rabbits), though neither of them knew of my interest in angels. But the gift they gave me was perfect. It was a porcelain Christmas tree ornament in the shape of a white rabbit's head and ears with angel's wings sprouting out the shoulders. It now hangs over Willow's hutch, keeping watch over him and reminding me every day that angels can take many forms.

Nancy Grimley Carleton, M.A., in addition to being the editor of this book, is a licensed Marriage, Family, and Child Counselor with a psychotherapy practice in Berkeley, California. Trained in transpersonal counseling, alchemical hypnotherapy, and bodywork, Nancy helps clients complete unfinished business from the past. She is particularly interested in working with clients who are grieving the loss of animal friends, many of whom are angels. She can be reached at:

Nancy Grimley Carleton
(510) 644-0172
FAX Line: (510) 843-4324

An Ode to Angels
by Alice Way

Angels bring good tidings of hope and joy and peace,
But also comfort when our spirits need release.
They also bring us visions in luminescent light—
Messages of forgiveness that stay forever bright;

A word, a name, a fragrance, or voices that we hear,
We do not always need these signs to know they're near.

Often they are using the skill of human hands,
And human prayers uplifted over many lands.
They help us make hard choices or help us courage find,
Or give us opportunities to be more kind.
We thank our guardian angels for their faithful care,
And for the ways that humankind can learn to share.

Whate'er our name for angels or what our name for God,
The network of the spirit pervades our earthly sod.
So let us join the angels in their joyful songs,
Never, though, forgetting to help to right the wrongs.

Alice Way was a Quaker educator who founded Pacific Oaks
College and the Ackworth Friends Elementary School in Pasa-
dena, California. For forty-seven years, she was codirector of
these schools, involving herself most extensively in special education; she never gave up on a child however difficult the case.
Her guiding light was giving compassionately to others. Visitors
to her house often noticed heavenly scents. Alice would explain,
"That just means the angels are back." She wrote "An Ode to
Angels" on Christmas day, 1986. She died in mid-1989, in her
late seventies, after a lifetime of service.

Living With Angels:
An Interview With Artist K. Martin-Kuri
 by Carol Kramer

Karyn Martin-Kuri's paintings are filled with light. Their shim-
mering colors glow with a vibrant intensity that would seem to
be impossible to create with mere paint and brush. An interna-
tionally known artist, Martin-Kuri's works are shown throughout

the world. She has been compared to William Blake but is most often called "The Angel Lady" by those who know her. It is not just the fact that she creates angel paintings that has brought her this title, however; it is also due to her extensive knowledge of angels. She is an "angelologist" who has studied angels for twenty-five years, and, as can be seen in her paintings, she has more than a passing acquaintance with them.

I spoke with her at her home, Angels' Cup, in Cape Cod, Massachusetts. She is an expert in the use of color, and every room glows with the same airy, spacious light that fills her paintings.

Her paintings, described as "Celestial Art," are sometimes done in oils, but most often are a combination of watercolor (using a wet-on-wet technique, followed by a layering of colored veils) and chalk pastel, which heightens the radiant effect. Her work does not stop with her paintings: she lectures, leads seminars, and provides angelic consultations. She also teaches the development of creativity in individuals as a path to higher consciousness. To encourage this flowering of sprituality and creativity, she and five others have created a cultural forum for spiritual development called Tapestry.

Carol Kramer: Does everyone have a guardian angel?

Karyn Martin-Kuri: Oh, very definitely! Everyone has a guardian angel. They are assigned to us prior to our birth, and they are with us continuously throughout our whole life. They are with us at our death and our return to the spiritual realms.

Kramer: You say "they" — do we all have only one or can we have more than one?

Martin-Kuri: You have one guardian angel, but you may have other angels helping you as well. The guardian angel is a protector, holds the destiny of the individual, and may be with you for many incarnations. You can also have special angels assigned who can help create a piece of music, perhaps, or inspire works in architecture or science.

Kramer: What prompted you to begin studying angels?

Martin-Kuri: When I was a teenager I wanted to help humanity

heal its ailments—both physical ills as well as those of consciousness. I became an expert on color and its effect on consciousness
and found that color is connected to very high levels of angelic
beings. It was through discovering the relationship of angelic
beings to color and energy that I realized there was no other
kind of work for me. How could I do anything else?

Kramer: Is there an angel for every color?

Martin-Kuri: The other way around; there are colors for every angel. Color is something we see only in certain dimensions,
but hues exist on the spiritual plane much finer than the colors
we experience. When we let color speak to us in its true celestial language, we begin to communicate with angelic beings.

Kramer: Is this how you can contact your guardian angel?

Martin-Kuri: Actually, there's no need to contact your angel
because you're *already* in contact. It's just a matter of realizing
it. It's like forgetting your left hand—it's still part of you, but
somehow you forgot it was there. Do you have to talk to your
left hand? No. But you can become conscious of it.

Kramer: When did that happen for you?

Martin-Kuri: I became very conscious of my guardian angel
from the time I was a little child. I was aware of the presence
of a being of great light and love who would watch over me and
protect me from harm. As I grew older, I became very involved
with flowers and nature and could see the presence of God in
the world around me—and I could also see that the world was
filled with angels! There were angels everywhere! There are more
angels than there are people. I learned to contact my guardian angel by remembering that presence.

Kramer: Can I discover the name of my angel?

Martin-Kuri: You can ask your guardian angel at night—give
it at least three nights—what name you could use in this incar-
nation. But, you see, languages in the spiritual world are different from languages here on earth. Angels are known by their
signs, not by their names, with the few exceptions of those names
given traditionally to archangels. Your guardian angel may have

a name in a language you couldn't even pronounce. What you want is just some way to address your angel.

Kramer: Could I get a visual image rather than a name?

Martin-Kuri: Yes! I would prefer a visual. Then you would know there's a private link between the two of you.

Kramer: What do you mean when you say they carry your destiny?

Martin-Kuri: Angels carry, as though they were holding a secret package, the destiny of each person. Only that angel knows what it is. Angels are God's representative and have long-term vision that spans eons, so they know the whole destiny of the soul. They are interested not just in helping you a year from now but in how your life can become a complete and wonderful component of the fulfilling experience of returning to God.

Kramer: While we're talking I'm getting a sense of that presence, and of companionship . . .

Martin-Kuri: Absolutely. And you'll find that when you become aware of the encompassing love that this being has as a representative of God—directly—in your life, you will not be the same. We can choose to ignore this being, or we can acknowledge it. Imagine an invisible being standing right by you that tries to guide you and prevent you from harm and is totally ignored! If we can realize what it is to give out of such purity of love and have it rejected over and over and over again, we can begin to glimpse some of the consciousness of the guardian angel.

Kramer: Is my angel a beautiful being with wings? A ball of light?

Martin-Kuri: It's a combination of both. Everything in creation has its source in light, so it is truly an experience of light, but it manifests to the degree that we can comprehend it. If you can comprehend it only as a little man in a blue suit with a briefcase, that's what you'll experience! If you can experience the concept as a being of light with appendages that move as if they were wings, that is exactly what you will be able to experience. However, as you ascend through the hierarchies, if we were to be in the presence of the seraphim, it would destroy us. We could not endure that amount of radiant light. You would need some kind of transformer to experience it.

Kramer: Are angels male and female?

Martin-Kuri: Angels are basically asexual beings, but they carry a male or female impulse. In the universe there are polarities that will manifest as masculine or feminine, and they may carry those energies, but it does not mean at all that they have human forms that we would identify as male or female.

Kramer: Do they match up to your gender?

Martin-Kuri: No, it makes no difference. You may have changed your own sex through incarnations, but your angel will still be the same as you evolve.

Kramer: Are they the same as spirit guides?

Martin-Kuri: Spirit guides are very different. Spirit guides are human beings who have left the physical body. Angels have never been in human form. Angels can superimpose themselves on an individual for a moment of enlightenment or great inspiration as was done in the ancient temples long ago.

Kramer: What exactly do you mean by superimpose?

Martin-Kuri: It's through inspiration; it's not a channeling situation. It's a matter of being divinely inspired, just as people's guardian angels inspire them, but they do not know it!

Kramer: Is there a difference between angels and devas?

Martin-Kuri: Many people get a little confused when they hear of sylphs, undines, salamanders, and gnomes—these are the helpers of nature. Gnomes have to do with the earth, sylphs with air, salamanders with fire, and undines with water. We think of these as separate beings, and many times people will see them working in the garden, especially in spring. Actually, they are like the fingers of the archai—there are angels, archangels, and then the archai—which have the responsibility of working on the development of the planet. The devic kingdom is an extension of them.

When you are in the presence of any of the elementals or

angels, you can perceive them with other senses through the heart—for example, when you see the incredible perfection of a rose! Shouldn't that humble every one of us? Or the face in a pansy. If you go about trying to see them visually, you won't do it. What you have to do is open your heart and you'll feel them. Then whenever you're around them, you'll also feel wisdom. It's because the wisdom of God flows through them.

Kramer: What tradition of knowledge are you drawing from with this information?

Martin-Kuri: Multiple sources. The delineation of spiritual hierarchies I prefer originated in ancient times and was brought to life again at the turn of the century by Rudolph Steiner.

The words may change, but there are three major divisions of hierarchies and within each of these there are three more levels. Closest to humanity are the angels, archangels, and archai. Angels are responsible for the development of the human being, archangels are responsible for cultures, and the archai are responsible for the planet. Michael, one of the seven archangels is, since the end of the last century, now in a situation where he is also the leading archai. This means that the archangel Michael is responsible for planetary development and the whole family of humanity. You will find that there's a tremendous impulse toward individual freedom in the world; this is a Michaelic influence, as well as the impulse to develop consciousness. It leads to the understanding of the Christ.

Kramer: Angels are referred to in Hebrew, Christian, and Islamic texts. Are they called by other names in other religions?

Martin-Kuri: In the American Indian tradition they are called spirits. For example, the spirit of a river would be an angel spirit connected to the angels.

Kramer: What about Hindu culture? I don't remember coming across any mention of angels in the Vedas.

Martin-Kuri: No, but the Vedas were probably written from angelic inspiration overshadowing human beings. It's so common to have the presence of these beings working through great spiritual teachers that they didn't have to sit down and write a handbook about it.

Kramer: In the current environmental crisis — people destroying nature — is the archangel Michael the link to helping us save ourselves and the earth?

Martin-Kuri: Absolutely. And it's not just the physical pollution we have to worry about — it's the mental dumping of negativity into the spiritual bodies of the earth. If we could stop that, it would make the work of the angels so much easier. They have a great capacity to purify; they know what's going to happen with a planet. Negativity jars the work of the angels.

Kramer: How should one transmute negativity?

Martin-Kuri: First, no matter how difficult you may perceive your life to be, begin to live every day with the quality of gratitude. That will immediately connect you with your guardian angel. Gratitude will open the doorway, and then your guardian angel can begin to transform you. Once the conscious closeness is deepened between one's guardian angel and oneself, then all sorts of creativity will awaken. Before long the individual will flower — no longer caught in negativity.

One of the important things to remember is that the way we attract angels is by becoming the qualities that are of interest to them. When we focus on such qualities as compassion, faith, or tolerance, we attract angelic beings that are trying to help develop that in all humanity. The more we focus on these qualities, the more we can help them.

Kramer: In what way?

Martin-Kuri: We have free will; the angels don't. They are on assignment, operating out of love, to help humanity turn to God out of love. So it's their work to awaken that in us. They keep the order, they keep the planet spinning, they keep the nature forces working, they keep us in our bodies! There is such tremendous order.

Kramer: That's reassuring. Sometimes the world seems very chaotic.

Martin-Kuri: It's we who are chaotic.

Kramer: So why do they bother with us?

Martin-Kuri: Because we're an incredible cosmic experiment, to see if we can consciously develop this form of love. It's time for us to respond with our own creativity, our own inner nature, to the heavens.

Kramer: I have heard a lot of people claiming to be angels. Can people become angels?

Martin-Kuri: It's very possible for anyone to learn to *behave* like an angel, but it's only by the will of God that one is an angel. Angels are not born and they do not die: they're eternal. Humans are born and die. Our spirits are different. They originate at a different point of creation. They precede us.

The more you enhance your own light, the more interest you engender in the higher beings. It gets their attention. You have to have pretty strong light to get the attention of those high in the hierarchy.

Martin-Kuri: I would think so. But it seems that once you get it going it would work like a loop—you help them, they help you, and it must build.

Martin-Kuri: Exactly, it does, and pretty soon you find yourself behaving like an angel—*serving* the universe rather than taking from it.

Kramer: People talk about sending angels with messages.

Martin-Kuri: Your angel loves you and will want to make your life easier, but you cannot demand and you cannot command. You can't suddenly say, "Oh, angel, will you go do this? I need to have this commissioned painting; go get one for me." That's a violation. What you can do is say, "Help me to become a better person so that I can help this process." If you stop and become centered in a state of inner peace, your angel will give you the inspiration.

There is an "angel etiquette": as you would treat any loving friend, so you would treat your angel. That means appreciation is a very important part of the relationship. If you find that you have suddenly had help, healing, etc., immediately acknowledge it. That has tremendous power.

You can do something once in a while for the angels in your life. You can put some flowers in your house as a love link, or listen to a beautiful piece of music. Every time you see or hear something beautiful, consciously give it to your angel to distribute. Then it can be given to somebody who may be in need of it. It's a form of energy: you translate an experience into energy, which can then go into the care of your angel and be used.

Also, this is where creativity comes in; it is a truly intimate time between you and your angel. You can feel your angel so close!

Another thing you can do is, when you go to bed at night, visualize your angel lifting you in his or her wings and carrying you into other dimensions of consciousness. We expand out into the universe at a very rapid rate when we go to sleep. Also, if you're ill, when you go to sleep, ask your angel to come close and help you understand why you're ill.

Kramer: How can we work with angels around relationships?

Martin-Kuri: We can listen to their loving guidance. They love to bring harmony. Since they know about destiny, they have many tasks, one of which is bringing people together.

Kramer: Is that why I will suddenly get up and walk across a room to talk to a total stranger who later turns out to be a very important person in my life?

Martin-Kuri: Yes! And conversely, when you hold back and just can't bring yourself to talk to someone, the angels are perhaps saying, "Not now." Your angel would never say no—they don't speak that way except in life-threatening situations.

Kramer: I've had people tell me of being pushed back onto a sidewalk just before a speeding car went by.

Martin-Kuri: Angels have the ability to access different dimensions and can manifest right down to the level of gravity and force. So they could literally stop a train, if need be.

Kramer: Does prayer allow an angel to intercede?

Martin-Kuri: Oh yes, but never pray to an angel—always pray to God! The angel listens. The angel many times responds, but the angel only gets its orders from one place, and that's God.

Kramer: When I sense that presence, it seems the more I have, the more I want. Is there such a thing as being angel-greedy?

Martin-Kuri: What you really want is to become more of who you truly are. The more you are that, the more angels will be attracted to you. They'll be there by their own natural right. It's like they look down from heaven and say, "Oh, how very interesting! Look what's happening with her. Let's go see." The more you are in service to humanity, the more angels will be there.

Kramer: How do you do your commissioned paintings?

Martin-Kuri: There's tremendous preparation for each type of commission, whether a guardian angel painting or a life destiny painting. Life commissions may take many months of deep preparation. I always work out of a meditative state. It's not just a matter of portraying in color and form the image of an angel or the realms of heaven. It is a matter of improving the relationship between individuals and the higher worlds so that the moment they see the image, their hearts are already open.

Kramer: Do you see a visual image in your mind?

Martin-Kuri: I experience it. It's a state of consciousness that is really beyond prayer because there are no words. I'm at a level where the angel can access me very easily. The guardian angel of the other individual, myself, and my guardian angel are all together. I become the vehicle with the paintbrush of the image that the angel would like the indivdual to see. The colors come as we begin to work.

Kramer: If I'm working on a creative project, how can I go about getting the inspiration I need to complete it?

Martin-Kuri: All creativity, in my opinion, comes from one source and it's in the word *Creator*. There's no other way we can create in a truthful way. We can create a lot of garbage, a lot of illusions, and think we're doing a great thing, but if we're truly creating, we have to work with the Creator. In order to do that, we need to be in a state of inner peace. We need to quiet ourselves and let go of the attachment to the future. Most anxiety originates from an overfixation on the future, and that will not bring you closer to the angels or to the Creator. It is possible the Creator may, through the angels, be giving you an act of the will of God to do. You have to be in a timeless space, and you have to forget everything you've ever done and also not worry about anything you're going to do.

Kramer: Creativity is very much connected to spiritualty.

Martin-Kuri: Yes, I don't think they can be separated. Not if we're talking about truth. If we're talking about creativity that originates in darkness, that's another story. The lack of discernment in our times really needs our immediate attention.

Kramer: I guess we all see enough of that! You teach a course in "Creativity as a Path to Enlightenment."

Martin-Kuri: I try to teach people to fall in love with themselves in a very healthy way so they can see that through their own creativity they can develop absolutely beautiful things far beyond their imaginations. That is one of the most meaningful things in my life, to reveal that to a person. Because that's what God wants us to do, to really love ourselves, and then we have enough to share and can love others. We can get a real glimmer of the heaven within through our own creative acts.

The finest art of all is creating beautiful relationships. That interests me the most. My art form has moved through many different spheres these many years; I still paint and teach, but what truly amazes me is to see people use their creativity to develop a whole new life.

This contribution was excerpted from *Body Mind & Spirit* with kind permission. You may contact K. Martin-Kuri at:

> (800) 28-ANGEL or
> Tapestry
> P.O. Box 3032
> Waquoit, MA 02536

She may be commissioned to create paintings for individuals, organizations, or those in need of special help.

Other Comments on Angels

The following is contributed by Linda Hayden: "Angels can appear when a person's body is very ill. Usually they don't say much. Sometimes they do. A rebirth experience follows."

A letter I received, from an angelic being named Filomena stated: "I am an Angel. My purpose is to reveal the flame of light that I am, and to enlighten you with the sheer innocent delight of expressing the I am in my physical body. In my personal process of integrating body, heart, and soul, I'm revealing what I see and feel. I'm balancing out the seeking of my own wonder."

My friend Shannon Boomer asked her son Gideon to tell us what he thought angels were. He answered, "Oh, they're just plain old air!"

Quotations About Angels

Angels are aspects of God that touch us in mysterious and subtle ways and on many levels of the mind. They are divine messengers of God that can transform our attitudes, change our thought patterns and renew our ideals if we open ourselves to their heedings.

Harvey Humann

Though angels are both the messengers and the message of God, that makes them no easier to receive. For one thing, we almost never recognize them, even when they knock at our door.

F. Forrester Church

It is not because Angels are holier than men or devils that makes them Angels, but because they do not expect holiness from one another, but from God alone.

William Blake

Millions of spiritual creatures walk the earth unseen, both when we sleep and when we wake.

Milton

I throw my selfe downe in my Chamber, and I call in and invite God, and his Angels thither, and when they are there, I neglect God and his Angels, for the noise of a Flie, for the rattling of a Coach, for the whining of a doore.

John Donne

Silently one by one, in the infinite meadows of Heaven, Blossomed the lovely stars, the forget-me-nots of the Angels

H.W. Longfellow

Chapter 36

Noteworthy
Angel Progaganda

Angel Bits and Glossary

GALLUP POLLS

According to the Gallup poll in 1978, *A Surprising Number of Americans Believe in Paranormal Phenomena,* a majority of fifty-four percent believe in angels, increasing to sixty-eight percent among people whose religious beliefs are important to them. The study found that those who believe in supernatural beings are generally younger and better educated.

According to the Gallup poll in 1988, *Teen Belief in Angels Is on the Rise,* more teens than ever believe in angels. Three teens in four believe in angels, or seventy-four percent nationwide.

GLOSSARY

Ange passe: This is French for "angel passing." When there is a lull or quieting in a conversation, the French say, "ange passe," because the quiet means an angel has passed overhead.

Angel satchel: This is a term coined by Mary Beth Crain for a place to put unwanted energy and personalities that are interfering in your life. The angels will pick it up for you and send it far away (possibly all the way to the planet Pluto).

Kairos: A moment of God's grace in which angels do their thing— an opportune time when conditions are right for the accomplishment of a crucial action. A decisive action.

AFFIRMATION OF ARCHANGEL MICHAEL:

Divine light of the highest order under the protection of the archangel Michael. [Repeat this three times for protection in any situation.]

THEMES AND SYMBOLS SURROUNDING ANGELS

Angels are often portrayed in portraits surrounded by the following symbols:

The lily flower: symbolizes purity

Bearing a palm: symbolizes victory

Musical instrument: symbolizes praise

Trumpet: the voice of God

Carrying a thurible (an incense burner): symbolizes adoration and prayer

Pilgrim's staff: symbolizes readiness

Wings: symbolize the speed and quickness with which they fulfill the divine command

Nimbus (plural, nimbi): refers to a bright cloud surrounding deities when they appear on earth—an aura that spiritual beings from the heaven plane have around them

Halo: the holy shining light that encircles an angel's head; the light streaming from the head

Aureola: the full aura of light outlining a person or angel

The glory: a combination of both the halo and aura

Diadem: a crown or headband symbolizing royal authority

ORDERS OF ANGELS

There are three orders of angels, each consisting of three choirs, making a total of nine choirs of angels.

Those closest to God

1. **The seraphim:** Purifying and enlightened powers, shown with six wings and flames of fire around them, they are led by Uriel and call out to one another the words: "Holy, Holy, Holy is the Lord of hosts" (see Isaiah 6:3).
2. **The cherubim:** With the power of knowing, they are shown with multieyed peacock's feathers symbolizing their all-knowing power. Their leader is Jophiel.
3. **The thrones:** With the simplicity from purification, they are shown as wheels of fire, the throne bearers of God, representing divine majesty. Their leader is Japhkiel.

Priest-princes of the court of heaven

4. **The dominions or dominations:** Aspiring to true lordship, they carry the scepter and sword to symbolize the divine power over all creation. Their leader is Zadkiel.
5. **The virtues or authorities:** Powerful assimilations of the will of God, they carry out the instruments of the passion of Christ. Their leader is Haniel.
6. **The powers:** Orderly authorities, they carry flaming swords to protect humankind. Their leader is Raphael.

The ministering angels

7. **The principalities:** Princely powers, they watch over the leaders of people, carrying scepters and crosses. Their leader is Chamael.
8. **The archangels:** Leaders among angels, their leader is Michael.
9. **The angels:** Beings of light who reveal the divine mysteries and who don't have special ranks or commissions in the celestial army.

WELL-KNOWN ANGELS FOR HELP OR INSPIRATION

Raphael

> Spring
> Hebrew *Rapha'* (to heal) and *'el* (God): God has healed
> Raphael means God heals or divine healer
> Leader of the powers
> He is charged with healing the earth, and through him the
>   earth furnishes an abode for humans, whom he also heals
> Healing and mercy: He directs spiritual beams into hospi-
>   tals, institutions, and homes where his healing beams are
>   needed
> Intellect, curiosity, and instruction in the sciences
> Guardian and treasurer of creative talents
> Symbol: a sword or an arrow that has been well sharpened
> He carries a golden vial of balm
> Time of day: the dawn
> Soft greens and all tints of blue
> Bible story: Tobias

Michael

> Autumn
> Hebrew *Mikha'el* means "Who is God?" His name is a bat-
>   tle cry
> Captain of the heavenly host, leader of the archangels,
>   viceroy of heaven
> Also known as St. Michael
> The lord of the way
> The slayer of the dragon of evil intentions
> Guardian of holy places
> Ruler of the fourth heaven
> Often equated with the Holy Ghost
> Midday angel clad in armor, with shield and weapon
> Fights first Satan and his demons, then all the enemies of
>   God's own people

Known as an angel who cleanses persons, groups, or localities of discord and evil
Represents the right, the creative, that which should be done
The master of the energy of balance
Element: fire, purification, perfection
Deep green, vivid blues, golden, and rose red
Invoked as a champion against all adversity and when you need courage and a strong defender; success
Direction to invoke: south
Red candle
Inspired Joan of Arc to help the king of France

Gabriel

Winter
Hebrew *gebher* means "man and el," or God
Gabriel means man of God or strength of God
Bible: announcing of Jesus to the Virgin Mary, and through the prophet Daniel
Presides over paradise
Sits on the left-hand side of God
Associated with a trumpet, symbolizing the voice of God
Usually portrayed as carrying a lily, olive branch, or torch
Bringer of good news and maker of changes
Annunciation, resurrection, mercy, truth
The potency of God
Procreation and resurrection
Love is his great force factor
Late afternoon; peaceful vibration
Fluidlike activity, water
Tans, browns, dark greens
Invoked toward the west
Favorite day: Monday
Important figure in Muslim religion: the guardian angel of the prophet Mohammed

Uriel

Summer

Hebrew: fire of God

Angel of prophecy who inspires and conveys ideas to writer and teachers

The angel of interpretation and salvation

Shown with a scroll as his symbol

Leader of the seraphim

The alchemist imparting transforming ideas for the realization of goals (especially those of the discouraged and weak)

Associated with the arts, with music in particular

Haniel

Glory or grace of God

All powers of love

Governor of Venus

Invoked as power against evil

Angel of the month of December

Metatron

King of angels

Prince of the divine face

Charged with the sustenance of mankind

Link between the human and divine

Tallest angel in heaven

Resides in seventh heaven (the dwelling place of God)

Highest power of abundance

When invoked, he can appear as a pillar of fire, his face more dazzling than the sun

Raziel

Secret of God

Angel of the mysteries

Knowledge; guardian of originality

Habitat Chokmah, the realm of pure ideas

Auriel

Angel of night
Associated with the earth
Winter: he is the creative force in the ebb period
The seed is in the earth and all is dark
Helps us contemplate the future
Winter colors: black, brown, gray

In brief

Michael: courage, strong defense, divine protection, shield and sword
Gabriel: bringer of news, maker of changes, trumpet
Haniel: all powers of love
Raphael: God has healed, golden vial of balm
Uriel: emergencies, judgment, scroll
Raziel: knowledge, guardian of originality, habitat Chokmah, the realm of pure ideas
Camael: power in interpersonal relationships, self-discipline
Metatron: highest power of abundance, chancellor of heaven

Annotated Bibliography

BOOKS OF GENERAL ANGEL INFORMATION

Adler, Mortimer J. *The Angels and Us.* New York: Macmillan Publishing Co., Inc., 1982.
Written by a prolific contemporary philosopher/thinker, this book contains original thinking, artfully addressing the age-old questions about angels.
Church, F. Forrester. *Entertaining Angels: A Guide to Heaven for Atheists and True Believers.* San Francisco: Harper and Row, 1987.
Very fun and thought provoking. An honest look at heaven, including the paradoxical nature of the Christian viewpoint

on heaven. Lots of humorous scenarios. Contains true angelic insight.

D'Angelo, Dorie. *Living With Angels.* Carmel, CA: First Church of Angels, 1980.
Written by a human angel with simple angelic wisdom and true angel stories. Inspirational. Includes some methods for contacting angels.

Davidson, Gustav. *A Dictionary of Angels (Including the Fallen Angels).* New York: The Free Press, 1971.
One of the most bizarre and amazing compilations of data on angels. It had to have taken a lifetime to collect all the information. An angel archive, dictionary style.

Gilmore, G. Don. *Angels, Angels, Everywhere.* New York: Pilgrim Press, 1981.
Contains historical perceptions of angels, from the world's great religions and cultures, and describes the various forms angels have taken and their roles in history. Real-life accounts of experiences with angels, including some well-known personalities.

Graham, Billy. *Angels: God's Secret Agents.* Waco, TX: Word Books, 1986.
Angels are discussed as "spiritual creatures created by God for the service of Christendom and the church." Based on accounts from the Bible.

Hodson, Geoffrey. *The Brotherhood of Angels and Men.* Wheaton, IL: Theosophical Publishing House, 1982.
Written by a clairvoyant, this book consists of messages he received direct from the angelic kingdom.

Humann, Harvey. *The Many Faces of Angels.* Marina del Rey, CA: DeVorss and Co., 1986.
Described as an introduction or overview on the subject of angels, from a metaphysical standpoint. The author is quite a wordsmith and conveys the beauty and essence of angels in a fitting way.

MacGregor, Geddes. *Angels: Ministers of Grace.* New York: Paragon House, 1988.

The author is a theologian and philosopher. The book is scholarly, confronting the age-old questions about angels. Examines the role of angels in art (contains about forty illustrations), music, mythology, and the Bible. Very complete compared to other books of its kind.

Moolenburgh, H.C. *A Handbook of Angels.* Great Britain: C.W. Daniel Co. Ltd., 1984.

A very interesting book written by a Dutch medical doctor, who started his own survey by asking patients about their experiences with angels. Ahead of its time in many ways.

Parente, Fr. Pascal P. *Beyond Space: A Book About the Angels.* Rockford, IL: Tan Books and Publishers, Inc., 1973.

Catholic viewpoint and references, mostly dealing with angelic hierarchy.

Ronner, John. *Do You Have a Guardian Angel?* Indialantic, FL: Mamre Press, Inc., 1985.

Answers to eighty-three questions on angels, imparting interesting folklore and age-old wisdom, along with current interest and information.

BOOKS ABOUT THE DEVIC KINGDOM

Bloom, William. *Devas, Fairies and Angels (A Modern Approach).* Somerset, England: Gothic Image Publications, 1986.

Short pamphlet; contains a lot of insightful information.

Maclean, Dorothy. *To Hear the Angels Sing.* Issaquah, WA: Lorian Press, 1987.

This is my personal favorite of all angel books. It is inspiring and contains actual messages recorded from the angels. After reading it, you get a real sense of who and what angels are, and what your connection to nature is, and how important the devic kingdom is.

Newhouse, Flower A. *Rediscovering the Angels and Natives of Eternity.* Escondido, CA: The Christwatch Ministry, 1976.

Written by a Christian mystic who set out to bring angels back
into Christian teaching. Covers a wide range of mystical angel
information, with emphasis on the devic kingdom.

BOOKS FOR "SENSITIVES" AND SEEKERS

Bowers, Barbara. *What Color Is Your Aura?* New York: Pocket
Books, 1989.

This book includes a test that not only tells you the color of
your aura but also gives you tremendous insight into your personality when you read about the color or colors in your aura.

Calhoun, Marcy. *Are You Really Too Sensitive?* Nevada City,
CA: Blue Dolphin Press, Inc., 1987.

Sensitives need to understand themselves, so that they won't
think that something is wrong or vastly different about them.
This book is written to help the true sensitive in all aspects
of his or her life—from money to love.

Fields, Rick. *Chop Wood, Carry Water.* Los Angeles: Jeremy P.
Tarcher, Inc., 1984.

A book you probably either own or have seen in your favorite
bookstore. A very valuable handbook for spiritual seekers regardless of their level of awareness or stage.

Roman, Sanaya. *Spiritual Growth.* Tiburon, CA: H.J. Kramer,
Inc., 1989.

This is the best book I know for understanding your higher
self, and developing ways to *become* your higher self in your
everyday life.

PROSPERITY AND ABUNDANCE

Ponder, Catherine. *The Prospering Power of Love.* Marina del
Rey, CA: Devorss and Co., 1966.

Has a great section about writing to angels.

Roman, Sanaya, and Packer, Duane. *Creating Money.* Tiburon,
CA: H.J. Kramer, Inc., 1988.

By far the most complete book on abundance and prosperity.
Many helpful techniques, affirmations, and exercises are included that are known to produce results.

HUMOR AND HEALING

Cousins, Norman. *The Anatomy of an Illness as Perceived by the Patient.* New York: Norton, 1979.

This famous journalist was stricken with a mysterious inflammatory and degenerative illness, which doctors were at a loss to treat. He cured himself through a program of laughter, in a nonstressful environment.

Samra, Cal. *The Joyful Christ: The Healing Power of Humor.* San Francisco: Harper and Row, 1985.

A study of humor in the Bible — holy humor. Also looks at joy and humor as the true healing powers the universe (God) provides.

Swami Beyondananda. *Driving Your Own Karma: Swami Beyondananda's Tour Guide to Enlightenment.* Rochester, Vermont: Destiny books, 1989.

Steve Bhaerman (a.k.a. Swami) is a genius! This book is must reading for anyone who wants to "enlighten up", have a good laugh and promote anti-seriousness.

TALES OF SPIRITUAL ADVENTURE

Harricharan, John. *When You Can Walk on Water, Take the Boat.* New York: Berkeley/Putnum, 1990.

John is a true motivational teacher and we are fortunate that he wrote this book. It is an uplifting story, practical, mystical and fun. And one of the main characters is an angel named Gideon.

Millman, Dan. Way of the Peaceful Warrior. Tiburon, CA: H.J. Kramer, Inc., 1984.

The angels made me (long story) read this and I'm glad they did.

ALSO FROM H J KRAMER

THE ALCHEMY OF PRAYER
Rekindling Our Inner Life
by Terry Lynn Taylor
The Alchemy of Prayer is an original, inspiring,
empowering, and loving look at a timeless subject
by best-selling angel expert Terry Lynn Taylor.

THE LAWS OF SPIRIT:
Simple, Powerful Truths for Making Life Work
by Dan Millman
From the author of *Way of the Peaceful Warrior,*
a book of timeless values, containing twelve universal
principles for living and loving well.

CREATING MIRACLES:
Understanding the Experience of Divine Intervention
by Carolyn Miller, Ph.D.
Discover the book where science and miracles meet!
The first scientific look at creating miracles in your life.
These simple practices and true stories offer new wisdom
for accessing the miraculous in daily life.

UNDERSTAND YOUR DREAMS:
1500 Dream Images and How to Interpret Them
by Alice Anne Parker
The essential guide to becoming your own dream expert—
makes dreaming a pleasure and waking an adventure.

WAY OF THE PEACEFUL WARRIOR:
A Book That Changes Lives
by Dan Millman
A spiritual classic! The international best-seller that
speaks directly to the universal quest for happiness.

If you are unable to find these books in your favorite bookstore,
please call 800-833-9327.

ALSO FROM H J KRAMER

TARA'S ANGELS:
One Family's Extraordinary
Journey of Courage and Healing
by Kirk Moore
The singular account of a father's journey through grief
and the awakening of the soul of a family to profound
love and spiritual purpose.

HEALING YOURSELF WITH LIGHT:
How to Connect With the Angelic Healers
by LaUna Huffines
The complete guide to the healing power of light
for physical, mental, and emotional health.

RECLAIMING OUR HEALTH:
Exploding the Medical Myth and
Embracing the Source of True Healing
by John Robbins
In his rousing and inspiring style, John Robbins,
author of *Diet for a New America*, turns his attention
to the national debate on health care.

TALKING WITH NATURE
by Michael J. Roads
The startling revelations of one man's
journey into the heart of nature's wisdom.

THE LIFE YOU WERE BORN TO LIVE:
A Guide to Finding Your Life Purpose
by Dan Millman
Dan Millman's popular Life-Purpose System features
key spiritual laws to help understand your past, clarify
your present, and change your future.

If you are unable to find these books in your favorite bookstore,
please call 800-833-9327.